This book provides an excellent addition to the current international education literature in providing a robust European theoretical perspective on student mobility within European higher education.

Darla K. Deardorff, Association of International
Education Administrators, USA.

Joana Almeida has done a great service to research about study abroad in this book. She has combined an admirably comprehensive and systematic analysis of the field – and a characterisation of its evolution – with her own mixed-methods study of contrasting experiences of varied study groups. Her book provides both a handbook-like introduction and a revealing and challenging empirical study.

Mike Byram, Professor Emeritus, School of Education,
University of Durham, UK.

Student mobility is on the rise both in Europe and around the world and currently plays a major role in contemporary higher education at educational, policy and research levels. However, few studies provide appropriate theorisation of student mobility as an area of study and professional practice. This work makes a major contribution to the field by advancing a comprehensive conceptual framework, resulting in an interdisciplinary approach to student mobility. The study suggests outcomes in three important areas: (a) personal, (b) linguistic and (c) intercultural, and concludes with suggestions for important activities to enrich the intercultural sojourn. This work is of value to all educators concerned with the quality design and implementation of effective study abroad experiences for their students.

Alvino E. Fantini, Professor Emeritus, School for International
Training, Vermont, USA.

This is a valuable book that brings together in a highly original way the conceptual, educational and methodological foundations and practical applications of interdisciplinarity within the complex and multifaceted field of student mobility. In doing that, the author – Joana Almeida – challenges assumptions and argues convincingly for adopting an interdisciplinary approach which can have implications at both conceptual and methodological levels. Scholars, students, practitioners and policy-makers should read this innovative and accessible monograph in order to expand their awareness and understanding of study abroad, and make sustained contributions to improve the field.

Mattia Baiutti, Researcher, Fondazione Intercultura, Italy.

Understanding Student Mobility in Europe

Understanding Student Mobility in Europe interprets student mobility in European higher education through an active dialogue between disciplines, voices and variables of interest. Providing the conceptual, methodological, pedagogical and empirical foundations, this book advances readers' understanding of the student exchange experience, whilst outlining guidelines and resources for approaching student mobility and considering how students can gain from cross-border education.

Intersecting voices from different disciplines and sojourners, including exchange students, international students and highly skilled immigrants, the book outlines practical guidelines for intercultural curriculum development and assessment, and provides insights, practical ideas, useful terminology and resources to maximise the learning gains of this student population. Split into three distinct parts, the book initially lays the foundational substructure in which an interdisciplinary approach is based. It then addresses questions of practical application by considering the experiences of 50 sojourners in Portugal and the UK through an interdisciplinary lens, and summarises the implications of interdisciplinarity with regards to student mobility in European tertiary-level education.

This book is essential reading for academics and postgraduate students interested in student mobility, education abroad practitioners, and policy-makers at institutional, national and international levels.

Joana Almeida is a Research Fellow at the University of Minho, Portugal.

Internationalization in Higher Education

Series Editor: Elspeth Jones, Emerita Professor, Leeds Beckett University, UK

This series addresses key themes in the development of internationalisation within Higher Education. Up to the minute and international in both appeal and scope, books in the series focus on delivering contributions from a wide range of contexts and provide both theoretical perspectives and practical examples. Written by some of the leading experts in the field, they are vital guides that discuss and build upon evidence-based practice and provide a clear evaluation of outcomes.

Titles in the series:

The Future Agenda for Internationalization in Higher Education
Next Generation Insights into Research, Policy and Practice
Douglas Proctor and Laura E. Rumbley

Online Intercultural Education and Study Abroad
Theory into Practice
Jane Jackson

Internationalization and Employability in Higher Education
Robert Coelen and Cate Gribble

Educational Approaches to Internationalization through Intercultural Dialogue
Reflections on Theory and Practice
Edited by Ulla Lundgren, Paloma Castro and Jane Woodin

Understanding Student Mobility in Europe
An Interdisciplinary Approach
Joana Almeida

For more information about this series, please visit: https://www.routledge.com/Internationalization-in-Higher-Education-Series/book-series/INTHE

Understanding Student Mobility in Europe

An Interdisciplinary Approach

Joana Almeida

LONDON AND NEW YORK

First published 2020
by Routledge
2 Park Square, Milton Park, Abingdon, Oxon OX14 4RN

and by Routledge
52 Vanderbilt Avenue, New York, NY 10017

Routledge is an imprint of the Taylor & Francis Group, an informa business

© 2020 Joana Almeida

The right of Joana Almeida to be identified as author of this work has been asserted by her in accordance with sections 77 and 78 of the Copyright, Designs and Patents Act 1988.

All rights reserved. No part of this book may be reprinted or reproduced or utilised in any form or by any electronic, mechanical, or other means, now known or hereafter invented, including photocopying and recording, or in any information storage or retrieval system, without permission in writing from the publishers.

Trademark notice: Product or corporate names may be trademarks or registered trademarks, and are used only for identification and explanation without intent to infringe.

British Library Cataloguing-in-Publication Data
A catalogue record for this book is available from the British Library

Library of Congress Cataloging-in-Publication Data
Names: Almeida, Joana, author.
Title: Understanding student mobility in Europe: an interdisciplinary approach/Joana Almeida.
Description: Abingdon, Oxon; New York, NY: Routledge, 2020. | Series: Internationalization in higher education | Includes bibliographical references and index. | Identifiers: LCCN 2019058860 (print) | LCCN 2019058861 (ebook) | ISBN 9781138298958 (hardback) | ISBN 9781138298972 (paperback) | ISBN 9781315098265 (ebook)
Subjects: LCSH: College student mobility–European Union countries. | Foreign study–European Union countries. | University cooperation–European Union countries. | Education and globalization–European Union countries.
Classification: LCC LB2376.6.E85 A56 2020 (print) | LCC LB2376.6.E85 (ebook) | DDC 378.1/98–dc23
LC record available at https://lccn.loc.gov/2019058860
LC ebook record available at https://lccn.loc.gov/2019058861

ISBN: 978-1-138-29895-8 (hbk)
ISBN: 978-1-138-29897-2 (pbk)
ISBN: 978-1-315-09826-5 (ebk)

Typeset in Galliard
by Deanta Global Publishing Services Chennai, India

To my loving father, José Manuel Almeida,

who did not see this book come through completion but with whom I have learned so much.

Contents

List of figures	xi
List of tables	xii
Series forward	xiii
Acknowledgements	xv
Notations	xvi

Introduction	1

PART I
Foundations of an interdisciplinary approach   **7**

1	Conceptual foundations	9
2	Educational foundations	53
3	Methodological foundations	88

PART II
Applications of an interdisciplinary approach   **115**

4	Pre-departure	117
5	Adaptation	149
6	Outcomes and transformations	183

PART III
Implications of an interdisciplinary approach

217

7 Conclusions

219

Index

239

Figures

1.1	Conceptual diagram: macro organisers	15
1.2	Conceptual diagram: learning domains abroad	16
1.3	Conceptual diagram: variables informing study abroad	27
1.4	Conceptual diagram: global student dynamics and internationalisation of higher education	31
1.5	Conceptual diagram: long-term impact of study abroad	36
1.6	Conceptual diagram of student mobility research and scholarship in European higher education	41
2.1	Descriptor 5: direction of academic movement	59
3.1	Empirical studies: case study component	100
3.2	Empirical studies: procedural diagram	101
4.1	All sojourners: foreign languages learnt before the sojourn	120
4.2	Mobile students: motivations to study abroad	123
4.3	Mobile students: motivations to study in the host country	125
5.1	Mobile students: social contacts	153
5.2	Mobile students: social activities	164
5.3	All sojourners: host culture facilities	166
5.4	All sojourners: extent sojourners felt at home in the local community	167
5.5	Adaptation continuum	170
6.1	All sojourners: learning and developmental domains abroad	186
6.2	All sojourners: host language proficiency in the pre-experience questionnaire	190
6.3	All sojourners: host language proficiency in the post-experience questionnaire	191
6.4	Campus Europae students: host language learning variables	193
6.5	Intercultural curriculum development	199
6.6	Teaching and assessment frameworks	201
6.7	Compound development of intercultural sensitivity	208
6.8	Integrated or holistic view of intercultural communicative competence	210
7.1	Conceptual diagram of student mobility research and scholarship in European higher education	220
7.2	Major dichotomies of an interdisciplinary approach to understand student mobility	230

Tables

2.1	Common types of physical student mobility in European higher education	63
2.2	Objectives of the different iterations of Erasmus	74
2.3	Typological features of intercultural competence models	78
3.1	Features of mixed methods research	95
4.1	Operationalisation of mobility capital	127
4.2	Post-experience questionnaire: reliability of the intercultural competence scale	128
4.3	Mobility capital correlation matrix	129
4.4	Steps into mobility	133
4.5	Mobile students: perceptions about steps into mobility	134
5.1	Immigrants: social contacts	153
5.2	Mobile students: number of sojourner and hosts friends	154
5.3	All sojourners: level of difficulty in making friends with hosts	155
5.4	Mobile students: social activities offered by volunteer organisations	163
5.5	Mixed methods matrix: extent to which sojourners felt at home	171
6.1	All sojourners: ratings of the sojourn experience	185
6.2	*Campus Europae*, *Erasmus* and highly skilled immigrants: motivation to learn language issues	193
6.3	*Campus Europae*, *Erasmus* and highly skilled immigrants: intercultural impact of the intervention	204
6.4	Intercultural impact of the intervention: absence or paucity of intercultural gains	207

Series forward

This series addresses the rapidly changing and highly topical field of internationalisation in higher education. Increasingly visible in institutional strategies as well as national, regional and international agendas since the latter part of the twentieth century internationalisation has, in all its forms, been informed by diverse disciplines but continues to vary in interpretation. In part its rise can be seen as a response to globalisation and growing competition among higher education institutions. Indeed, use of the term 'internationalisation' itself is not uncontested, particularly when interpreted as neo-liberal, anglophone or post-colonial in orientation.

There are compelling drivers for university leaders to adopt an integrated approach to internationalisation. Intensifying competition for talent, changes in global student flows, international branch campuses and growing complexity in cross-border activity, along with the rising influence of institutional rankings, all provide economic impetus and reputational consequences of success or failure. However, interest in more values-driven rationales is increasingly evident, in part recognising the need to prepare students for changing local as well as global environments in both personal and professional life.

Student demand for international and intercultural experiences reflects growing employer interest in the knowledge, skills, attitudes and competencies which can result from these experiences. University leadership, academics and support staff must respond accordingly, with programmes and activities appropriate to societal change and a complex global landscape. Internationally informed research and collaborative partnerships can support teaching and learning processes which will help develop skills relevant for global contexts but which are equally important for living and working in diverse multicultural societies. Internationalisation thus has both global and more local intercultural interests at its heart.

Internationalisation as a powerful force for change and the enhancement of quality is an underlying theme of this series. It addresses the complex and varied topics arising as internationalisation continues to develop and grow. The series aims to reflect current concerns, with volumes written or edited by leading thinkers and authors from around the world, while giving a voice to emerging researchers. It examines some of the critical contemporary issues in the field of internationalisation, and offers theoretical perspectives with practical applications for higher education leaders, academics and practitioners alike.

This volume in the series advances a comprehensive theorisation of student mobility across Europe. Playing a key role in international higher education, mobility is frequently practised but has rarely been framed as a field of study in itself. The book takes a range of perspectives on the topic of mobility and provides a systematic analysis of the field. It also presents varied empirical research as the basis for its conclusions. The resulting conceptual and methodological framework provides a compelling case for taking an interdisciplinary approach to student mobility and signifies a step forward for both research and practice. Its focus on emphasising the educational value of mobility, and the importance of making learning outcomes clear and rewarding, offers a vital lesson for programme designers in an aspect of higher education which continues to dominate the internationalisation discourse in universities around the world.

Elspeth Jones, Series Editor
Emerita Professor of the Internationalisation of
Higher Education
Leeds Beckett University, UK

Acknowledgements

I would like to express my appreciation to Elspeth Jones and Routledge for making this opportunity possible. I am especially grateful to four people in particular for their support and invaluable insights in different aspects of this book. To: Elspeth Jones, series editor, my loving partner, Rui Aristides, who drew the illustrations symbolising Chapters 4 to 6, and my dear colleagues and friends, Mattia Baiutti and Cláudia Figueiredo.

I am also grateful to Mike Byram and Cultnet colleagues for their insights.

I would also like to thank my friends for their encouragement and for making Newcastle or the UK feel like home: Martyn Barrett, Michael Ramsay, François Sançon, Thais Oliveira, Cristina Becker Lopes, Conceição Pereira, Sarina Theys and Lydia Wysocki.

A final thank you goes to the Portuguese Foundation for Science and Technology and the Luso-American Development Foundation for the funding provided to carry out Study no.1 in this book, and to my PhD co-supervisor, Alvino Fantini, for his friendship and for being a huge reference in my academic career (Grazie mille!).

Last but not least, to the sojourners in this book without whom this book would not be possible. May the experiences of our students always inspire us to do better!

Notations

N	Frequency distribution
n	Number of valid responses
M	Mean
Mdn	Median
SD	Standard Deviation
Max	Maximum value
Min	Minimum value
α	Cronbach's alpha
p	Probability value
ρ	Spearman's rho
χ^2	Chi-square

Introduction

About this book

Understanding Student Mobility in Europe: An Interdisciplinary Approach is about interpreting student mobility in European higher education through an active dialogue between disciplines, voices and variables of interest.

Like intertextuality, a term popularised by Julia Kristeva to signify the ways in which (literary) texts are inescapably related to other texts, this book draws on a matrix of multiple meanings and was developed as a site of intersection of voices from different disciplines and sojourners (exchange students, international students and highly skilled immigrants). In a sense, then, in this volume I do not propose a new interpretation of student mobility per se; rather, a reinterpretation that seeks to find firm conceptual and methodological footing by contextualising the frames of reference through which we interpret student mobility.

This book can therefore be placed at a space between disciplines (hence the prefix 'inter' in interdisciplinary) that pushes the boundaries of disciplinary thinking to reinterpret the phenomenon of student mobility more comprehensively. Its ultimate goal is to produce an integrated account of this phenomenon by laying the foundations, practical applications and implications of an interdisciplinary approach. This approach is presented in the three parts in which the book is organised. Part I lays the foundational substructure in which an interdisciplinary approach is housed. Part II addresses questions of practical application by considering the experiences of 50 sojourners in Portugal and the United Kingdom (UK) through an interdisciplinary lens. Finally, Part III summarises the implications of interdisciplinarity for further reasoning and critical evaluation of the stock of knowledge about student mobility in European tertiary-level education.

Why an interdisciplinary approach?

Interdisciplinarity frames the approach to (physical) student mobility in this book. It responds to two immediate needs. First, it responds to the compartmentalisation of thought about student mobility by tracing the range of knowledge production and scholarship on this phenomenon. Second, it illuminates

2 Introduction

the blind spots or questions falling between disciplinary cracks by developing a more systematic and comprehensive understanding of student mobility. This comprehensive understanding is the ultimate goal of interdisciplinarity (Repko & Szostak, 2017), offering a broad base for an expanded agenda for theorising student mobility.

The need for this sort of approach is commensurate with the very essence of interdisciplinarity. Broadly speaking, interdisciplinarity offers a critical idiom that aims to produce a comprehensive account of complex multifaceted problems and/or phenomena wherein the host of different variables requires integrating insights from two or more disciplines (Lattuca, 2001; Moran, 2010; Repko & Szostak, 2017).

If we think about student mobility, and as the book will show, there are more than two disciplines interested in it, more than a single variable of interest and more than one legitimate way to look at it. The main argument behind this book is, thus, that the phenomenon of student mobility can be considered in an interdisciplinary sense because it is a complex problem (with multiple facets) and at least two disciplines have studied it or some aspect of it. Stated another way, a mono-disciplinary approach is insufficient to advance our understanding of student mobility as a complex whole.

Central to how interdisciplinarity is perceived in this book is the concept of integration[1] which is, in turn, key to distinguishing *interdisciplinarity* from *multidisciplinarity* and *transdisciplinarity*. While the intellectual essence of the academic field of interdisciplinary studies is outside the remit of this book, a few words regarding the use of these three terms are needed. Building on the work of the interdisciplinarians Repko and Szostak (2017), I use integration as the line of demarcation between the three terms, employed in this book with the following meanings:

- *interdisciplinarity* points to an integrated account of different disciplinary insights on complex problems and/or phenomena (in our case, this integrated account comes in the form of a renewed understanding of student mobility);
- *multidisciplinarity* involves the (mere) concatenation of different disciplinary insights, based on a relationship of proximity instead of integration;
- *transdisciplinary* involves integration of insights from inside and outside academia and often points to a unified meta-synthesis.

To frame these terms in the context of this book, student mobility is as yet just an area of multidisciplinary interest insofar as the perspectives from relevant disciplines eschew forms of close engagement or integration. In contrast, the interdisciplinary account that is sought aims to create a common ground between varied (and, at times, conflicting) disciplinary insights to speak with a joint voice on a problem of mutual interest – student mobility. While transcending disciplinary knowledge via integration, this monograph does not claim one single all-inclusive

Introduction   3

synthesis as in transdisciplinarity. My point is that the synthesis offered in the chapters that follow is not the only possible combination of disciplinary perspectives as, although I strove for the greatest degree of integration, the insights provided are also bound to the disciplines I can navigate across and may, thereby, be further expanded.

How?

The argument of this book is delivered across seven chapters which together lay the *foundations, applications* and *implications* of an interdisciplinary approach to student mobility. Hence the book's organisation into three interconnected parts. The underpinnings of this approach are laid in Part I and divided into *conceptual, educational* and *methodological* foundations, i.e., Chapters 1, 2 and 3, respectively.

The second part builds on the foundations set in early chapters by combining disciplinary theories to analyse the sojourn of 22 exchange students and 9 highly skilled immigrants in Portugal, and 19 international students in the UK. The integration of different theoretical frames, coupled with mixed methods (Chapter 3), aims to provide sustained responses to questions raised by the chronological instances of the sojourn. Specifically, Pre-departure (Chapter 4), Adaptation (Chapter 5) and Outcomes and Transformations (Chapter 6). These specific questions are, in turn, intertwined with a more general questioning about student mobility in European post-secondary education. The dialectic interplay between theories, methods and sojourner voices attests to the explanatory power of interdisciplinarity while illustrating how an interdisciplinary understanding of student mobility can be constructed, validated and communicated. The seventh and concluding chapter, in Part III, builds on this conception by identifying ten core premises that can leverage an interdisciplinary agenda for theorising student mobility in European higher education.

So that readers can easily follow the sequential nature of the narrative, summaries of individual chapters are provided and expanded with summary vignettes unpacking key points or offering additional information to the one contained in the body of the text. Readers will also be able to ascertain the usefulness of the chapters' key ideas to their own contexts and/or investigations through reflective questions and/or points at the end of each chapter. These questions and/or points can be also used by instructors of postgraduate courses addressing student mobility and the internationalisation of higher education.

For whom and by whom?

This book is intended for four audiences: academics and postgraduate students from any discipline who are interested in student mobility; education abroad practitioners; and policy-makers involved in cross-border higher education at institutional, national and supranational levels.

Through intertwining theoretical perspectives with practical applications, this monograph is of appeal to researchers and practitioners alike. However, academic audiences will likely be the ones reaping the most gains given the fast-evolving and self-contained repositories of disciplinary knowledge on student mobility accumulated from the mid-1990s on through the current decade. The breaking down of disciplinary knowledge into pockets of information is attuned to the integrative habit of mind needed for an interdisciplinary appreciation of student mobility. As a result, the book may be useful in the context of the burgeoning master's and doctoral programmes on the internationalisation of higher education (especially those programmes calling on their students to cross disciplinary boundaries). Its early chapters in particular may serve as a primary text for introductory courses on student mobility, its theorisation and role within the internationalisation of higher education.

The systematising of knowledge in this volume does not mean little attention is paid to what is happening in terms of practice. The contrary is true because besides deriving from the concrete experiences of 50 sojourners in two different countries, the book is designed to offer a guide on what should become the practice of theorising study abroad and, through it, more informed ways to promote quality study abroad experiences. The practical applications of an interdisciplinary approach in this book therefore mean the impact of (interdisciplinary) research on education abroad practice.

As education abroad evolves into an area of study, it becomes critically important to bridge the gap between theory and practice. Practitioners, in this book, are therefore not necessarily study abroad programme designers and implementers but all those professionals who have an interest in the practice of study abroad. They may also be scholar-practitioners in international higher education (Streitwieser & Ogden, 2016) who want to improve education abroad beyond the validation of disciplinary theories or the performance of routine administrative chores.

Given this backdrop, it comes as no surprise to the reader that this narrative is also a culmination of personal and professional reflections about student mobility over the 17 years that elapsed since I was an exchange student in England.

Social theory is not developed in a social vacuum and can involve something we know closely in our social lives. This has definitely been my case and, I believe, of a new generation of scholars who, having lived the experience of studying abroad, are now bringing new angles to student mobility and ways of interpreting it. In my case, these lenses have been formal, as a participant in the *Erasmus* programme, and informal as a former volunteer of the Erasmus Student Network.

Ten years into my exchange experience I had the opportunity to become a visiting scholar in the US and learn about study abroad beyond Europe. Four years later, I (re)entered England as an immigrant fleeing from unemployment in my home country, where the labour market is still at odds with ensuring returns on education to a highly qualified youth. The circumstances through which I entered England in 2003 and 2017 put me in a very different position towards the same host society, allowing me to see migration in a different light.

The 16,620 incoming *Erasmus* students I joined in 2003/2004 were certainly in a position of privilege compared to the circa 226,000 EU immigrants with whom I entered the UK in 2017.

All of this and the fact that I have family and friends who pursued PhDs in high-ranking institutions in the UK and secured stable careers abroad, made me question the extent to which my 'mobility capital' was suffice to pursue an international academic career. My temporary mobility experiences, while public funded, appeared not to be enough to cross the divide between credit and degree-seeking mobility and the type of career opportunities offered to each. A further question has been left in my mind ever since – in addition to social inequalities in enabling student mobility for all, are not there certain types of student mobility only accessible to some? In a way, this questioning justifies the comparison between the three types of sojourn the reader will come across in this book.

The other side of the story and the kaleidoscope of disciplinary mirrors readers will find throughout the book were, in part, triggered by my cultural immersion experiences. They gave me a sense of what to look for but also made me put the questions and variables relating to student mobility before my own disciplinary interests. The other part stems from my upbringing and academic choices. I was raised by a civil engineer and a language teacher, having started my professional career as a language teacher just like my mother. Coincidence or not, my sister followed my father's footsteps and studied civil engineering. In being closer to my mother's positioning and my sister to my father's, I always questioned the extent to which meaning-making is influenced by academic training.

This questioning was further heighted during my PhD in general education which allowed me to connect with colleagues with an interest in education but from varied academic backgrounds, from applied linguistics to physics, from educational psychology to biology, to mention but a few. With the restructuring of higher education qualifications introduced by the Bologna process in Europe, my PhD also encompassed a three-year doctoral programme in (educational) evaluation and, through my own initiative, I pursued international education as a visiting scholar in the US. Albeit germane, these disciplines (and their disciplinary statuses) produced conflicting normative and institutional expectations which I learned to reconcile by creating what in interdisciplinary research is commonly known as common ground. My experiential interest in student mobility did the rest by instilling in me the necessary perspective to look into as many disciplinary windows as determined by student mobility itself. To a certain extent, just like in intertextuality a text only exists in relation to other texts, interdisciplinarity comes about through its relation to disciplines. The same can be said about this book and the confluence of disciplinary views on student mobility it houses.

I hope you enjoy reading it.

J. A.

Nelas, Portugal

Note

1 Although integration is considered a marker of interdisciplinarity, it is also interpreted differently by interdisciplinarians – e.g., Moran (2010) sees integration loosely as any form of interaction or dialogue, whereas Lattuca (2001) defines it according to the sort of questions asked by those pursuing interdisciplinarity. There are also interdisciplinarians who contest integration on the grounds that epistemological divides between disciplines impede an all-inclusive synthesis or that different disciplinary combinations would lead to multiple syntheses (see Repko & Szostak, 2017 for further information). My personal understanding is closer to Repko and Szostak's (2017), since I see integration as an explicit process whereby conceptual and methodological assumptions can be purposefully dismantled and/or modified to create new meaning.

References

Lattuca, L. (2001). *Creating interdisciplinarity: Interdisciplinary research and teaching among college and university faculty*. Nashville, TN: Vanderbilt University Press.

Moran, J. (2010). *Interdisciplinarity*. Oxon: Routledge.

Repko, A., & Szostak, R. (2017). *Interdisciplinary research: Process and theory* (3rd ed.). Thousand Oaks, CA: Sage.

Streitwieser, B., & Ogden, A. (2016). *International higher education's scholar-practitioners: Bridging research and practice*. Southampton: Symposium Books.

Part I

Foundations of an interdisciplinary approach

Chapter 1

Conceptual foundations

About Chapter 1

Student mobility plays a major role in contemporary higher education at educational, policy and research levels.

The millions of students on the move worldwide has sparked interest in the academic, demographic, psychological and socio-cultural variables that characterise student mobility in higher education, bringing about a plethora of publications, resources and professional forums. However, this host of new publications has not been accompanied by appropriate theorisation of student mobility as an area of study and professional practice. This is particularly notable in European higher education.

Given this backdrop, this chapter outlines the conceptual lenses for approaching student mobility comprehensively from a theoretical standpoint. To this end, I propose a fourfold conceptual diagram to account for the variables characterising student mobility in European post-secondary education. This conceptual diagram is organised into four macro descriptors which also correspond to the chapter sections: (1) Learning domains abroad, (2) Variables informing study abroad, (3) Global student dynamics and higher education internationalisation and (4) Long-term impact of study abroad. Each descriptor unfolds into variables or research foci that build from a range of disciples and subject areas to produce an interdisciplinary account of student mobility in European higher education. Summary vignettes will be provided across chapter sections to systematise the variables informing the conceptual descriptors.

To conclude, a summary of the main key points is provided. This is followed by a number of reflective questions and/or points that will help readers apply the chapter ideas to their own contexts and review their work or professional practice (see Box 1.6).

Student mobility: a kaleidoscope of different images

Like a kaleidoscope that produces multiple images by means of mirrors reflecting constantly changing patterns, student mobility calls for multiple perspectives.

10 Foundations of an interdisciplinary approach

The different modalities of student mobility and the complexity of the study abroad experience requires transcending the limits of disciplinary boundaries and normative reasoning through a wide-angle lens that captures the polymorphous nature of this phenomenon. Not that disciplinary boundaries are unimportant, but they may confine how wide our reading lens is.

In this book I make the case that while the ideologies shaping disciplinary discourses and knowledge presentation are a prerequisite for examining social phenomena, they may as well restrict the cross-fertilisation of perspectives, theories and ideas. One of the major goals of this book is to develop an awareness of the multifarious disciplines and theories informing knowledge about student mobility. Ultimately, I seek to show to the reader how and why such interconnectedness should become part of an expanded agenda for theorising student mobility.

Although the call that I advocate here is not exactly new, it is generally forgotten in specialised publications about the internationalisation of higher education, in general, and student mobility, in particular. From a research standpoint, throughout the two past decades or so scholars from different scientific fields and geographical contexts stressed the need to theorise and/or approach academic mobility (student and staff) from different perspectives (e.g., Barber, Altbach, & Myers, 1984; Byram & Dervin, 2008; Murphy-Lejeune, 2002, 2008; Streitwieser, 2012; Teichler, 1996; Wächter, Lam, & Ferencz, 2012; Whalen, 2012). And yet, the question of how student mobility can be analysed more comprehensively remains to be answered. The present chapter aims to provide sustained responses to this question while the chapters in the second part of the book offer practical applications of this interdisciplinary approach. To this end, I now lay the conceptual foundations for understanding student mobility comprehensively, turning to its educational and methodological underpinnings in Chapters 2 and 3, respectively. Before laying the conceptual groundwork, another few words of contextualisation are needed.

In the Western world, the demand to understand student mobility in collaborative and multi-modal ways has been emphasised at either side of the Atlantic. From a North American–based perspective, in 1984, Barber and colleagues called upon practitioners, policy-makers and academic researchers to combine forces in examining foreign study and its ramifications in more complex ways. More recently, in Canada, Larsen (2016) proposed a theoretical framework based on spatial, network and mobilities theories to shift from a linear account of higher education internationalisation to a multi-centred one. This analytical shift underlines the spatial and relational dimension of student mobility. Similarly, in Europe, Van Mol (2014) employed a systems approach theory (of migration) to provide a relational understanding of the nexus between social context and individual agency in intra-European student mobility.

Earlier, in Europe, Teichler (1996) voiced the urge for systematic research on the international dimension of higher education and academic mobility. Twelve years later, the interculturalists Michael Byram and Fred Dervin edited two volumes to develop a more focused field of study concerned with student and staff mobility (Byram & Dervin, 2008; Dervin & Byram, 2008). In the former book,

Murphy-Lejeune's (2008) chapter argues that student mobility is a transdisciplinary domain where different disciplinary voices may be heard. She exemplifies with 'voices' from sociology, international politics, economics and social anthropology; that is, the first generation of studies (in the 1990s) about student mobility in European higher education.

In 2012, the monograph series of the Academic Cooperation Association, in Brussels, released a book (Wächter et al., 2012) underscoring the need to avoid a 'single-issue view' of international higher education by tying together academic mobility, excellence, social inclusion and funding. In that same year, Streitwieser (2012) edited a special issue, in the *Journal of Research in Comparative and International Education*, warranting more articulation between international and comparative education to approach global student mobility in theoretical and empirically sound ways. In this same issue, the founding editor of the first academic journal on study abroad (*Frontiers: The Interdisciplinary Journal of Study Abroad*) called for more scholarly analyses of education abroad to advance the field (see Whalen, 2012).

While international education matters and study abroad are active areas of professional practice and research inquiry, its knowledge base is scattered among a bewildering plethora of specialised and non-specialised resources. An overview of specialised resources is provided in Box 1.1.

Inquiries about student mobility can also be found in non-specialised outlets, including academic journals publishing occasional papers or special issues on international education matters. The array of journals publishing research about student mobility is as wide as the disciplines feeding this area of study. While this may enrich inquiries about international education and student mobility, it makes it difficult for the reader to take stock of relevant publications and studies. From an academic standpoint, it is challenging to identify a pool of scholars devoted solely to this field as much research is produced by scholars who have an interest in this area but whose field of scientific inquiry is another. In practical terms, this leads to publications which do not always have continuation or bring about implications for further research and practice.

Box 1.1 – Specialised resources on the internationalisation of higher education and academic mobility (student and staff)

1. Academic journals devoted to different aspects of the internationalisation of higher education (e.g., *Journal of Studies in International Education*) or focusing on study abroad in particular (e.g., *Frontiers: The Interdisciplinary Journal of Study Abroad* and, more recently, the *Journal of International Students*).
2. Books series about the internationalisation of higher education (e.g., the Routledge series this book is part of), individual books and handbooks addressing topics related to student and staff mobility (e.g., Bista, 2019;

Blumenthal, Goodwin, Smith, & Teichler, 1996; Byram & Dervin, 2008; Byram & Feng, 2006; Dervin & Byram, 2008; Lewin, 2009; Murphy-Lejeune, 2002; Papatsiba, 2003; Streitwieser, 2014; Velliaris & Coleman-George, 2018) as well as to international education in general (e.g., Hayden, Thompson, & Levy, 2015) and international higher education in particular (e.g., Deardorff, de Wit, Heyl, & Adams, 2012).

3. Listservs for study abroad professionals (e.g., SECUSS-L, www.secussl. info), online newspapers reporting on international higher education (e.g., University World News, www.universityworldnews.com).

4. Professional organisations dedicated to international education matters in general (e.g., The Association of International Educators and the Association of International Education Administrators in the USA – NAFSA and AIEA, respectively, The European Association for International Education in Europe – EAIE) and study abroad in particular (e.g., the Forum on Education Abroad – FEA – in the USA).

5. Academic associations (e.g., the Academic Cooperation Association – ACA, the European University Association – EUA), research networks (e.g., the International Education Research Network – IERN) and databases (e.g., the Database of Research on International Education – IDP). Both academic and professional associations host conferences, seminars and trainings on various international education issues. These associations often have blogs, newsletters, professional textbooks or resources and paper series, some of which are available for download – e.g., the ACA Papers on International Cooperation in Education.

6. Master's and doctoral programmes, research institutes and centres.

7. Intergovernmental organisations (like the OECD, UNESCO) and their overview publications about the state of education, its international dimension and statistics of student mobility flows.

8. Student organisations like the Erasmus Student Network (ESN, www. esn.org) and the European Students' Union (ESU, www.esu-online. org) overview publications and research projects on various student mobility-related issues.

9. Annotated bibliographies developed by individuals or organisations – e.g., The FEA bibliography on education abroad outcomes assessment (www.forumea.org), the NAFSA education abroad bibliography (www. nafsa.org), the Global Center for Education Abroad annotated bibliography (http://globaledresearch.com/). There are also discipline-specific bibliographies or reference lists like the selected reference list *on study abroad and language learning* provided by the Research Foundation for English Language Education (TIRF, www.tirfonline.org/).

10. Blogs by education abroad professionals or scholars (e.g., David Comp's blog, https://davidcomp.wordpress.com/).

As Box 1.1 demonstrates, there is no dearth of literature on the internationalisation of higher education and student mobility. The list provided is not exhaustive but illustrative. For a more comprehensive review of specialised resources on international education research, primarily from a European perspective, the reader is referred to de Wit and Urias (2012). An overview of research devoted to education abroad is only available from a North American perspective (see Ogden, 2015; Ogden & Streitwieser, 2017).

The point here is that altogether specialist and lay resources mirror the diversity of themes, conceptual organisers, methodologies and findings relevant to understanding higher education internationalisation and academic mobility. This is particularly evident in edited volumes and, to some extent, special issues of academic journals. In fact, the range of edited volumes about academic mobility cannot pass unnoticed. For instance, all but two of the ten books about academic mobility in Point 2 of Box 1.1 are edited volumes.

Notwithstanding the value of edited books in reading academic mobility from different conceptual and methodological standpoints, these compilations often fail to theorise student mobility as an area of study. Added to this, the cartography of the conceptual maps offered by edited books is frequently left to interpretation, not to mention that many volumes tend to combine study abroad with other conceptual organisers. For example, the well-known handbook about study abroad in higher education (see Lewin, 2009) is coupled with the quest for global citizenship, which conceptual organiser assumes more prominence leaves ample room for discussion.

Against this backdrop, it is crucial that some edited volumes go beyond a goal unto themselves or an outcome of a given conference or preset research agenda. Edited books about academic mobility are at their best when the sum is greater than the parts; more specifically, when they offer novel syntheses or advance the knowledge base of student mobility. While the aggregation of chapters or papers can help establish the presence of an emerging area of study in the primary literature, once such a field achieves considerable maturity it becomes important to systematise what has been accomplished so far. The paucity of literature about student mobility is seldom a problem. If anything, the opposite is normally the case, with individuals (I include myself here) finding it hard to keep up with the widely dispersed sources. Secondary literature and systematic literature reviews can be very helpful in this respect as shown by large-scale reviews of research into the internationalisation of higher education (e.g., Bedenlier, Kondakci, & Zawacki-Richter, 2018; Yemini & Sagie, 2016). This leads me to questioning the following:

> If research on the internationalisation of higher education has grown into a distinct field in recent decades, should not student mobility be further theorised as well?

I argue the case for a positive answer, not least because in the absence of appropriate theoretical innovation and analytical categories, we run the risk of providing

14 Foundations of an interdisciplinary approach

ill-articulated analyses of student mobility. It is also here where an interdisciplinary approach has a role to play via the intertwinement of disconnected literatures and theoretical strands, discussed next.

An interdisciplinary approach in student mobility

Given the dispersed knowledge of student mobility, a systematic way of finding relevant literature is to map key themes. Identifying these thematic areas is crucial to change the mono-disciplinary lenses through which we tend to interpret student mobility. First, because it allows us to systematise its knowledge base more comprehensively while breaking normative umbrellas. The second reason derives from the first in that the rupture with disciplinary reasoning can amplify our analytical capacity and enable a more relational understanding of student mobility. It is in this relational understanding where the analytical power of an interdisciplinary approach resides. Part of this understanding entails systematising and categorising existing literature about student mobility.

European literature reveals notable gaps in this regard, with little or no attempts to compile and review studies of student mobility. The same cannot be said regarding study abroad in the US, since much research has been compiled and reviewed as demonstrated by the examples in Point 9 in Box 1.1. Also noteworthy is the bibliography by Comp, Gladding, Rhodes, Stephenson, and Vande Berg (2007) for the Forum on Education Abroad. This bibliography groups studies of education abroad assessment into research foci and variables of interest.

Given the knowledge gaps in European literature, and building on some of the categories advanced by Comp et al. (2007) and Ogden (2015), in this chapter I propose a conceptual diagram that can assist readers, whether practitioners or scholars, in charting the variables characterising (physical) student mobility in European post-secondary education. The ultimate goal is to produce an interdisciplinary account of student mobility that draws from a broad range of disciplines and subject areas. To this end, I will bring together sample studies from various disciplinary perspectives and research foci to abstract from that very literature and set a framework for continued abstracting.

Sample studies will be identified according to variables of interest and posited against the multifarious theories and disciplines feeding research and practice about study abroad. Examples stem from North American and European literature to foster a dialogue of interest to both readerships. For readers based outside Europe, it is hoped this comparative perspective enhances their grasp of the particulars of student mobility in Europe. For those readers based in the European continent, the systematic comparison of the knowledge base on either side of the Atlantic may stimulate a more fine-grained understanding of student mobility beyond European higher education (as part of an expanded agenda for its theorisation). Historical synopses will thread throughout the discussion to put studies in context while reflecting upon study abroad developments on both sides of the ocean.

Conceptual foundations 15

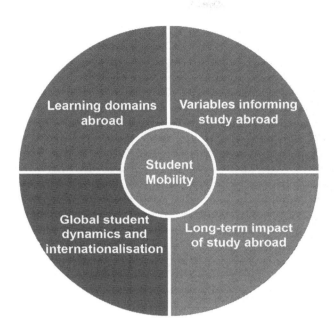

Figure 1.1 Conceptual diagram: macro organisers.

The overarching conceptual diagram in Figure 1.1 is structured into four macro organisers: (1) Learning domains abroad, (2) Variables informing study abroad, (3) Global student dynamics and higher education internationalisation and (4) Long-term impact of study abroad.

In each macro organiser the reader will find different themes or variables related to the student experience across the study abroad cycle, i.e., pre-departure, in-country and re-entry phases. Due to the confluence of a large number of variables, the conceptual organisers will be broken down into four pieces corresponding to four individual but interdependent figures (see Figures 1.2, 1.3, 1.4 and 1.5). The full conceptual diagram is provided in Appendix 1.1.

Learning domains abroad

Learning domains abroad tend to address three key spheres: second language acquisition, intercultural and disciplinary learning. The last component stems primarily from North-American literature as will be discussed later in this section.

Language learning in study abroad is a widely studied topic insofar as enhanced foreign language abilities are posited as a key learning outcome of studying in another country.

Research on language learning abroad is usually rooted in language education or pedagogy (foreign and second), applied linguistics and theories of second

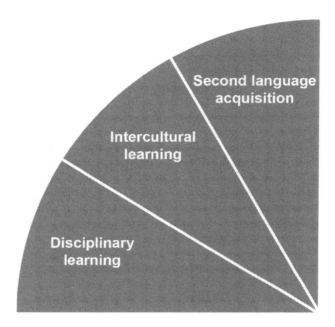

Figure 1.2 Conceptual diagram: learning domains abroad.

language acquisition (SLA). These kinds of study grew considerably in the mid-1990s, mostly since Freed's (1995) volume *Second Language Acquisition in a Study Abroad Context* brought attention to this strand of SLA research. More recently, the strong interest of applied linguists and language professionals in study abroad led to an SLA journal on the role of study abroad in language learning and educational development – *Study Abroad Research in Second Language Acquisition and International Education* (Amsterdam: John Benjamins). Another outlet of reference work within this research strand is made available by the Research Foundation for English Language Education (TIRF, www.tirfonline.org/) through its reference list on study abroad and language learning (on TIRF's webpage click on the tabs 'Resources & References'→ 'Reference lists'→ select the letter 'S'→ scroll down until you find *Study Abroad and Language Learning*).

As noted by Kinginger (2017), research on language learning in study abroad varies in scope but can be broadly divided into two research foci: outcomes and process-oriented research. In other words, two lines of research coexist focusing on the type of linguistic abilities acquired by mobile learners, and how the host context and socialisation processes shape language learning.

Investigations span the four modalities of language learning – listening, speaking, writing and reading – and underlying abilities, with early studies addressing primarily gains of proficiency and fluency via quantitative methods and standardised instruments as demonstrated by the work of Carrol (1967), in the US, and Willis (1977) in Europe. Recent research brings heightened attention to the contextual conditions in which language learning takes place, the individual variables and learning pathways of mobile learners (e.g., Collentine & Freed, 2004; Dufon & Churchill, 2006; Jackson, 2008; Kinginger, 2013; Mitchell, Tracy-Ventura, & McManus, 2017, 2015; Pellegrino Aveni, 2005; Regan, Howard, & Lemée, 2009; Segalowitz et al., 2004). Qualitative research methods are, thus, preferred.

These 'extra-linguistic' factors can comprise learning strategies and socio-cognitive constructs like learner self-esteem, anxiety, motivation, as well as socio-cultural aspects relating to socio-cultural theory and language socialisation in study abroad. Examples include studies ascertaining the socio-cultural variables influencing sojourner language gains, such as: contact with hosts (e.g., Freed, Segalowitz, & Dewey, 2004), social circles (e.g., Coleman, 2015) and type of social networks (e.g., Isabelli-García, 2006), difficulties in cultural adaption (e.g., Beaven & Spencer-Oatey, 2016), the effect of communities of practice (e.g., Bracke & Aguerre, 2015), the 'advantage' of the homestay (e.g., Diao, Freed, & Smith, 2011). This second generation of SLA studies about study abroad is usually guided by socio-cultural perspectives and post-communicative approaches following the cultural turn in the latter half of the twentieth century. This shift brought culture and socially oriented approaches to the centre of academic debates in the humanities and social sciences. Naturally, this brought implications for study abroad research.

One implication is the strand of studies intersecting language and intercultural learning in sojourner contexts. In Europe and North America, these kinds of study have been commonly developed by interculturalists, applied linguists and language educators with an interest in study abroad. Among these studies one can find investigations adopting communicative models of intercultural competence. The aim of these models is to explore language and intercultural learning in tandem on the assumption that these types of learning are inextricably linked. These and other intercultural constructs will be taken up in the next chapter. For now, suffice it to say that intercultural communicative models like the ones advanced by Byram (1997), in Europe, and Fantini (2006a), in the US, brought about investigations across different contexts where this competence can be acquired, including in immersion contexts (e.g., Almarza, Martínez, & Llavador, 2015; Alred & Byram, 2002; Alred, Byram, & Fleming, 2003; Byram & Feng, 2006; Fantini, 2006b, 2019).

Intercultural learning and development in study abroad spans various disciplines, from applied linguistics to language education, anthropology, business and management, psychology, intercultural education, comparative and international education, to name but a few. Numerous are the investigations addressing intercultural learning in immersion contexts, whatever the targeted construct may be (e.g., intercultural maturity, intercultural sensitivity, intercultural communicative competence, intercultural communication competence, cross-cultural effectiveness). Examination of these constructs in study abroad has varied from exploratory, to explanatory and intervention purposes. For some scholars and practitioners, study abroad offered a rich context to understand or explain intercultural learning and development. For others, it was more than a rich context but an endeavour that required intervening in student intercultural learning (e.g., Jackson, 2018; Jackson & Oguro, 2017; Vande Berg, 2007; Vande Berg & Paige, 2009; Vande Berg, Paige, & Lou, 2012a). Among the earliest strands of study abroad research, intervention studies go beyond scholarly wok given their roots in cross-cultural training.

These studies enjoy a long tradition in the US, dating back to the 1950s and 1960s particularly through the work of the Foreign Service Institute and the Peace Corps. From the 1970s on through the 1990s, these approaches were increasingly utilised when intercultural studies expanded to include academic and study abroad programmes. As a result, the need to develop intercultural competence among mobile students flourished across tertiary institutions and study abroad organisations in North America (Sinicrope, Norris, & Watanabe, 2006). It is no coincidence that the first edition of the *Handbook of Intercultural Training* was released in 1983 (see Landis & Brislin, 1983a, 1983b).

An early example of study abroad trainings at tertiary-level education in the US is the University of the Pacific's *Cross-Cultural Training Program*. Designed by the cultural anthropologist Bruce La Brack, in the 1970s, this programme sought to address the intercultural challenges faced by university students upon studying abroad (see La Brack, 1993), and is still offered today as two pre-departure and re-entry courses for credit. These courses also provided the basis for the online intercultural resource *What's Up with Culture?* (https://www2.pacific.edu/sis/culture/).

Another early example encompasses the School for International Training (SIT Graduate Institute) intercultural academic programmes and its field-based study abroad programmes for undergraduate students (SIT Study Abroad). The academic arm of one of the earliest student exchange organisations in the US and forerunner of the homestay – The Experiment in International Living (World Learning Inc.) – this graduate institute continues to extend the philosophy of intercultural contact and world peace of the Experiment since its foundation in 1932 (World Learning, 2000).

Throughout time, other intercultural initiatives within study abroad emerged in North American post-secondary education, either at individual level or under the scope of research projects like *Maximizing Study Abroad through Language and Culture Strategies* (MAXSA). Dating back to the 1990s, this research project was developed at the University of Minnesota. As with many other intervention studies, *Maximizing Study Abroad* was centred on curriculum development to support and enhance the linguistic and intercultural gains of mobile students. Hence the instructional materials developed which include three different textbooks targeting: (a) students (see Paige, Cohen, Kappler, Chi, & Lassegard, 2002b), (b) study abroad professionals (see Paige, Cohen, Kappler, Chi, & Lassegard, 2002a) and (c) language instructors (see Cohen et al., 2003).

Maintaining the calendar in the 1990s, we can also find intercultural learning courses at Willamette and Bellarmine universities. Initially focused on offering intercultural curricula for US outbound students, these courses paved the way for the development of the Bosley/Lou Intentional Targeted Intervention Model in 2004. This model came to address the intercultural learning needs of both incoming and outgoing mobile students (see Lou & Bosley, 2012). To this end, Gabrielle Bosley and Kris Lou interlocked face-to-face and online modes of delivery through learning communities of instructors and students situated in different cultural contexts around the world.

In the European continent the calls to rethink policies and practices in student mobility and view intercultural learning as foundational are essentially an outcome of the current and past decade. To the best of my knowledge, among the first European systematic initiatives of this kind is a series of three research projects funded by the Higher Education Funding Council for England, from 1997 to 2001, and collectively known as *Residence Abroad Matters*. Led by three British universities, these projects sought to identity, evaluate and promote best practices in residence abroad, including in intercultural learning (Coleman & Klapper, 2005). They were: *Learning and Residence Abroad* (LARA), the *Interculture Project* (ICP), the *Residence Abroad Project* (RAPORT). Embedded in modern language degrees in countries like the UK, residence abroad can be a slippery term and a deeper analysis of it and related terminology will be conducted in Chapter 2.

More recently, research efforts like the *Intercultural Educational Resources for Erasmus Students and their Teachers* (IEREST, www.ierest-project) and *Erasmus Mundus Intercultural Competence* (EMIC, www.emic-project) were designed to develop pedagogical outputs and/or learning toolkits to enhance the intercultural abilities of mobile learners. Both efforts are multilateral projects funded by the European Commission and addressing its education abroad programmes. Whereas the IEREST addresses *Erasmus* students' needs (and their teachers), EMIC caters for *Erasmus Mundus* students. Both are also relatively recent projects which began in 2012 and 2013, respectively, and finished in 2015. The timing here is no coincidence as these kinds of initiative are relatively new in Europe.

While purposeful intercultural pedagogy in student mobility is advocated by a growing number of European scholars (e.g., Almeida, Fantini, Simões, & Costa, 2016; Anquetil, 2006; Baiutti, 2017, 2018; Beaven & Borghetti, 2015, 2016; Byram & Feng, 2006; Carroll, 2015; Dervin, 2008; Shaules, 2007; Strong, 2011), intercultural interventions in Europe tend to happen haphazardly, making it extremely difficult to trace them. Two edited volumes in the Routledge series of which this book is part make a valuable contribution in this regard by aggregating case studies promoting intercultural learning in higher education in general (Deardorff & Arasaratnam-Smith, 2017) and study abroad in particular (Jackson & Oguro, 2017). Although the scope of these volumes is worldwide, examples of intercultural interventions with mobile students in Europe can be found across both. Also noteworthy is the monograph by Jackson (2018), centred on online

20 Foundations of an interdisciplinary approach

intercultural interventions, and the edited volume by Borghetti and Beaven (2018) with studies developed within the IEREST project.

To summarise, whereas in Europe the counter-narrative to the view that mobile students learn interculturally by simply going abroad seems to be taking its first steps, in the US this narrative has grown to a point wherein Vande Berg, Paige, and Lou (2012b) advocate a paradigm shift in study abroad. Posited as a three-paradigm progression, this shift of assumptions is based on evolving accounts of the nature of knowing, teaching and learning in study abroad – from positivism to relativism, to the current experiential/constructivist narrative. The positivist paradigm is premised on the notion that learning occurs by exposure to cultural difference, whereas the relativist narrative acknowledges structure in study abroad design, namely by employing cultural immersion strategies (e.g., homestays) that maximise contact with the host environment (ibid.). The current experiential/constructivist paradigm views intercultural learning in study abroad as experiential, developmental and holistic, requiring a balance between challenge and effective educational support.

Altogether, sample studies of language acquisition and intercultural learning remind us of two types of learning gains studying abroad should produce: linguistic and intercultural. Nevertheless, both lines of inquiry do also cast doubt on the traditional view that mobile learners typically make remarkable gains in these learning dimensions. Two questions arise:

Is the sole purpose of study abroad mostly linguistic and intercultural?
What about the disciplinary dimension and discipline-specific skills?

In answering these questions, in the last paragraphs of this section I will explore this other dimension of student learning abroad. As a learning domain, disciplinary achievement abroad is often overshadowed by personal development. The specialised and lay literature provides us with a handful of student statements emphasising the transformative power of study abroad and how personal growth and autonomy can outweigh proficiency in a given subject matter.

Student satisfaction surveys do also forefront the broad division of the study abroad experience into personal and academic gains. In Europe, early *Erasmus* survey studies reflect this rough division or slightly finer categorisations of personal, academic, linguistic and cultural achievements (see Teichler & Maiworm, 1997). According to the evaluation conducted by Teichler and Maiworm of the first eight years of the European Union (EU) flagship exchange scheme, the academic front is depicted as an increase of the knowledge base, in terms of theories, methods and enhanced reflection. However, many surveys funded by the EU to evaluate *Erasmus* have measured academic attainment via logistic and administrative aspects of recognition of the period of studies abroad. The longitudinal evaluation by Teichler and Maiworm reflects this conception in using the formal integration of learning results from the period abroad into home study programmes as a measure of academic success. This measure is coupled with student self-ratings of academic

Conceptual foundations   21

progress at the host institution (compared to study at home) as well as subsequent study and employment opportunities. And yet, two fundamental questions remain:

> What are mobile students learning academically abroad? Or, are they meant to be academically adrift?

The paucity of investigations seeking to answer these questions reflects my inability to point out sample studies assessing the academic gains of student mobility in European higher education. This is particularly true for credit-seeking student mobility, i.e., students moving across national borders to pursue credits as recognition of the period of studies abroad. Two unstated assumptions underlie this reality. First, the academic value of student mobility is often taken for granted, overshadowed by participant metrics or anecdotal accounts of personal maturation. A deeper analysis of this assumed value will take place in Chapter 2, where I argue that the academic value of student mobility in European higher education should be clarified and acted upon.

The second assumption relates to policy discourse and how it has shaped public perceptions of course accreditation in study abroad as a synonym for academic success. There is something fundamentally different between positing academic recognition as a variable with a bearing on learning abroad and as a measure of educational attainment. In its simplest form, academic recognition is a mechanism used to facilitate the award of academic credits when studying abroad. I take this argument up in the next section where I outline other variables informing the three major learning domains of studying abroad. Before doing so, and to systematise knowledge, a summary vignette of key terminology and/or points in this section is provided in Box 1.2.

Box 1.2 – Summary vignette: learning domains abroad

- **Second language acquisition/language learning** – acquisition of knowledge, skills and/or experiences relevant to learn a language (typically, the host language) throughout the study abroad cycle. It involves predispositions and mediating variables.
- **Intercultural learning** – acquisition of knowledge, skills and/or experiences relevant to learn (inter)cultural aspects, either culture-specific (dealing with a given culture, typically the host culture) or culture-general (dealing with several cultures) throughout the study abroad cycle. It involves predispositions and mediating variables.
- **Academic learning** – acquisition of knowledge, skills and/or experiences related to learning a given subject matter throughout the study abroad cycle. In credit-seeking student mobility, this type of learning is usually bound to a student's home study programme (e.g., an undergraduate degree in psychology). It involves predispositions and mediating variables.

22 Foundations of an interdisciplinary approach

Variables informing study abroad

As discussed in the previous section, there are tensions between the purpose, function, delivery and assessment of study abroad. Note that by delivery I mean the ways in which study abroad is enacted.

These tensions affect the identification of variables informing study abroad and their relative importance across disciplines and scholarly communities interested in education abroad. For instance, the delivery and assessment of programmatic types of study abroad in higher education are largely under-researched in Europe where exchange programme design and delivery does not even emerge as a line of inquiry. This is possibly because exchange schemes in European higher education are yet to go beyond bi/multilateral institutional agreements.

In making this case, I am relying not only on the vast North American literature on study abroad programme design, but also on the voices of the 50 sojourners behind this book. I will disclose the literary premises first and then foreground them in the words of participants in Part II of this book.

Different design features or components of study abroad programmes may influence student learning and experiences abroad. These features encompass:

1. programme duration;
2. interventions, trainings and/or orientations;
3. programme evaluation and assessment;
4. curriculum design and integration;
5. grading policies and recognition of studies;
6. opportunities for contact with hosts and/or the host culture;
7. type of housing.

All programme components are here discussed and illustrated with sample studies retrieved primarily from the specialised North American literature.

Programme duration is a widely held piece of conventional wisdom about study abroad, often translated into the adage 'more is better'. Simply put, the longer the sojourn abroad, the greater the personal and academic gains reaped by mobile learners. Framed as a question: Does programme duration necessarily translate into more learning? To explore the role of this programmatic feature in student learning, Dwyer (2004) compared the impact of study abroad programmes of varying length on the learning outcomes of 3,700 alumni from the Institute for International Education of Students. Results from this longitudinal study confirm that although the premise 'more is better' holds true, shorter duration programmes can also enhance sojourner gains when properly designed. Recent research (e.g., McGourty, 2014; Mellors-Bourne, Jones, Lawton, & Woodfield, 2015) challenges further this adage by demonstrating that programme duration does not necessarily correlate positively with (more) gains as short and longer mobility periods can yield similar impacts.

Another (sub)group of studies on programme duration includes: the expansion of short-term study abroad in the US (e.g., Chieffo & Griffiths, 2009) and elsewhere (e.g., the increase of short-term outbound mobility from Australia to the Indo-Pacific Region – see Malicki, 2012), comparison between the learning gains of participants in short programme durations and their home counterparts (e.g., Chieffo & Griffiths, 2004) and specialist resources for designing these programmes (e.g., Chieffo & Spaeth, 2017; Pasquarelli, Cole, & Tyson, 2018).

With respect to the second component – interventions, trainings and/or orientations – interventions have traditionally addressed intercultural learning (as demonstrated in the previous section). In university education in the US, designing and embedding interventions, trainings and/or orientations into study abroad programming gained prominence from the 1970s on through the 1990s. The importance of intervening in student learning abroad gained renewed emphasis in recent years. The edited volume by Vande Berg et al. (2012a) has been instrumental in this regard by providing the conceptual foundations for an interventionist approach in US study abroad.

By contrast, European higher education intervention studies (particularly in the intercultural domain) are relatively recent and focused mainly on the development of pedagogical materials or learning pathways. Ironically, programmatic student mobility in Europe constitutes a fertile ground for implementing intentional intercultural teaching-and-learning as it is closely bound to EU supranational exchange schemes and its participant countries.

The third component of programmatic study abroad in our list is programme evaluation and assessment. That is, the extent to which study abroad programmes incorporate monitoring and evaluation systems that: (1) judge the overall quality of study abroad programmes, and (2) assess how well student learning goals and/or outcomes are achieved as result of participation in these programmes. Rooted in educational evaluation theory, programme evaluation and outcomes assessment in education abroad is a burgeoning line of inquiry emerging in response to the calls for accountability and accreditation in higher education and its internationalisation processes (Aerden, 2015, 2017; de Wit, 2009; Deardorff, 2015; Green, 2012; Hudzik & Stohl, 2009; Jones, 2013). This growing interest in evaluation processes is common to tertiary education in the US and Europe, even if in the latter it has not led to an active area of research in study abroad. But before moving forward, I need to clarify what I mean by evaluation which I see as an applied inquiry process, and transdisciplinary domain, entailing an empirical and normative aspect in order to determine the value of something (Fournier, 2005).

In the US, the seminal work of Engle and Engle (2003) gave impetus to evaluation in education abroad and assessment of its learning outcomes by classifying study abroad programmes according to independent variables. Their classification enabled the transition from a mono-centred study abroad classification system, organised into programme types, to a multi-centred one (Comp et al., 2007; Ogden, 2015). Based on the premise that the extent to which programme design facilitates interaction with the host culture is what most distinguishes one study

24 Foundations of an interdisciplinary approach

abroad programme from another, Engle and Engle identified seven programme characteristics squarely grounded on student learning. In doing so, they facilitated the comparison of learning outcomes fostered by study abroad programmes according to a common measurement system (Comp et al., 2007). This new classification, coupled with the increasing pressure for post-secondary institutions to document what students are learning, triggered an array of studies about study abroad assessment (e.g., Bolen, 2007; Engle, 2013; Savicki & Brewer, 2015; West, 2015). The diversity of these studies is such that the Forum on Education Abroad created an Outcomes Assessment Toolbox which includes a bibliography of studies assessing education abroad outcomes (see the Forum's site, https://forumea.org/→ Resources→ Outcomes Assessment and Research→ Outcomes Assessment Bibliography).

And yet again, research in this area is scant in Europe. As emphasised through part of the discussion in the previous section and elsewhere (e.g., Byram, 2008), student mobility in Europe needs to go beyond student satisfaction or rudimentary metrics like study abroad enrolments. This knowledge gap translates into another – curriculum design and integration – i.e., programme component 4 in our list.

In study abroad, at the heart of curriculum development is the integration of the period of studies abroad into home campus curricula, both at institutional, programme study and modular levels. The relevance of curriculum integration in study abroad prompted the Forum on Education Abroad and the Association of International Educators (NAFSA) to advance definitions for it:

> a variety of institutional approaches designed to fully integrate study abroad options into the college experience and academic curricula for students in all majors (NAFSA, as in Brewer & Cunningham, 2009, p. xii).
>
> Incorporating coursework taken abroad into the academic context of the home campus. It involves weaving study abroad into the fabric of the on-campus curriculum through activities such as course matching, academic advising, departmental and collegiate informational and promotional materials, and the structuring of degree requirements. It often requires the review of coursework by the home institution's academic departments.
>
> (Forum on Education Abroad, 2011, p. 11)

Historically, according to Brewer and Cunningham (2009) curriculum integration in study abroad received heightened attention in the US after the University of Minnesota undertook a major initiative, in the 1990s, to incorporate study abroad within the disciplines of the university schools and departments. Specialist publications and professional resources on curriculum integration have flourished since then. NAFSA, for instance, offers several professional resources to embed study abroad programmes across disciplines as well as best practices and case studies of curriculum integration in education abroad (see NAFSA website, www.nafsa.org→ Professional Resources→ Curriculum Integration: Best Practices).

Additionally, one can find publications written by individuals (e.g., Brewer & Cunningham, 2009), organisations (e.g., Woodruff & Henry, 2012 on behalf of NAFSA) or reflecting institutional case studies (e.g., Parcells, 2011).

A central concern of curriculum integration is the academic value of study abroad and how it can benefit disciplinary learning. This involves grading policies and recognition of studies (programme component 5 in our list), but it is not confined to such activities. There is a difference in simply aligning curricula between home and host institutions (to make study abroad possible) and in actually integrating study abroad into home campus curricula.

Clarifying such overlap is crucial in Europe where curriculum integration is often used as a synonym for academic recognition (through course matching). As previously discussed, supranational policy has put academic recognition at the centre of the few debates about educational attainment among mobile students in European higher education. Early and recent *Erasmus* evaluation and monitoring studies (like the aforementioned study by Teichler & Maiworm, 1997, or the ADMIT project – see West, 2002) echo the importance of academic recognition in European policy discourse. A more recent example is the two-edition project *Problems of Recognition in Making Erasmus* (PRIME, https://esn.org/prime). Conducted by the European student association Erasmus Student Network,[1] in 2009 and 2010, this project addressed the challenges of recognition procedures for *Erasmus* student mobility.

Other EU funded projects like *Facilitating Student Mobility's Service including Quality Insurance Dimension* (FASTQUAD) and *Erasmus Mobility Quality Tools* (EMQT) forefront this understanding of study abroad assessment as *recognition* and *accreditation* of degrees and study periods abroad. FASQUAD, which ran from 2007 to 2010, sought to improve exchange services to ease outbound cross-border flows of students from the Russian Federation to European higher education. The EMQT (2009–2011) had a less managerial approach by targeting organisational models, benchmarking procedures and tools for *Erasmus* student mobility. While these two projects addressed quality assurance and evaluation, the benchmarking mechanisms put in place targeted the structural-organisational level rather than the micro, that is, the learners and the assessment of learning outcomes reaped abroad.

This is quite telling as continental European policy on student mobility (*Erasmus* in particular) has been mostly centred on making study abroad accessible to an ever-increasing number of higher education students – the (in)famous 10 and 20 per cent milestones. I will go over these benchmarks in Chapter 2. For now, the point I want to make is that the quantitative imperative in supranational, intergovernmental and national discourses may have contributed to assigning a pivotal role to recognition and accreditation (as a lever to increase student participation). As a result, the academic benefits of student mobility were pushed to a subsidiary level. The empirical evidence base about academic gains is, *de facto*, rather thin. An exception is a few studies with postgraduate degree–seeking students in British higher education, although often tinted with issues of

26 Foundations of an interdisciplinary approach

socio-cultural adjustment and integration (e.g., Bamford, 2008; Spencer-Oatey & Dauber, 2019; Spencer-Oatey & Xiong, 2006; Young & Schartner, 2014).

Investigations on academic learning outcomes in student mobility in Europe are scarce, reflecting my inability to pin down such stu..lies (particularly in credit-seeking student mobility), at least not to the same extent as study abroad in the US. Here, there is an array of investigations examining the impact of studying abroad on various academic outputs: general academic success (e.g., Raby, Rhodes, & Biscarra, 2013; Sutton & Rubin, 2004), academic engagement (e.g., Hadis, 2005), time to graduate and graduation rates (e.g., Hamir, 2011), retention (e.g., Metzger, 2006), institutional perceptions and/or loyalty (e.g., Maggio, 2019), to name but a few.

The sixth programmatic feature of study abroad in our list is opportunities for contact with hosts and/or the host culture. While these opportunities can be sought on one's own (i.e., by the sojourner), if engagement with the host culture is to be at the heart of study abroad, possibilities for contact with hosts should not be left to accidental outcomes. They should be also integrated into the design of study abroad programmes. This incorporation is fundamental because the quantity and quality of host–sojourner interactions is a factor that can intensify the experience of living and working in another culture. Moreover, sojourner ability or willingness to engage with hosts can be hampered by socio-cultural factors that could be mitigated (at least to some extent) by study abroad programme design and delivery. These factors are numerous: from the tightly knit social networks sojourners tend to form, which can hinder entry into host social circles, to lack of proficiency in the host language or even housing options (as also demonstrated by Second Language Acquisition, SLA, research in the previous section).

Whereas a usual premise in SLA and language education research is that the quantity and quality of contact with hosts can influence language acquisition, study abroad programming assumes that the manipulation of design features can also shape such opportunities. Simply put, programme-related factors can mediate the degree of sojourners' cultural immersion. Type of housing is one of these factors (programme component 7 in our list). However, this line of inquiry applies primarily to US study abroad. This is perhaps unsurprising considering that homestays are not a common feature of study abroad in European higher education (although in some programmes they may be offered as an extra-curricular option). In any case, more research is needed to understand how learning outcomes can be influenced (positively or negatively) by accommodation abroad as will be demonstrated in Part II of this book. Among the outcomes related to accommodation abroad are language gains (e.g., Diao et al., 2011), intercultural gains (e.g., Ilino, 2006), attitudes and behaviour (e.g., Langran, Langran, & Ozment, 2009), socialisation and interaction (e.g., Coleman, 2015). Disciplinary takes in these studies, and in the study abroad literature in general, vary by research foci and primary research outcomes. For instance, the impact of living arrangements on language outcomes is likely to be examined from a SLA or language education perspective, whereas behavioural outcomes and sojourner

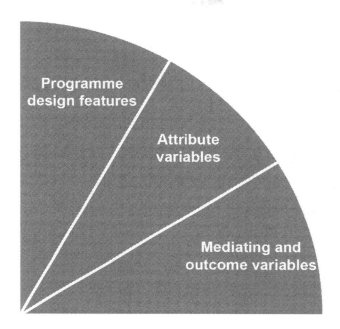

Figure 1.3 Conceptual diagram: variables informing study abroad.

functioning in the host society are most commonly addressed in psychology, namely social, cross-cultural and acculturation psychology.

This brings me to the remaining two categories in the second piece of our conceptual organiser (see Figure 1.3): Attribute and Mediating variables. The strength of the broad division into Attribute and Mediating variables is the possibility of pinning down the variables shaping the study abroad experience first to then posit them against theoretical and disciplinary frameworks. In doing so, I seek to reverse the prevailing normative thinking about student mobility in European higher education wherein the application of disciplinary frameworks usually precedes the identification of the variables of interest. That said, our category Attribute variables refers to individual background characteristics or attributes which, despite being inherent to the sojourner, can have a bearing on study abroad outcomes. These kinds of variable cannot be manipulated by the researcher because they are the characteristics or attributes describing our population (i.e., student mobility). In study abroad, some attention has been devoted to analysing attribute variables like gender (e.g., Anderson, 2003), previous international experiences or attributes (termed 'mobility capital' in the work of Murphy-Lejeune, 2002), socio-economic status – both for credit (e.g., Ballatore & Ferede, 2010) and degree-seeking students (e.g., Brooks & Waters, 2011), personality traits (e.g., Miao & Harris, 2012), motivations and/or decision-making (e.g., Krzaklewska, 2008, 2013). This set of personal characteristics

28 Foundations of an interdisciplinary approach

and/or experiences sojourners bring with them can influence the experience of living abroad.

By contrast, Mediating and outcome variables attend to determinants and effects of the study abroad experience, with mediating variables being used to determine expected outcomes, i.e., the gains or losses from studying abroad. For conceptual purposes, these variables are represented under the same category.

Within this category, one can locate the typical four gains of studying abroad – personal, linguistic, intercultural and academic. An important question arises:

> But was not it argued before that linguistic, intercultural and academic outcomes are learning domains?

They are indeed, but they are also variables informing the study abroad experience. For instance, intercultural gains are inextricably linked to socio-cultural/environmental variables, some of which have already been identified throughout our discussion. I am referring in particular to variables such as: social networks and friendship patterns, cultural adjustment, adaptation, degree of cultural immersion and isolation, institutional receptivity, type of accommodation abroad or even, as demonstrated by recent studies, social media (e.g., Hofhuis, Hanke, & Rutten, 2019). Many of these variables can function as predictors and outcomes, depending on the focus of analysis.

The examination of a given variable over another often varies according to researchers' disciplinary backgrounds. Additionally, the same variable can be investigated in different ways depending on the disciplinary and theoretical umbrellas used. By way of example, studies of cultural adjustment (also known as cross-cultural, intercultural and socio-cultural adjustment) and adaptation are commonly found in social, cross-cultural and acculturation psychology and frequently examined according to acculturation theory. These kinds of theory explore the process of cultural and behavioural change accruing from contact between cultural groups, eventually leading to long-term outcomes of adaptation (Berry, 2015). Within cross-cultural and/or acculturation psychology, mobile students are just one group of interest following various attempts to categorise travellers in order to facilitate the analysis of acculturation processes. The cross-cultural psychologist John Berry, for example, developed a fourfold taxonomy in 1997 according to travellers' motive to move, namely: (1) expatriate employees, (2) migrants, (3) international students and (4) refugees. Another cross-cultural psychologist, Stephen Bochner, categorised travellers based on their psychological response to the host culture: (1) passing, (2) chauvinistic, (3) marginal and (4) mediating. Within sociology and economic theory of migration, travellers tend to be categorised according to skilling or degree of specialisation of the labour force they represent: *unskilled, skilled* and *highly skilled*. Despite the different taxonomies, the division into groups of travellers (also known as acculturating groups in psychology) may be useful in accounting for similarities and differences

Conceptual foundations   29

in the cultural immersion of the groups under scrutiny in this book (as will be illustrated in Part II).

The analysis of the immersion experience of travellers according to group taxonomies is a common practice in cross-cultural psychology. In a systematic literature review, employing Berry's (1997) taxonomy to 222 adaptation studies, Bierwiaczonek and Waldzus (2016) found that the adaptation literature about international students was the most eclectic conceptually. Yet, this scientific *corpus* fell short in defining a common direction. The authors also note that in cross-cultural psychology student travellers are not usually studied by subpopulations. The tendency is to study degree-seeking students only, typically moving from East to West English-speaking countries. More importantly, findings from this systematic literature review demonstrate that adaptation studies with mobile students tend to report both socio-cultural and psychological adaptation and/ or adjustment. In terms of antecedents, social interaction and support as well as social stressors (like perceived discrimination and language barriers) prevail over cultural distance.

To put disciplinary views into perspective, let us now look at adaptation and/ or adjustment studies conducted by applied linguists and educators in European higher education (e.g., Gu, Schweisfurth, & Day, 2010; Spencer-Oatey & Xiong, 2006; Young & Schartner, 2014; Young, Sercombe, Sachdev, Naeb, & Schartner, 2013). A comparison between these studies and investigations in psychology illustrate my point by demonstrating how research foci and variables vary by disciplinary allegiances.

For the studies just cited, language learning, intercultural competence, social contact and support are seen as predictors of psychosocial and academic adjustment. Additionally, in all of them the learning condition of language acquisition is forefronted as an outcome of studying abroad. In contrast with these studies, cross-cultural, social and acculturation psychology generally depict language acquisition as a contact variable predicting sojourner functioning in the host society and, at times, a source of acculturative stress.

Another variable examined differently across disciplines is sojourner social networks. In applied linguistics and SLA research, this variable is often related to language outcomes (e.g., Gautier & Chevrot, 2015; Isabelli-García, 2006; Jackson, 2008; Kinginger, 2008). From a psychological perspective, social networks are often examined according to the type of social support provided (e.g., instrumental, emotional) and its relationship with higher levels of socio-cultural and psychological well-being (e.g., Kashima & Loh, 2006; Smith & Khawaja, 2011) on the assumption that sojourners' social networks may reflect their degree of emotional investment in the host society. To develop my argument further, let us now look at research from a sociological-migration perspective (e.g., Brooks, 2005; de Federico la Rúa, 2003; Van Mol & Michielsen, 2015). Once again research foci change, with human agency, the formation of sojourner networks across social spaces and their role in student decision-making at the heart of investigations. Put differently, whereas research on social networks from a sociological-migration

30 Foundations of an interdisciplinary approach

perspective posits sojourners as social agents against the interplay between social structures and individual agency, SLA and language education research sees them as language learners. Psychology, in turn, tends to emphasise individual mental functioning and social behaviour (hence terms like culture contact-induced behavioural changes).

To summarise, social network research exemplifies how disciplinary umbrellas inform knowledge presentation, often, at the expense of a broad dialogue between disciplines and their lines of inquiry. Part of the problem resides in the very compartmentalisation of thought and knowledge, hindering possibilities for connecting different conceptual and methodological approaches. Hopefully, the broad division of the second piece of our conceptual diagram – (1) Programme design features, (2) Attribute and (3) Mediating and outcome variables (Figure 1.3) – brought attention to another group of variables shaping the study abroad experience while facilitating a more relational understanding of it (see Box 1.3).

Box 1.3 – Summary vignette: variables informing study abroad

- **Programme design features** – design components of study abroad programmes like: (1) programme duration, (2) interventions, trainings and/or orientations across pre-departure, in-country and re-entry phases (3) programme evaluation and assessment, (4) curriculum design and integration, (5) grading policies and recognition of studies, (6) opportunities for contact with hosts, (7) type of housing.
- **Attribute variables** – background demographic and socio-cultural variables that characterise mobile students as a specific student population. These kinds of variable cannot be manipulated by the researcher as they account for the individual characteristics or attributes describing our population prior to the mobility experience (e.g., gender, socio-economic status, prior mobility capital, personality traits).
- **Mediating and outcome variables** – results of the study abroad experience (outcomes) and the variables mediating these outcomes (mediating variables). Note that mediating variables are used in this book in a broad sense without specifying their measurement role (e.g., as predictors, moderators).

Global student dynamics and higher education internationalisation

The third piece of our conceptual diagram in Figure 1.4 addresses the processes of growth and activity of student mobility. To specify further, this conceptual piece attends to studies of cross-border flows of mobile students (where they move from and to), push-and-pull factors, the typologies or modalities of student mobility (Taxonomies) and its role within the landscape of internationalising higher education.

Conceptual foundations 31

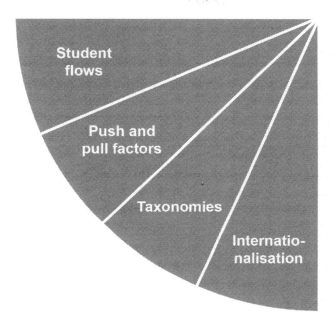

Figure 1.4 Conceptual diagram: global student dynamics and internationalisation of higher education.

Within the first strand of studies (Student mobility flows), we can locate grey literature and secondary analyses of quantitative metrics and trends of cross-border flows of students, focusing on specific countries and world regions or with a global scale. Typically conducted by third-party organisations, specialised agencies and research centres, these studies compile and explain quantitative data and/or indicators of the number of students on the move. This information is usually made available on an annual basis through reports and/or web-available statistics accounting primarily for the movement of degree-seeking students, that is, students moving across national borders to pursue a whole academic degree abroad.

At international level, the statistical standards for measuring student mobility are mainly set by the following three international organisations:

- Organisation for Economic Co-operation and Development (OECD);
- United Nations Educational, Scientific and Cultural Organisation (UNESCO) Institute for Statistics (UIS);
- EUROSTAT, the statistical office of the EU.

A publication we are, perhaps, all familiar with is the annual report *Education at a Glance* by the OECD Directorate for Education and Skills which aggregates comparable indicators in different areas of education across OECD member countries. This includes indicators of the profile of internationally mobile students (see Indicator B6 in OECD, 2019). The UIS also collects worldwide indicators of in- and outbound tertiary student mobility that can be downloaded by the interested reader. A relatively recent innovation of the UIS is an interactive map of global flows of tertiary-level students.[2] At European level, EUROSTAT has a portal on learning mobility statistics that analyses the mobility of tertiary education students in the EU.[3]

At national level, an endless list of agencies collecting data of student mobility flows could be pointed out. These data inform international data collectors like the OECD, UIS and EUROSTAT. The picture is, however, quite different for credit student mobility in absence of a comprehensive database on this type of student mobility and the little distinction made between credit and degree-seeking students by data collectors (Teichler, 2015, 2017). In Europe, available data are usually specific to mobility programmes like *Erasmus* by the EU (currently under Key Action 1 of *Erasmus+*) or the *Nordplus Higher Education Programme*[4] by the Nordic Council of Ministers. In the case of *Erasmus+*, part of the responsibility falls under the managing agencies of *Erasmus+* participant countries (usually known as National Agencies). These agencies are decentralised EU bodies responsible for the indirect management of *Erasmus+*, including managing national statistical information (see COM, 2019 for further information). General statistics of this programme and its predecessors are centralised by the European Commission.[5]

The depth of information accompanying quantitative indicators of global student flows varies substantially. Reports like *Education at a Glance* by the OECD provide some information on the push-and-pull factors prompting students to undertake international study. The focus of analysis in these meta-studies is macro-economic via outbound-push and inbound-pull models of the factors propelling and attracting students to study abroad, respectively. That is, the factors shaping individuals' decision to study or not to study abroad (push factors) and those influencing the choice of country and host institution (pull factors) (Woodfield, 2010). These factors are usually posited as the global macro context of international student mobility within the interplay of supply and demand for education abroad.

At a more intermediate level of analysis is the role of place in study abroad, namely how destination cities and their distinctive urban qualities influence mobility decision-making (e.g., Beech, 2014; Prazeres et al., 2017; Van Mol & Ekamper, 2016). Linking to this intermediate level of analysis is the need to take into consideration the micro individual perspective in addition to external push-and-pull factors to which some individuals may choose not to respond to. There is an intricate sway of global, national, local and personal drivers in mobility decision-making as the next section will also show.

Another important aspect of global student dynamics is the reliability of the indicators measuring cross-border student flows and the extent to which these figures account for the different types or modalities of student mobility (here termed Taxonomies of student mobility). As argued by Kelo, Teichler, and Wächter (2006b), and Wächter (2014), numerical patterns of student mobility in Europe (and worldwide) remain methodologically blurred. Terminologies can vary from country to country, ultimately affecting the analyses conducted by international data collectors, since national agencies may report data based on varying definitions of what a mobile student is (see Verbik & Lasanowski, 2007 in this regard). These caveats came to justify two major studies of student mobility trends and data definition issues in Europe – EURODATA I (Kelo, Teichler, & Wächter, 2006a) and II (Teichler, Ferencz, & Wächter, 2011a, 2011b); and more specifically, trends of in- and outbound credit and degree-seeking student mobility (and to a lesser extent staff mobility) across 32 European countries: the then 27 EU Member States, the 4 countries of the European Free Trade Association and Turkey.

Led by the European think thank ACA (see Box 1.1), the two EURODATA studies were pivotal in building a bigger picture view of student mobility flows in Europe. Findings revealed that Europe is a net importer world region, even though there are stark differences between individual countries. One of the major findings, in my opinion, went beyond student mobility trends. I am referring in particular to the contribution made to developing reliable data collection indicators on genuine/real student mobility and a taxonomy for its different modalities. In Wächter's (2014) words, statistics on real student mobility requires using criteria other than foreign nationality, namely mobile students' country of prior residence or education. In the end, and as Chapter 2 will demonstrate, the key challenge is how we define a mobile student.

To the best of my knowledge, the EURODATA studies are among the few systematic contributions in Europe bringing to light the semantic ambiguity permeating knowledge production of student mobility. Also noteworthy is the project *Mapping University Mobility of Staff and Students* (MAUNIMO) conducted by another European think tank – the European University Association (EUA, see Box 1.1) – to assist European higher education institutions in defining their approaches to student and staff mobility, including in data collection. This project was, however, more centred on mobility administration and data management issues than on terminology. The EURODATA studies, in turn, contributed substantially to advancing a taxonomy of the different modalities or types of student mobility in Europe, namely: 'credit', 'temporary' or 'horizontal' student mobility which is typically set in opposition to 'degree', 'diploma' or 'vertical' (although this opposition may not always be watertight).

I will go over this terminology in Chapter 2, but suffice it to say here that an expanded agenda for theorising student mobility requires clarifying semantic ambiguities. The relevance of this endeavour prompted the Forum on Education Abroad, in the US, to develop a glossary for education abroad (see Forum on Education Abroad, 2011). This task proves harder to accomplish in European higher education where student mobility is more recognised as a field of research inquiry than of professional practice. In addition to the work of international

34 Foundations of an interdisciplinary approach

education organisations and data collectors in furthering student mobility typologies, there are also individual academic studies.

International and comparative educators are amongst those who have strongly contributed to developing frameworks of higher education internationalisation and the role of student mobility in it. Conceptual and empirical analyses of student mobility within the internationalisation of higher education thread through the literature on the topic. Conceptually, the framework by Jane Knight (2004) is an often-cited definition of higher education internationalisation. In this framework, exchange programmes and study abroad are broadly defined as an activity and/or strategy at institutional level, as well as an approach at national/sector level promoting opportunities for institutions and individuals to take part in international activities.

Ten years later, Knight (2014) proposed a threefold taxonomy for cross-border education, considering that academic mobility has moved from people (students, faculty, scholars), to programme (movement of education/training programmes and courses – e.g., double degrees, twinning programmes, distance/online learning) and provider mobility (movement of education providers – e.g., branch campuses, bi-national universities). Naturally, terminology can be permeated by authors' conceptualisations of higher education internationalisation as will be discussed in Chapter 2. In any case, it is perhaps fair to say that the clarification of terminology on student and staff mobility (and cross-border education in general) has been primarily bolstered by studies in higher education research and policy (e.g., de Wit, 2002; Knight, 2014; Teichler, 2009; Woodfield, 2010), comparative and international education (e.g., Banks & Bhandari, 2012; Bhandari & Blumenthal, 2011), sociology, human geography and migration research (e.g., Findlay, 2010; Raghuram, 2013; Van Mol, 2014) as well as youth studies (e.g., Cairns, 2014; Krzaklewska, 2013).

Once again, the range of disciplines producing research about student mobility makes it difficult for someone outside these disciplines to pin down the plethora of publications. For instance, within migration and youth studies one can find publications about student mobility across journals like the *Journal of Youth Studies, Journal of Ethnic and Migration Studies, Mobilities, Comparative Migration Studies* and *Population, Space and Place* (see Cairns, 2014 for further information). The migration literature about student mobility is sometimes subsumed under what can be referred to as 'international student mobility' (e.g., Brooks & Waters, 2011; Cairns, 2014; Sussex Centre for Migration Research, 2005) or 'international student migration' (e.g., Findlay, Stam, King, & Ruiz-Gelices, 2005; King & Ruiz-Gelices, 2003; Raghuram, 2013). Within this body of knowledge, one is likely to find studies exploring the relationship between student mobility and professional development, migration aspirations and, more recently, migration policy and the role of place in student mobility. These research strands will be discussed in the next section. Before delving into them, a summary vignette of key terminology and/or points in this section is provided (see Box 1.4).

Conceptual foundations 35

> **Box 1.4 – Summary vignette: global student dynamics and internationalisation**
>
> - **Student mobility flows or trends** – indicators (typically quantitative) of the in- and outbound cross-border movement of students for education purposes. These trends analyse where students move from to (and to what effect) and can be posited at national, regional and global levels.
> - **Push-and-pull factors** – push factors are variables that influence individuals' decision to study or not to study abroad, whereas pull factors relate to the choice of country, city and host institution.
> - **Taxonomies of student mobility** – different types or modalities of student mobility within the broader landscape of higher education internationalisation.
> - **Internationalisation of higher education** – empirical and conceptual studies and/or analyses of the role of student mobility within the internationalisation of higher education. Different foci can be adopted, from a macro meta-governance perspective to a meso institutional view, for example.

Long-term impact of study abroad

The fourth and last piece of our conceptual diagram concerns the long-term impact, effects or fundamental changes happening as a result of having studied abroad. These effects can be of varying nature: from personal to professional development, from the nexus between student mobility and migration (including the influence of migration policies) to host community impact (see Figure 1.5).

The large stock of knowledge on the nexus between student mobility and migration aspirations interlocks with the equally vast literature on the professional value of study abroad, either for degree- or credit-seeking forms of student mobility.

With regard to credit-seeking student mobility, there are studies devoted specifically to the professional impact of *Erasmus* (e.g., Bracht et al., 2006; Brandenburg, Berghoff, & Taboadela, 2014; Cammelli, Ghiselli, & Mignoli, 2008; Janson, Schomburg, & Teichler, 2009; Teichler, 2011). Considering the promotion of the European labour market has been a key rationale across the iterations of *Erasmus*, it is no surprise that three of the five cited studies were funded by the European Commission. Employment prospects in *Erasmus* decision-making have also long been scrutinised in EU-funded survey research like *Erasmus* monitoring and evaluation studies (see Teichler & Maiworm, 1997) and the Europe-wide survey by the Erasmus Student Network (ESN, https://esn. org/ESNsurvey).

Conducted annually since 2005, the ESN survey has shown that career opportunities and employability skills do not necessarily rank first in the decision-making of credit-seeking students. This contrasts with students studying towards a degree

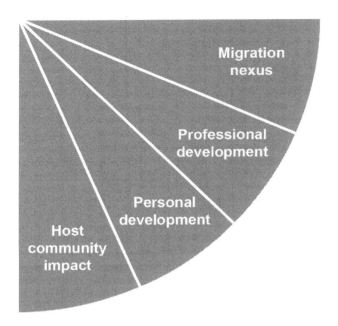

Figure 1.5 Conceptual diagram: long-term impact of study abroad.

for whom professional prospects are a clear driver. Typically, these students seek a return on their investment by studying in attractive destinations and/or institutions worldwide, particularly Western English-speaking destinations (Woodfield, 2010). This does not invalidate heterogeneity among this student population, including those striving to access education unavailable at home.

Despite the ever-present interest in the professional value of student mobility, the nexus between student mobility and future migration aspirations needs to be probed further from an empirical standpoint (Van Mol, 2014, 2017; Wiers-Jenssen, 2008). As yet, findings regarding the causal relationship between student mobility and subsequent migration remain inconclusive. This may be in part due to the selective nature of this student population which is likely predisposed towards the idea of becoming mobile in the first place (Cairns, 2014; Rodrigues, 2013).

As discussed before, in Europe studies investigating the migration nexus and issues of brain circulation in student mobility are mainstays of migration studies within sociology and human geography. Unsurprisingly, these studies address primarily degree-seeking students as the normative expectations of their return home are smaller than for credit-seeking students. The geographical lens is usually focused on degree-seeking students from outside Europe studying in international student hubs like the United Kingdom, Germany and France. Given the large national export international students represent, these countries loosened legal procedures to integrate them in their labour markets. The current climate of political unrest and anti-migration movements has, nonetheless, challenged some of these migration policies. For instance, with the Brexit vote the British government has oscillated between the tightening and loosening of work visas for international students (from four months to two years upon graduation) to prevent further damage to the international student sector.

The duality of migration policy discourses in student mobility coexists with the marketisation of international higher education insofar as degree-seeking students are both sources of revenue, ensuring the financial sustainability of some national higher education systems, and prospective migrants. This comes at the expense of a steep competition for the most talented students and a net effect of accelerating the brain drain from developing to developed countries. Hence the increasing scholarly attention to mobile students in international skilled migration literature (e.g., Van Riemsdijk & Wang, 2017) and the increasing interest in the link between migration policy and student post-migration (e.g., Riaño & Piguet, 2016; Riaño, Van Mol, & Raghuram, 2018).

The transition from education to work and migration aspirations are even more difficult to document among credit-seeking students, as yet, with no convincing evidence on the causal effect between credit student mobility and migration; but that is not to say that positive correlations are not possible. In a survey research with non-mobile and mobile graduates for credit across 16 European countries, Rodrigues (2013) found a positive correlation between short-term student mobility[6] and the probability of becoming mobile five years after graduation. This effect is larger the more time spent abroad. However, Rodrigues cautions about the inconclusive causal effect between this type of student mobility and migration as well as about differences across countries and fields of study.

In a country-specific study with Polish outgoing *Erasmus* alumni, Bryła (2018) reported that subsequent migration does not differ significantly by mobility type but by the number of times one has been mobile, students' fields of study, host country and involvement in student associations. Despite gaining a 'mobility capital' (Murphy-Lejeune, 2002) and becoming 'Eurostars' (Favell, 2008) with an enhanced social awareness of other EU Member States, credit-seeking student mobility appears to be more strongly driven by personal development. Evidence of this can be found in *Erasmus* survey research and evaluation studies previously mentioned, as well as individual studies (e.g., Papatsiba, 2005; Teichler, 2004; Tsoukalas, 2008; Van Mol & Timmerman, 2014). Not that international professional ambitions are irrelevant for these students, but they may play a secondary role (in the face of experiential pursuits) and vary according to students' fields of study and employability opportunities in home and host countries (Bryła, 2019; Cairns, 2014; Van Mol, 2017). Social-economic conditions are reproduced by student mobility. As result, some scholars argue that inequalities in student mobility should be debated in terms of access and outcomes (Bilecen & Van Mol, 2017) as well as the societal expectations of becoming mobile among the youth population (Cairns, 2014, 2017). The latter aspect is striking in societies with

38 Foundations of an interdisciplinary approach

high youth unemployment rates where labour markets do not offer high returns on education.

Societal aspects in student mobility should be also understood in the context of host communities and the extent to which they are impacted by the presence of mobile students. This brings us to the last category – Host community impact.

Within this category, we can find studies gauging the *socio-cultural, economic* and *spatial* impacts of mobile students on host communities. Each type of impact tends to be addressed by specific disciplines and/or scholarly communities. Socio-cultural effects of education abroad on host communities, for instance, is a burgeoning line of inquiry often centred on community-based study abroad programmes like international service-learning, volunteering and field work. Research in this area is still little, with a couple of studies available primarily from a North American perspective (e.g., Gaul, 2015; Tonkin & Quiroga, 2004; Wood, Banks, Galiardi, Koehn, & Schroeder, 2011). While the implications of the presence of foreign visitors in local communities has long been a topic of interest in anthropology and tourism, only recently did it start garnering attention in education abroad. Here, the focus of the extant literature on community-based study abroad stems from the nature of these programmes which require students to immerse themselves within a community. Part of the ethical practice of these kinds of programme, the implications of study abroad for host communities gain greater attention as international service-learning and volunteering embrace more vulnerable communities in developing countries (Tonkin & Quiroga, 2004; Wood et al., 2011).

Economic effects on host communities are also considered, although this type of impact appears to be less frequently documented in the education abroad literature. Browsing through disciplines like tourism economics yields studies in which mobile students are depicted as academic tourism with economic impact on local and regional economies (e.g., López, Fernández, & Incera, 2016).

Finally, with regard to spatial impacts on host communities, an increasing number of scholars in (e.g., Malet Calvo, 2018) and outside Europe (Collins, 2010) are unlocking the role of place in student mobility, including the intended and unintended effects of mobile students on urban spaces and their host communities. This group of studies cuts across scholarly contributions from disciplines like human geography, architecture, sociology and urban anthropology. The foci of analysis are destination cities on the assumption that mobile students can transform urban places, but they can also be transformed by these places as a new class of urban transnational consumers.

The attention to the city in student mobility research and scholarship may be related to the shift in the ways space is theorised in student migration literature (see Raghuram, 2013 in this regard) and how migration flows link distinctive places (e.g., South–North; East–West; rural–urban; small–large cities). Both material and symbolic aspects of host cities are considered to analyse student involvement in urban processes like the tourism industry, gentrification, entrepreneurial

Conceptual foundations 39

creativity, recreational and cultural activities (Malet Calvo, 2018). These analyses disclose the complex urban lifestyles and changes induced by mobile students in these social settings, beyond the housing-centred literature[7] examining the effects of student housing in urban areas (Malet Calvo, 2018).

To summarise, the use of the city as a spatial framework of analysis in studies exploring the urban impacts (and dynamics)[8] of student mobility comes to amplify our understanding of the local dimension of mobile students' transitions into and impacts on a given place and its local communities, as well as student spatialised identities and lifestyles.

Box 1.5 summarises key terminology and/or points of the fourth conceptual piece in our conceptual diagram.

Box 1.5 – Long-term impact of study abroad

- **Personal development** – opportunities for self-development accruing from studying abroad (e.g., enhanced self-awareness, maturity, identity, emotional self-resilience, personal fulfilment).
- **Professional development** – employability opportunities and enhanced career prospects that accrue from studying abroad.
- **Migration nexus** – link between studying abroad and future migration aspirations. It can include the analysis of the role of migration policies in cross-border flows of students and their decision to stay in the host country.
- **Host community impact** – the extent to which host communities are impacted by the presence of mobile students. This presence can produce impacts of varying nature (socio-cultural, economic and spatial) on local host communities, with both positive and negative implications (intended or unintended).

Summary

The discussion in this chapter forefronted the need to develop an expanded agenda for theorising student mobility in European higher education.

The several research areas, theoretical perspectives and disciplinary accounts in this chapter have also indicated that this agenda should be interdisciplinary, at least if the purpose is to understand student mobility relationally and transcend the limits of disciplinary reasoning through a wide-angle lens that captures the polymorphous nature of student mobility and the colourful set of images it is made of.

This colourful set of images was represented by a conceptual diagram that integrates different knowledges. This diagram is organised into four macro descriptors, each of which is informed by different variables and/or thematic areas and illustrated by sample studies of major research strands. The four macro descriptors – (1) Learning domains abroad, (2) Variables informing study abroad, (3) Global student dynamics and higher education internationalisation, (4) Long-term impact of study abroad – and underlying variables of interest or research foci set a framework for continued abstracting (see Appendix 1.1 for the full conceptual diagram). It is hoped this framework will assist researchers and practitioners in pining down the multifarious facets of student mobility from an interdisciplinary perspective. This framework should not be seen as an end in itself, but a roadmap that can guide those interested in furthering their knowledge about student mobility in European higher education. It would be of particular value to develop systematic literature reviews to test this conceptual diagram further, and perhaps add other areas of research interest.

Such systematisation is crucial to making connections between the various ways of knowledge. Or, in the words of George Eliot in her novel *Daniel Deronda*, in understanding what is our key of interpretation.

Box 1.6 – Reflective questions and/or points of Chapter 1

To help you review critically the content of this chapter, ask yourself the following questions and discuss them with colleagues from other disciplines.

1. What topics and disciplines fall within the purview of student mobility?
2. How does your discipline (and scholarly community) interpret student mobility?
3. Does your discipline influence what you study and how you study student mobility?
   3.1. And, to what extent does it expand and confine your understanding of it?
4. What might an interdisciplinary approach add to your knowledge of student mobility?
5. Take a variable grouping you are interested in and use the interdisciplinary diagram to analyse it.
   5.1. How would you start your analysis? By reading studies focused only on your variable of interest? Or by brainstorming the range of related variables and studies?
6. To want extent might an interdisciplinary approach improve education abroad practice?
7. Who should be responsible for improving education abroad?

Conceptual foundations 41

Appendix 1.1

Figure 1.6 Conceptual diagram of student mobility research and scholarship in European higher education.

Notes

1 The Erasmus Student Network (ESN) was established in 1990 to support and develop student exchange. In 2020, ESN was present in more than 1,000 higher education institutions from 42 countries and involved 15,000 acti... members based mainly on a volunteer regime (ESN, www.esn.org/about).
2 For the UNESCO Institute for statistics please see http://uis.unesco.org/en/uis-student-flow
3 For the EUROSTAT portal on Learning Mobility Statistics please see http://ec.europa.eu/eurostat/statistics-explained/index.php/Learning_mobility_statistics
4 The Nordplus Higher Education Programme is a 'mobility and network programme in the higher education sector, at Bachelor and Master's levels, for the Nordic and Baltic countries' (www.nordplusonline.org/).
5 For statistical figures on *Erasmus+* please see http://ec.europa.eu/programmes/erasmus-plus/about/statistics_en
6 In Rodrigues' (2013) study, short-term mobility is defined as mobility ranging from 3 to more than 12 months. It should be noted that the use of short and longer-term to classify student mobility durations can be ambiguous as discussed in Chapter 2.
7 This type of literature is also called 'studentification' literature. Studentification is a term coined by Darren Smith (2002) to understand the effects the influx of students can have in urban processes. The studentification literature has been developed primarily from a UK-based perspective given that university accommodation in the UK has been insufficient to cater to the large international student intake, leading students to turn to the private rental sector for accommodation.
8 While studies addressing urban impact fall under the category Host community impact, there are also studies that use the city as a spatial framework of analysis but are more concerned with the role of urban places in mobility decision-making. For this reason, I categorised this last group of studies under Push-and-pull factors.

References

Aerden, A. (2015). Frameworks for the assessment of internationalization. *ECA Occasional Paper*. Retrieved from www.ecahe.eu

Aerden, A. (2017). The guide to quality in internationalization (2nd ed). *ECA Occasional Paper*. Retrieved from www.ecahe.eu

Almarza, G., Martínez, R. D., & Llavador, F. (2015). Identifying students' intercultural communicative competence at the beginning of their placement: Towards the enhancement of study abroad programmes. *Intercultural Education*, 26(1), 73–85.

Almeida, J., Fantini, A. E., Simões, A. R., & Costa, N. (2016). Enhancing the intercultural effectiveness of exchange programmes: Formal and non-formal educational interventions. *Intercultural Education*, 27(6), 517–533.

Alred, G., & Byram, M. (2002). Becoming an intercultural mediator: A longitudinal study of residence abroad. *Journal of Multilingual and Multicultural Development*, 23(5), 339–352.

Alred, G., Byram, M., & Fleming, M. (2003). *Intercultural experience and education*. Clevedon: Multilingual Matters.

Anderson, A. (2003). Women and cultural learning in Costa Rica: Reading the context. *Frontiers: Interdisciplinary Journal of Study Abroad*, 9(Fall), 21–52.

Anquetil, M. (2006). *Mobilité Erasmus et communication interculturelle: Une recherche action pour un parcours de formation* (Vol. 17). Berne: Peter Lang.

Baiutti, M. (2017). *Competenza interculturale e mobilità studentesca: Riflessioni pedagogiche per la valutazione*. Pisa: ETS.

Baiutti, M. (2018). Fostering assessment of student mobility in secondary schools: Indicators of intercultural competence. *Intercultural Education, 29*(5–6), 549–570.

Ballatore, M., & Ferede, M. K. (2010). The Erasmus programme in France, Italy and the United Kingdom: Student mobility as a signal of distinction and privilege. *European Educational Research Journal, 12*(4), 525–533.

Bamford, J. (2008). Strategies for the improvement of international students' academic and cultural experiences of studying in the UK. *The Enhancing series case Studies: International learning experience*, 1–10. Retrieved from https://www.hea cademy.ac.uk/system/files/e2_strategies_for_improvement.pdf

Banks, M., & Bhandari, R. (2012). Global student mobility. In D. K. Deardorff, H. de Wit, J. D. Heyl & T. Adams (Eds.), *The Sage handbook of international higher education* (pp. 379–397). Thousand Oaks, CA: Sage.

Barber, E., Altbach, P. G., & Myers, R. (1984). Introduction: Perspectives on foreign students. *Comparative Education Review, 28*(2), 163–167.

Beaven, A., & Borghetti, C. (2015). Editorial. *Intercultural Education, 26*(1), 1–5.

Beaven, A., & Borghetti, C. (2016). Interculturality in study abroad. *Language and Intercultural Communication, 16*(3), 313–317.

Beaven, A., & Spencer-Oatey, H. (2016). Cultural adaptation in different facets of life and the impact of language: A case study of personal adjustment patterns during study abroad. *Language and Intercultural Communication, 16*(3), 349–367.

Bedenlier, S., Kondakci, Y., & Zawacki-Richter, O. (2018). Two decades of research into the internationalization of higher education: Major themes in the Journal of Studies in International Education (1997–2016). *Journal of Studies in International Education, 22*(2), 108–135.

Beech, S. E. (2014). Why place matters: Imaginative geography and international student mobility. *Area, 46*(2), 170–177.

Berry, J. W. (1997). Immigration, acculturation, and adaptation. *Applied Psychology, 46*(1), 5–34.

Berry, J. W. (2015). Acculturation. In J. M. Bennett (Ed.), *The Sage encyclopedia of intercultural competence* (pp. 1–5). Thousand Oaks, CA: Sage.

Bhandari, R., & Blumenthal, P. (Eds.). (2011). *International students and global mobility in higher education: National trends and new directions*. New York, NY: Palgrave Macmillan.

Bierwiaczonek, K., & Waldzus, S. (2016). Socio-cultural factors as antecedents of cross-cultural adaptation in expatriates, international students, and migrants: A review. *Journal of Cross-Cultural Psychology, 47*(6), 767–817.

Bilecen, B., & Van Mol, C. (2017). Introduction: International academic mobility and inequalities. *Journal of Ethnic and Migration Studies, 43*(8), 1241–1255.

Bista, K. (Ed.). (2019). *Global perspectives on international student experiences in higher education*. New York, NY: Routledge.

Blumenthal, P., Goodwin, R. M., Smith, A., & Teichler, U. (Eds.). (1996). *Academic mobility in a changing world: Regional and global trends*. London: Jessica Kingsley Publishers.

Bolen, M. C. (Ed.). (2007). *A guide to outcomes assessment in education abroad*. Carlisle, PA: The Forum on Education Abroad.

Borghetti, C., & Beaven, A. (Eds.). (2018). *Study abroad and interculturality: Perspectives and discourses*. London: Routledge.

44 Foundations of an interdisciplinary approach

Bracht, O., Engel, C., Janson, K., Over, A., Schomburg, H., & Teichler, U. (2006). The professional value of Erasmus mobility Retrieved from https://www.par lement.com/9353210/d/belang%20erasmus%20onder%20professionals.pdf

Bracke, A., & Aguerre, S. (2015). Erasmus students: Joining communities of practice to learn French? In R. Mitchell, N. Tracy-Ventura & K. McManus (Eds.), *Social interaction, identity and language learning during residence abroad* (pp. 139–168). Amsterdam: European Second Language Association.

Brandenburg, U., Berghoff, S., & Taboadela, O. (2014). Erasmus impact study: Effects of mobility on the skills and employability of students and the internationalisation of higher education institutions. Retrieved from http://ec. europa.eu/dgs/education_culture/repository/education/library/study/201 4/erasmus-impact_en.pdf

Brewer, E., & Cunningham, K. (Eds.). (2009). *Integrating study abroad into the curriculum: Theory and practice across the disciplines.* Sterling, VA: Stylus.

Brooks, R. (2005). *Friendship and educational choice: Peer influence and planning for the future.* Basingstoke: Palgrave Macmillan.

Brooks, R., & Waters, J. (2011). *Student mobilities, migration and the internationalization of higher education.* Basingstoke: Palgrave Macmillan.

Bryła, P. (2019). International student mobility and subsequent migration: The case of Poland. *Studies in Higher Education, 44*(8), 1386–1399.

Byram, M. (1997). *Teaching and assessing intercultural communicative competence.* Clevedon: Multilingual Matters.

Byram, M. (2008). The value of student mobility. In M. Byram & F. Dervin (Eds.), *Students, staff and academic mobility in higher education* (pp. 30–45). Newcastle upon Tyne: Cambridge Scholars Publishing.

Byram, M., & Dervin, F. (Eds.). (2008). *Students, staff and academic mobility in higher education.* Newcastle upon Tyne: Cambridge Scholars Publishing.

Byram, M., & Feng, A. (Eds.). (2006). *Living and studying abroad: Research and practice.* Clevedon: Multilingual Matters.

Cairns, D. (2014). *Youth transitions, international student mobility and spatial reflexivity.* Basingstoke: Palgrave Macmillan.

Cairns, D. (2017). Exploring student mobility and graduate migration: Undergraduate mobility propensities in two economic crisis contexts. *Social & Cultural Geography, 18*(3), 336–353.

Cammelli, A., Ghiselli, S., & Mignoli, G. (2008). Study experience abroad: Italian graduate characteristics and employment outcomes. In M. Byram & F. Dervin (Eds.), *Students, staff and academic mobility in higher education* (pp. 217–236). Newcastle upon Tyne: Cambridge Scholars Publishing.

Carrol, J. B. (1967). Foreign language proficiency levels attained by language majors near graduation. *Foreign Language Annals, 1*(1), 131–151.

Carroll, J. (2015). *Tools for teaching in an educationally mobile world.* London: Routledge.

Chieffo, L., & Griffiths, L. (2004). Large-scale assessment of student attitudes after a short-term study abroad program. *Frontiers: The Interdisciplinary Journal of Study Abroad, 10*(Fall), 165–177.

Chieffo, L., & Griffiths, L. (2009). Here to stay: Increasing acceptance of short-term study abroad programsLewin. In R. In & R. Lewin (Ed.), *The handbook of practice and research in study abroad: Higher education and the quest for global citizenship* (pp. 365–380). New York, NY: Routledge.

Chieffo, L., & Spaeth, C. (2017). *NAFSA's guide to successful short-term programs abroad*. Washington, DC: NAFSA: Association of International Educators.

Cohen, A. D., Paige, R. M., Kappler, B., Demmessie, M., Weaver, S. J., Chi, J. C., & Lassegard, J. P. (2003). *Maximizing study abroad: A language instructor's guide to strategies for language and culture learning and use*. Minneapolis, MN: Center for Advanced Research on Language Acquisition – University of Minnesota.

Coleman, J. A. (2015). Social circles during residence abroad: What students do and who with? In R. Mitchell, N. Tracy-Ventura & K. McManus (Eds.), *Social interaction, identity and language learning during residence abroad* (pp. 33–51). Amsterdam: European Second Language Association.

Coleman, J. A., & Klapper, J. (2005). *Effective learning and teaching in modern languages*. London: Routledge.

Collentine, J., & Freed, B. (2004). Learning context and its effects in second langauge acquisition. *Studies in Second Language Acquisition, 26*(2), 153–171.

Collins, F. L. (2010). International students as urban agents: International education and urban transformation in Auckland, New Zealand. *Geoforum, 41*(6), 940–950.

COM. (2019). Erasmus+. Programme Guide. Retrieved from https://ec.europa.eu/pro grammes/erasmus-plus/resources/documents/erasmus-programme-guide-2019_en

Comp, D., Gladding, S., Rhodes, G., Stephenson, S., & Vande Berg, M. (2007). Literature and resources for education abroad outcomes assessment. In M. C. Bolen (Ed.), *A guide to outcomes assessment in education abroad* (pp. 97–135). Carlisle, PA: The Forum on Education Abroad.

de Federico la Rúa, A. (2003). *Réseaux d'identification à l'Europe: Amitiés et identités d'étudiants/ Redes de identifiación con Europa: Amistad e identidades de estudiantes europeos* (Doctoral thesis). Université des Sciences et Technologies de lille/ Universidad pública de Navarra, Pampeleune. Retrieved from http://www.sudoc.fr/07786803X

de Wit, H. (2002). *Internationalization of higher education in the United States and in Europe: A historical, comparative, and conceptual analysis*. Westport, CT: Greenwood Press.

de Wit, H. (2009). Measuring success in the internationalization of higher education. *EAIE Occasional Paper 22*. Amsterdam: European Association for International Education.

de Wit, H., & Urias, D. (2012). An overview and analysis of international education research, training and resources. In D. K. Deardorff, H. de Wit, J. D. Heyl & T. Adams (Eds.), *The Sage handbook of international higher education* (pp. 101–110). Thousand Oaks, CA: Sage.

Deardorff, D. K. (2015). *Desmystifying outcomes assessment for international educators: A practical approach*. Sterling, VA: Stylus Publishing.

Deardorff, D. K., & Arasaratnam-Smith, L. A. (Eds.). (2017). *Intercultural competence in higher education: International approaches, assessment and application*. London: Routledge.

Deardorff, D. K., de Wit, H., Heyl, J. D., & Adams, T. (Eds.). (2012). *The Sage handbook of international higher education*. Thousand Oaks, CA: Sage.

Dervin, F. (2008). *Métamorphoses identitaires en situation de mobilité* (Doctoral thesis). Université de Turku, Turku. Retrieved from http://www.theses.fr/2008PA030027

Dervin, F., & Byram, M. (Eds.). (2008). *Échanges et mobilités académics: Quel bilan?* Paris: L'Harmattan.

Diao, W., Freed, B., & Smith, L. (2011). Confirmed beliefs or false assumptions? A study of home stay experiences in the French study abroad context. *Frontiers: The Interdisciplinary Journal of Study Abroad, XXI*(Fall), 109–142.

Dufon, M. A., & Churchill, E. (Eds.). (2006). *Language learners in study abroad contexts*. Clevedon: Multilingual Matters.

Dwyer, M. M. (2004). More Is better: The impact of study abroad program duration. *Frontiers: The Interdisciplinary Journal of Study Abroad, 10*(Fall), 151–163.

Engle, L. (2013). The rewards of qualitative assessment in study abroad. *Frontiers: The Interdisciplinary Journal of Study Abroad, XXII*(Winter/Spring), 11–126.

Engle, L., & Engle, J. (2003). Study abroad levels: Toward a classification of program types. *Frontiers: The Interdisciplinary Journal of Study Abroad, IX*(Fall), 1–20.

Fantini, A. E. (2006a). About intercultural communicative competence: A construct. *Appendix E*. Retrieved from World Learning. SIT Digital Collections website http://digitalcollections.sit.edu/worldlearning_publications/1/

Fantini, A. E. (2006b). Exploring and assessing intercultural competence: Final report of a research project conducted by the FEIL. Retrieved from http://digitalcollections.sit.edu/cgi/viewcontent.cgi?article=1001&context=worldlearning_publications

Fantini, A. E. (2019). *Intercultural communicative competence in educational exchange: A multinational perspective*. New York, NY: Routledge.

Favell, A. (2008). *Eurostars and Eurocities: Free movement and mobility in an integrating Europe*. Oxford: Blackwell Publishing.

Findlay, A. M. (2010). An assessment of supply and demand-side theorizations of international student mobility. *International Migration, 49*(2), 162–190.

Findlay, A. M., Stam, A., King, R., & Ruiz-Gelices, E. (2005). International opportunities: Searching for the meaning of student migration. *Geographical Helvetica, 60*(3), 192–200.

Forum on Education Abroad. (2011). Education abroad glossary. Retrieved from https://forumea.org/wp-content/uploads/2014/10/Forum-2011-Glossary-v2.pdf

Fournier, D. M. (2005). Evaluation. In S. Mathinson (Ed.), *Encyclopedia of evaluation* (pp. 139–140). Thousand Oaks, CA: Sage.

Freed, B. (Ed.). (1995). *Language learning in a study abroad context*. Amsterdam: John Benjamins.

Freed, B., Segalowitz, N., & Dewey, D. (2004). Context of learning and second language fluency in French: Comparing regular classroom, study abroad and intensive domestic immersion programs. *Language Acquisition, 26*, 275–301.

Gaul, E. (2015). *The American student abroad and the perceived impact in the local community* (Master's dissertation). Loyola University Chicago, Chicago, IL. http://ecommons.luc.edu/luc_theses/2889 database

Gautier, R., & Chevrot, J.-P. (2015). Acquisition of sociolinguistic variation in a study abroad context: The impact of social network. In R. Mitchell, N. Tracy-Ventura & K. McManus (Eds.), *Social interaction, identity and language learning during residence abroad* (pp. 169–184). Amsterdam: European Second Language Association.

Green, M. (2012). *Measuring and assessing internationalization*. Washington, DC: NAFSA. Retrieved from www.nafsa.org/epubs

Gu, Q., Schweisfurth, M, & Day, C (2010). Learning and growing in a "foreign" context: Intercultural experiences of international students. *Compare: A Journal of Comparative and International Education, 40*(1), 7–23.

Hadis, B. F. (2005). Why are they better students when they come back? Determinants of academic focusing gains in the study abroad experience. *Frontiers: The Interdisciplinary Journal of Study Abroad, 11*, 57–70.

Hamir, H. B. (2011). *Go abroad and graduate on-time: Study abroad practicipation, degree completion, and time-to-degree* (Doctoral thesis). University of Nebraska Lincoln, Lincoln, NE. Retrieved from http://digitalcommons.unl.edu/cehse daddiss/65

Hayden, M., Thompson, J., & Levy, J. (Eds.). (2015). *The Sage handbook of research in international education* (2nd ed.). Thousad Oaks, CA: Sage.

Hofhuis, J., Hanke, K., & Rutten, T. (2019). Social network sites and acculturation of international sojourners in the Netherlands: The mediating role of psychological alienation and online social support. *International Journal of Intercultural Relations, 69,* 120–130.

Hudzik, J., & Stohl, M. (2009). Modelling assessment of the outcomes and impacts of internationalization In H. de Wit (Ed.), *Measuring success in the internationalization of higher education. EAIE Occasional Paper 22* (pp. 9–21). Amsterdam: European Association for International Education.

Ilino, M. (2006). Norms of interaction in a Japanese homestay: Toward a two-way flow of linguistic and cultural resources. In M. A. Dufon & E. Churcill (Eds.), *Language learners in study abroad contexts* (pp. 151–176). Bristol: Multilingual Matters.

Isabelli-García, C. (2006). Study abroad social networks, motivation and attitudes: Implications for second language acquisition. In M. A. Dufon & E. Churchill (Eds.), *Language learning in study abroad contexts* (pp. 237–258). Clevedon: Multilingual Matters.

Jackson, J. (2008). *Language, identity and study abroad: Sociocultural perspectives.* London: Equinox Publishing.

Jackson, J. (2018). *Online intercultural education and study abroad.* London: Routledge.

Jackson, J., & Oguro, S. (Eds.). (2017). *Intercultural interventions in study abroad.* London: Routledge.

Janson, K., Schomburg, H., & Teichler, U. (2009). *The professional value of Erasmus mobility: The impact of international experience on former students' and on teachers' careers.* Bonn: Lemmens.

Jones, E. (2013). Internationalization and student learning outcomes. In H. de Wit (Ed.), *An introduction to higher education internationalisation* (pp. 107–116). Milan: Vita e Pensiero.

Kashima, E. S., & Loh, E. (2006). International students' acculturation: Effects of international, conational, and local ties and need for closure. *International Journal of Intercultural Relations, 30*(4), 471–485.

Kelo, M., Teichler, U., & Wächter, B. (2006a). *Eurodata: Student mobility in European higher education.* Bonn: Lemmens.

Kelo, M., Teichler, U., & Wächter, B. (2006b). Toward improved data on student mobility in Europe: Findings and concepts of the Eurodata study. *Journal of Studies in International Education, 10*(3), 194–223

King, R., & Ruiz-Gelices, E. (2003). International student migration and the European 'Year Abroad': Effects on European identity and subsequent migration behaviour. *International Journal of Population Geography, 9*(3), 229–252.

Kinginger, C. (2008). Language learning in study abroad: Case studies of Americans in France. *The Modern Language Journal, 92*(s1), 1–124.

Kinginger, C. (2013). *Social and cultural aspects of language learning in study abroad.* Amsterdam: John Benjamins.

Kinginger, C. (2017). Second language learning in a study abroad context. In N. Van Deusen-Scholl & S. May (Eds.), *Second and foreign language education* (pp. 125–136). Cham: Springer International Publishing.

Knight, J. (2004). Internationalization remodeled: Definitions, rationales, and approaches. *Journal of Studies in International Education, 8*(1), 5–31.

Knight, J. (2014). Three generations of crossborder higher education: New developments, challenges and issues. In B. Streitwieser (Ed.), *Internationalisation of higher education and global mobility* (pp. 43–58). Southampton: Symposium Books.

Krzaklewska, E. (2008). Why study abroad? An analysis of Erasmus students' motivations. In M. Byram & F. Dervin (Eds.), *Students, staff and academic mobility* (pp. 82–98). Newcastle upon Tyne: Cambridge Scholars Publishing.

Krzaklewska, E. (2013). Students between youth and adulthood: Analysis of the biographical experience. In B. Feyen & E. Krzaklewska (Eds.), *The Erasmus phenomenon – Symbol of a new European generation?* (pp. 79–96). Frankfurt: Peter Lang.

La Brack, B. (1993). The missing linkage: The process of integrating orientation and reentry In R. M. Paige (Ed.), *Education for the intercultural experience* (pp. 241–279). Yarmouth, ME: Intercultural Press.

Landis, D., & Brislin, R. W. (Eds.). (1983a). *Handbook of intercultural training: Area studies in intercultural training* (Vol. II). New York, NY: Pergamon.

Landis, D., & Brislin, R. W. (Eds.). (1983b). *Handbook of intercultural training: Issues in training methodology* (Vol. I). New York, NY: Pergamon.

Langran, I., Langran, E., & Ozment, K. (2009). The effect of the university roomate contact on ethnic attitudes and behavior *Journal of Experimental Social Psychology, 41*(4), 329–345.

Larsen, M. A. (2016). *Internationalization of higher education: An analysis through spatial, network and mobilities theories.* New York, NY: Palgrave Macmillan.

Lewin, R. (Ed.). (2009). *The handbook of practice and research in study abroad: Higher education and the quest for global citizenship.* New York, NY: Routledge.

López, X. P., Fernández, M. F., & Incera, A. C. (2016). The Economic impact of international students in a regional economy from a tourism perspective. *Tourism Economics, 22*(1), 125–140.

Lou, K. H., & Bosley, G. (2012). Facilitating intercultural learning abroad: The Intentional Targeted Intervention Model. In M. Vande Berg, R. M. Paige & K. H. Lou (Eds.), *Student leaning abroad: What our students are learning, what they're not, and what we can do about it* (pp. 335–359). Sterling, VA: Stylus Publishing.

Maggio, L. M. D. (2019). The connection of study abroad to students' positive feelings of institutional action. *Journal of College Student Retention: Research, Theory & Practice, 21*(3), 326–341.

Malet Calvo, D. (2018). Understanding international students beyond studentification: A new class of transnational urban consumers: The example of Erasmus students in Lisbon (Portugal). *Urban Studies, 55*(10), 2142–2158.

Malicki, R. (2012). *Outbound mobility best practice guide for Australian universities* Canberra: Australian Government – Department of Industry, Innovation, Science, Research and Tertiary Education.

McGourty, R. (2014). Does study abroad accelerate personal growth? *Trends & Insights for International Education Leaders*, 1–5. Retrieved from www.nafsa.org

Mellors-Bourne, R., Jones, E., Lawton, W., & Woodfield, S. (2015). Student perspectives on going international. Retrieved from https://www.british council.org/sites/default/files/iu_bc_outwd_mblty_student_perception_se pt_15.pdf

Metzger, C. A. (2006). Study abroad programming: A 21st century retention strategy? *College Student Affairs Journal, 25*(2), 164–175.

Miao, S. Y., & Harris, R. (2012). Learning and personality on study tours abroad. *Research in Post-Compulsory Education, 17*(4), 435–452.

Mitchell, R., Tracy-Ventura, N., & McManus, K. (2017). *Anglophone students abroad: Identity, social relationships, and language learning.* London: Routledge.

Mitchell, R., Tracy-Ventura, N., & McManus, K. (Eds.). (2015). *Social interaction, identity and language learning during residence abroad.* Amsterdam: European Second Language Association.

Murphy-Lejeune, E. (2002). *Student mobility and narrative in Europe: The new strangers.* London: Routledge.

Murphy-Lejeune, E. (2008). The student experience of mobility: A contrasting score. In M. Byram & F. Dervin (Eds.), *Students, staff and academic mobility in higher education* (pp. 12–30). Newcastle upon Tyne: Cambridge Scholars Publishing.

OECD. (2019). *Education at a glance 2019: OECD indicators.* Paris: OECD Publishing. doi:10.1787/f8d7880d-en.

Ogden, A. (2015). Toward a research agenda for U.S. education abroad. In E. Brewer (Ed.), *AIEA research agendas for the internationalization of higher educational and psychological measurement.* Retrieved from http://www.aieaworld.org/assets/doc s/research_agenda/ogden_2015.pdf

Ogden, A., & Streitwieser, B. (2017). Research on US education abroad: A concise overview. In D. M. Velliaris & D. Coleman-George (Eds.), *Handbook of research on study abroad programs and outbound* (pp. 1–39). Adelaide: IGI Global Press.

Paige, R. M., Cohen, A. D., Kappler, B., Chi, J. C., & Lassegard, J. P. (2002a). *Maximizing study abroad: A program professional's guide to strategies for language and culture learning and use.* Minneapolis, MN: Center for Advanced Research on Language Acquisition - University of Minnesota.

Paige, R. M., Cohen, A. D., Kappler, B., Chi, J. C., & Lassegard, J. P. (2002b). *Maximizing study abroad: A student's guide to strategies for language and culture learning and use.* Minneapolis, MN: Center for Advanced Research on Language Acquisition - University of Minnesota.

Papatsiba, V. (2003). *Des étudiants européens: "Erasmus" et l'aventure de l'altérité.* Berne: Peter Lang.

Papatsiba, V. (2005). Student mobility in Europe: An academic, cultural and mental Journey? Some conceptual reflections and empirical findings. In M. Tight (Ed.), *International Relations (International Perspectives on Higher Education Research)* (Vol. 3, pp. 29–65): Bingley, Emerald Group Publishing Limited.

Parcells, C. (2011). Institutional case studies of curriculum integration practices based upon the University of Minnesota model. Retrieved from https://global. umn.edu/icc/documents/institutional_case_studies.pdf

Pasquarelli, S. L., Cole, R. A., & Tyson, M. J. (2018). *Passport to change: Designing academically sound, culturally relevant short term faculty-led study abroad programs.* Sterling, VA: Stylus Publishing.

Pellegrino Aveni, V. A. (2005). *Study abroad and second language use: Constructing the self.* Cambridge: Cambridge University Press.

Prazeres, L., Findlay, A., McCollum, D., Sander, N., Musil, E., Krisjane, Z., & Apsite-Berina, E. (2017). Distinctive and comparative places: Alternative narratives of distinction within international student mobility. *Geoforum, 80*, 114–122.

Raby, R. L., Rhodes, G. M., & Biscarra, A. (2013). Community college study abroad: Implications for student sucess *Community College Journal of Research and Practice, 38*(2–3), 174–183.

50 Foundations of an interdisciplinary approach

Raghuram, P. (2013). Theorising the spaces of student migration. *Population, Space and Place, 19*(2), 138–154.

Regan, V., Howard, M., & Lemée, M. (2009). *The acquisition of sociolinguistic competence in a study abroad context.* Bristol: Multilingual Matters.

Riaño, Y., & Piguet, E. (2016). International student migration. In B. Wharf (Ed.), *Oxford bibliographies in Geography.* New York, NY: Oxford University Press.

Riaño, Y., Van Mol, C., & Raghuram, P. (2018). New directions in studying policies of international student mobility and migration. *Globalisation, Societies and Education, 16*(3), 283–294.

Rodrigues, M. (2013). Does student mobility during higher education pay? Evidence from 16 European countries. *European Commission Joint Research Centre: Scientific and Technical Reports.* Retrieved from http://www.jrc.ec.europa.eu/

Savicki, V., & Brewer, E. (Eds.). (2015). *Assessing study abroad: Theory, tools, and practice.* Sterling, VA: Stylus Publishing.

Segalowitz, N., Freed, B., Collentine, J., Lafford, B., Lazar, N., & Diaz-Campos, M. (2004). A comparison of Spanish second language acquisition in two different learning contexts: Study abroad and the domestic classroom. *Frontiers: The Interdisciplinary Journal of Study Abroad, 10*(Fall), 1–18.

Shaules, D. (2007). *Deep culture: The hidden challenges of global living.* Clevedon: Multilingual Matters.

Sinicrope, C., Norris, J. M., & Watanabe, Y. (2006). Understanding and assessing intercultural competence: A summary of theory, research, and practice. *Second Language Studies, 26*(1), 1–58. Retrieved from http://www.hawaii.edu/sls/uhwpesl/26(1)/Norris.pdf

Smith, D. (2002). Patterns and processes of studentification in Leeds. *Regional Review, 12,* 6–7.

Smith, R. A., & Khawaja, N. G. (2011). A review of the acculturation experiences of international students. *International Journal of Intercultural Relations, 35*(6), 699–713.

Spencer-Oatey, H., & Dauber, D. (2019). Internationalisation and student diversity: How far are the opportunity benefits being perceived and exploited? *Higher Education, 78,* 1035–1058.

Spencer-Oatey, H., & Xiong, Z. (2006). Chinese students' psychological and sociocultural adjustments to Britain: An empirical study. *Language, Culture and Curriculum, 19*(1), 37–53.

Streitwieser, B. T. (2012). Editorial. *Research in Comparative and International Education, 7*(1), 1–4.

Streitwieser, B. T. (Ed.). (2014). *Internationalization of higher education and global mobility.* Southampton: Symposium Books.

Strong, D. (2011). Discourse of bi-national exchange students: Constructing dual identification. In F. Dervin (Ed.), *Analysing the consequences of academic mobility and migration* (pp. 51–66). Newcastle Upon Tyne: Cambridge.

Sussex Centre for Migration Research. (2005). *International student mobility.* Brighton: Sussex Centre for Migration Research.

Sutton, R. C., & Rubin, D. L. (2004). The GLOSSARI Project: Initial findings from a system-wide research initiative on study abroad learning outcomes. *Frontiers: Interdisciplinary Journal of Study Abroad, 10*(Fall), 65–82.

Teichler, U. (1996). Research on academic mobility and international cooperation in higher education: An agenda for the future. In B. Blumenthal, R. M. Goodwin, A. Smith & U. Teichler (Eds.), *Academic mobility in a changing World: Regional and global trends* (pp. 338–358). London: Jessica Kingsley Publishers.

Teichler, U. (2004). Temporary study abroad: The life of Erasmus students. *European Journal of Education, 39*(4), 395–408.

Teichler, U. (2009). Internationalisation of higher education: European experiences. *Asia Pacific Education Review, 10*(1), 93–106.

Teichler, U. (2011). International dimensions of higher education and graduate employment. In J. Allen & R. Van der Velden (Eds.), *The Flexible Professional in the Knowledge Society: New Challenges for Higher Education* (pp. 177–197). Dordrecht: Springer Netherlands.

Teichler, U. (2015). The impact of temporary study abroad. In R. Mitchell, N. Tracy-Ventura & K. McManus (Eds.), *Social interaction, identity and language learning during residence abroad* (pp. 16–32). Amsterdam: European Second Language Association.

Teichler, U. (2017). Internationalisation trends in higher education and the changing role of international student mobility. *Journal of International Mobility, 1*(5), 177–216.

Teichler, U., Ferencz, I., & Wächter, B. (2011a). *Mapping mobility in European higher education: Case studies* (Vol. II). Brussels: A study produced for the Directorate General for Education and Culture (DGEAC), European Commission.

Teichler, U., Ferencz, I., & Wächter, B. (2011b). *Mapping mobility in European higher education: Overview and trends* (Vol. I). Brussels: A study produced for the Directorate General for Education and Culture (DGEAC), European Commission.

Teichler, U., & Maiworm, F. (1997). The Erasmus students' experience. Major findings of the Erasmus evaluation research project. Retrieved from http://bookshop.europa.eu

Tonkin, H., & Quiroga, D. (2004). A qualitative approach to the assessment of international service-learning. *Frontiers: Interdisciplinary Journal of Study Abroad, 10*(Fall), 131–149.

Tsoukalas, J. (2008). The double life of Erasmus students. In M. Byram & F. Dervin (Eds.), *Students, staff and academic mobility in higher education* (pp. 131–152). Newcastle upon Tyne: Cambridge Scholars Publishing.

Van Mol, C. (2014). *Intra-European student mobility in higher education systems: Europe on the move.* Basingstoke: Palgrave Macmillan.

Van Mol, C. (2017). Do employers value international study and internships? A comparative analysis of 31 countries. *Geoforum, 78*, 52–60.

Van Mol, C., & Ekamper, P. (2016). Destination cities of European exchange students. *Geografisk Tidsskrift-Danish Journal of Geography, 116*(1), 85–91.

Van Mol, C., & Michielsen, J. (2015). The reconstruction of a social network abroad: An analysis of the interaction patterns of Erasmus students. *Mobilities, 10*(3), 423–444.

Van Mol, C., & Timmerman, C. (2014). Should I stay or should I go? An analysis of the determinants of intra-European student mobility. *Population, Space and Place, 20*(5), 465–479.

Van Riemsdijk, M., & Wang, Q. (Eds.). (2017). *Rethinking international skilled migration.* New York, NY: Routledge.

Vande Berg, M. (2007). Intervening in the learning of U.S. students abroad. *Journal of studies in International Education, 11*(3–4), 392–399.

Vande Berg, M., & Paige, R. M. (2009). Applying theory and research: The evolution of intercultural competence in US study abroad. In D. K. Deardorff (Ed.), *The Sage handbook of intercultural competence* (pp. 419–437). Thousand Oaks, CA: Sage.

Vande Berg, M., Paige, R. M., & Lou, K. H. (2012a). *Student leaning abroad: What our students are learning, what they're not, and what we can do about it.* Sterling, VA: Stylus Publishing.

52 Foundations of an interdisciplinary approach

Vande Berg, M., Paige, R. M., & Lou, K. H. (2012b). Student learning abroad: Paradigms and assumptions. In M. Vande Berg, R. M. Paige & K. H. Lou (Eds.), *Student leaning abroad: What our students are learning, what they're not, and what we can do about it* (pp. 3–28). Sterling, VA: Stylus Publishing.

Velliaris, D. M., & Coleman-George, D. (Eds.). (2018). *Handbook of research on study abroad programs and outbound mobility.* Hershey, PA: IGI-Global.

Verbik, L., & Lasanowski, V. (2007). *International student mobility: Patterns and trends.* London: The Observatory on Borderless Education.

Wächter, B. (2014). Recent trends in student mobility in Europe. In B. Streitwieser (Ed.), *Internationalisation of higher education and global mobility* (pp. 87–97). Southampton: Symposium Books.

Wächter, B., Lam, Q. K. H., & Ferencz, I. (2012). *Tying it all together: Excellence, mobility, funding and the social dimension in higher education.* Bonn: Lemmens.

West, A. (2002). Higher education admissions and student mobility: The ADMIT research project. *European Educational Research Journal, 1*(1), 151–172.

West, C. (2015). Assessing learning outcomes for education abroad. *International Educator,* 36–41. Retrieved from https://www.nafsa.org/_/File/_/ie_novdec 15_ea.pdf

Whalen, B. (2012). Frontiers Journal and the Forum on Education Abroad: Building a research tradition on education abroad for the comparative education scholarship. *Research in Comparative and International Education, 7*(1), 61–69.

Wiers-Jenssen, J. (2008). Does higher education attained abroad lead to international jobs? *Journal of Studies in International Education, 12*(2), 101–130.

Willis, F. (1977). *Residence abroad and the student of modern languages: A preliminary survey.* Bradford: The University of Bradford, Modern Languages Centre.

Wood, C. A., Banks, S., Galiardi, S., Koehn, J., & Schroeder, K. (2011). Community impacts of international service-Learning and study abroad: An analysis of focus groups with program leaders. *Partnerships: A Journal of Service Learning & Civic Engagement, 2*(1), 1–23.

Woodfield, S. (2010). Key trends and emerging issues in international student mobility. In F. Maringe & F. Foskett (Eds.), *Globalization and internationalization in higher education: Theoretical, strategic and management perspectives* (pp. 109–123). London: Continuum.

Woodruff, G. A., & Henry, A. M. (2012). *Curriculum integration of education abroad.* Washington, DC: NAFSA: Association of International Educators Publication.

World Learning. (2000). About our institution. *SIT Occasional Papers: 4.* Retrieved from https://digitalcollections.sit.edu/sop/4/

Yemini, M., & Sagie, N. (2016). Research on internationalisation in higher education – exploratory analysis. *Perspectives: Policy and practice in higher education, 20*(2–3), 90–98.

Young, T. J., & Schartner, A. (2014). The effects of cross-cultural communication education on international students' adjustment and adaptation. *Journal of Multilingual and Multicultural Development, 35*(6), 547–562.

Young, T. J., Sercombe, P. G., Sachdev, I., Naeb, R., & Schartner, A. (2013). Success factors for international postgraduate students' adjustment: Exploring the roles of intercultural competence, language proficiency, social contact and social support. *European Journal of Higher Education, 3*(2), 151–171.

Chapter 2

Educational foundations

About Chapter 2

Millions of students are on the move. The UNESCO Institute for Statistics estimates that the number of students studying outside their country of origin to pursue tertiary-level education abroad rose from 2.1 million in 2000 to 5.3 million in 2017. For the European Union (EU), 26 years after the launch of *Erasmus*, in 1987, the programme reached 3 million students who had studied or worked abroad. However, the forces shaping these figures and the impacts accruing to those who study abroad (and the institutions hosting them) need to be further explored.

This second chapter begins by contextualising the push to internationalise higher education and how student mobility sits within it. In the second section, I advance a typology of contemporary taxonomies for student mobility in European higher education, while discussing the multifarious terms used and misnomers like 'international', 'foreign' and 'culturally and linguistically diverse' students.

The third section offers a chronological synopsis of student mobility and the internationalisation of European higher education, with an emphasis on the role of EU student mobility schemes and underlying objectives. In the section that follows I point to the flaws of using student metrics as the primary marker of success of studying abroad instead of its educational value. To illustrate this misconception at supranational level, an analysis of the objectives in the decisions establishing the different iterations of the *Erasmus* programme is provided. Among these objectives and expected learning gains is intercultural learning, often coupled with language learning as previously discussed in Chapter 1.

The last section of the chapter focuses on the contextual conditions behind the widening policy interest in Europe's language and cultural diversity since the 1990s and how it influences the rationales for developing intercultural abilities through student mobility. This historical synopsis is followed by a summary of intercultural constructs.

To conclude, a summary of the chapter's key points is provided. This summary is followed by a roadmap of reflective questions and/or points (see Box 2.1) to help the reader critically review the content of the chapter.

54 Foundations of an interdisciplinary approach

Student mobility and internationalisation

Formerly of little concern, internationalisation became a major focus in European post-secondary education from the mid-1980s on, especially since the implementation of *Erasmus* in 1987.

This move from marginality to centrality was accompanied by the broadening of the meaning of internationalisation in the higher education sector. Since then, much has been written about it as reflected in the burgeoning number of specialised academic journals and books (see Chapter 1); less, however, about how student mobility permeates higher education internationalisation and how its different modalities sit within these discourses. To facilitate such an understanding, it is crucial to pin down the ways in which student mobility grows out of the process of internationalising higher education and is mediated by its different meanings and purposes.

To this end, this section begins by situating the epistemological shift, in the 1990s, from a conceptualisation of higher education internationalisation as an institutional list of activities (i.e., as an outcome) to a national/sector/institutional process (Knight, 2004; Larsen, 2016; Yemini, 2015). This shift in meaning cannot be overlooked as conceptualisations of higher education and its internationalisation processes can have implications as to how student mobility is theorised. My premise here is straightforward; by being clear about how I position myself regarding contemporary definitions of higher education internationalisation, I hope to be equally clear about the brushstrokes I use to paint a picture of student mobility within the internationalisation of higher education landscape. For this reason, only after clarifying how internationalisation is understood in this book will I delve into the taxonomies of student mobility in European higher education (more on this later).

As discussed in Chapter 1, in 2004 Jane Knight advanced a widely cited definition of internationalisation in the higher education sector. This definition derives from an earlier one developed by this Canadian scholar in 1994. Neither the time lapse nor the focus of the 2004 paper (Internationalization remodeled: definitions, rationales, and approaches) are a mere coincidence. Historical synopses cannot be put aside here. It was in the last decade of the twentieth century that the liberalisation of trade, including in education, took place following the ratification of the General Agreement on Trade in Services (GATS) in 1995. As asserted by Maringe (2010), internationalisation quickly became a buzzword in post-secondary education and a springboard for neo-liberal globalisation agendas across the sector. Unsurprisingly, the scope of Knight's (1994) definition was widened in 2004 to embrace the national/sector level in addition to the institutional. Hence the reformulated definition as 'the process of integrating an international, intercultural, or global dimension into the purpose, functions and delivery of post-secondary education' (p. 11).

Despite the widespread use of Knight's (2004) definition in academic circles, this conceptualisation is not consensual (e.g., Larsen, 2016; Yemini, 2015).

Miri Yemini (2015), for example, argues that this definition lacks clarity over the relationship between its three characterising dimensions and how the four rationales (political/economic/academic/socio-cultural) of internationalisation sit within it. Moreover, Yemini contends that Knight limits the process of internationalisation to higher education, ignoring the end impacts on lifelong learning of previous educational levels. Clarifying these aspects is critical to set the desired direction for internationalisation, a critique shared by a European Parliament report on the internationalisation of higher education in the European context (see de Wit, Hunter, Howard, & Egron-Polak, 2015).

The number of conceptualisations of higher education internationalisation and the web of related concepts would require a book of its own (see Maringe, 2010 for a summary of influential definitions). As a result, Teichler (2017) argues that only a few elements of internationalisation are shared by all actors and experts. Agreeing with this argument, my goal in this chapter is not to delve into the flurry of conceptualisations but to be clear about how I understand higher education internationalisation and, most of all, how student mobility sits in it. Notwithstanding the need to clarify some aspects in Knight's (2004) definition, her conceptualisation offers guiding principles to how higher education internationalisation is understood in this book, namely:

1. the integration of an international/intercultural/global dimension in tandem to reflect the breadth and depth of internationalisation;
2. the comprehensiveness of the process (in terms of activities, rationales, levels and pillars/streams);
3. the notion of an evolutionary change in shaping the activities and/or strategies of this very process;
4. the interdependence of internationalisation 'at home' and 'abroad'.

Student mobility emerges as one of these activities. Agreeing, however, with de Wit et al. (2015) that Knight's (2004) conceptualisation needs to specify the end goal of internationalisation in higher education, I would also add that it should be an: '**intentional** process' so as to 'enhance the quality of education for all students and staff, and to make a meaningful contribution to society' (p. 282 [boldface in the original]). To elaborate further, another element is added to the four elements previously outlined: (5) purpose. And when we add purpose, we need to bear in mind the ideologies, means, values and agency to leverage institutional and societal change. Clarifying the purpose of post-secondary internationalisation should address internal and external levels, in terms of institutional quality and contributions to society (Egron-Polak & Marmolejo, 2017).

By the same token, student mobility is more than a means to an end, but part of the end goal of internationalisation in that it should also lead to quality educational experiences. Clearly, 'all students' and 'all staff' are fundamental in this process, both as agents and beneficiaries of change (Robson, Almeida,

& Schartner, 2018). Moreover, the 'at home' dimension should be considered when facilitating internationalised university experiences for all students within domestic learning environments (Beelen & Jones, 2015) according to an inclusive approach to internationalisation that takes into account local conditions and needs (Almeida, Robson, Morosini, & Baranzeli, 2019).

Within Knight's (2004, 2012) taxonomy, the 'abroad' and 'at home' dimensions have an interdependent relationship, even if the implications each pillar has on the other are not specified. This interdependence is also assumed in this book. The reason is straightforward and transcends conceptual categorisations. Student mobility does not happen in a vacuum. It happens in a new academic and cultural setting – a new home which mobile students should adjust to, but a home that should also integrate them along with their domestic counterparts (Almeida, 2018). As will be demonstrated in Chapter 5, part of this integration can be facilitated by extra-curricular activities on campus and enhanced links to the local community.

To summarise, isolating student mobility from internationalisation efforts would ultimately ignore a major force shaping higher education today and the contextual scenarios student mobility is part of. The types of student mobility under examination in this book, and related terminology, are discussed next.

Typological synopsis

Two types of physical student mobility, within the European higher education context, are analysed in this book from an interdisciplinary perspective. Both imply the physical movement of students across national boundaries to study in a higher education institution located in a country other than students' countries of origin or prior education. Yet, they differ, among other things, on the purposes of studying abroad, more specifically, the pursuit of:

1. academic credits as recognition of a period of study abroad;
2. a whole academic degree abroad.

In both situations, students left their countries of origin or prior education to study abroad, but the drivers were different. In the first situation, students left on a temporary basis as part of a degree programme. This type of student mobility is usually framed by exchange programmes and/or bi- or multilateral agreements (like *Erasmus*). At the end of the mobility period, students return to the home institution to complete their studies, with the home institution having to recognise the academic marks obtained abroad. Hence the term 'exchange student', which points to the principle of reciprocity, i.e., student inflows should balance the outflows. Simply put, for a student sent abroad another is (or should be) received. In European literature, this programmatic type of student mobility can be referred to by a variety of terms; from 'credit-seeking' or 'non-degree' to 'temporary', 'short-term' or 'horizontal' student mobility (see Table 2.1 for a list of terms). As argued in Chapter 1, fluctuations in terminology can be a slippery slope and affect knowledge production in absence of an agreed-upon set of definitions for the different modalities of student mobility.

The second type of student mobility is often described in opposition to the first given that in this modality students have to complete a whole cycle or level of study to obtain a degree abroad (see Wächter, 2008 or the EURODATA studies). As in the first type of student mobility, terminology varies but amongst frequent terms are: 'degree-seeking', 'diploma', 'long-term', 'vertical' and 'international' student mobility (see Table 2.1 for a list of terms). Once again, terminology can be misleading as, albeit different, credit- and degree-seeking students are often referred to interchangeably as 'international' or 'foreign' students. This happens because the study abroad status is equated with foreign citizenship, ignoring prior student trajectories and heterogeneity amongst student cohorts. As a result, some scholars and practitioners consider the label 'international student' not fit for purpose, advancing alternatives like: 'culturally and linguistically diverse students' (e.g., Gonzalez, Pagan, Wendell, & Love, 2011), 'intercultural students' (e.g., Marginson & Sawir, 2011), 'diverse students' (e.g., Carroll, 2015).

Such labels can, nonetheless, be equally problematic by reproducing patterns of inequality that set off a standard: Diverse from whom? From their domestic counterparts? I therefore question whether these labels are not looking down the wrong end of the telescope by starting from students' identities and assuming a pattern of normality. But, are not all students diverse in their multiple identities?

Finding an innocuous lexicon for the different modalities of student mobility is certainly not an easy task, if attainable. In the end, I have opted to use 'mobile' or 'study abroad students' when I speak in broad terms (study abroad is used in the same sense).[1] To differentiate semantically between these two types of mobile students I use the academic purpose of their stay abroad – i.e., for credit or degree. Yet, as will be demonstrated throughout Part II of this book, these student groups are not only characterised by differences but also similarities. As much for the sake of simplicity than anything else, across this chapter and the remainder of the book I will use interchangeably credit-seeking students or exchange students, and degree-seeking or international students. When I refer to other types of student mobility this is explicitly stated in the text. The key of interpretation here is how we define: (1) mobile students, and (2) the different types of academic movement.

First, and as defined in the EURODATA studies described in Chapter 1, I define mobile students as 'students who cross national borders for the purpose or in the context of their studies' (Teichler, Ferencz, & Wächter, 2011, p. 27). My assumption is straightforward – in physical student mobility there is always a movement from at least one country or higher education institution to another, with other possible academic movements happening in-between.

58 Foundations of an interdisciplinary approach

The second layer of our definition – (2) different types of academic movement – involves outlining descriptors that characterise types of student mobility in European higher education. I advance five:

1. *academic purpose*: the academic goal of studying abroad (e.g., for credit and/or for a whole degree abroad);
2. *nature*: the type or sort of movement (e.g., within and/or across cycles/levels of study or both – i.e., horizontal, vertical and diagonal, respectively);
3. *duration*: the duration of the period of studies abroad (e.g., one semester);
4. *level of study*: the cycle or level of study in which the period of studies abroad takes place (e.g., as part of an undergraduate degree) and/or towards which it is geared (e.g., the award of an undergraduate degree);
5. *direction*: the end point(s) towards which the academic movement is aimed according to the acts of leaving (outbound) and/or arriving (inbound).

The use of and/or in descriptors 1, 2, 4, and 5 is intentional and aims to capture the combination of academic movements beyond binary logics. Positing credit and degree-seeking student mobility as contrasting scores neglects any intertwinement between the two.

To give an example, an international student (i.e., degree-seeking) might be mobile for a short period of time. Let us imagine a Portuguese student who is studying towards an undergraduate degree in another EU member state. This student can participate in 'mobility projects for higher education students' under Key Action 1 of *Erasmus+* (formerly *Erasmus*) and do a semester or an academic year abroad to gain academic credits. Thus, this student is mobile within and across levels of study.

These boundaries become increasingly blurred if we categorise the direction of the academic movement (Descriptor 5) made by our student. For instance, during the academic year our student participates in *Erasmus+* he/she can be categorised in three ways: (a) as an international student in Institution A, (b) an outgoing credit-seeking student in this very institution, and (c) an incoming credit-seeking student by the institution that receives temporarily our student (Institution B) (Figure 2.1).

The threefold categorisation of the student in Figure 2.1 is possible because the direction of academic movement depends on where (country + institution) the student is standing in the moment of our analysis, but also where he/she was before (country/ies + institution/s).[2] That is why categorising into binaries often disregards time and space logics underpinning student mobility, as forefronted by migration theorists (e.g., King & Raghuram, 2013; Raghuram, 2013) and international educators (e.g., Larsen, 2016).

This backdrop leads to a further consideration regarding Descriptor 2 – the nature of the academic movement – which I use to posit the type of academic movement against cycles/levels of study (e.g., Undergraduate/Bachelor, Master's and PhD). When the academic movement occurs across a level of study,

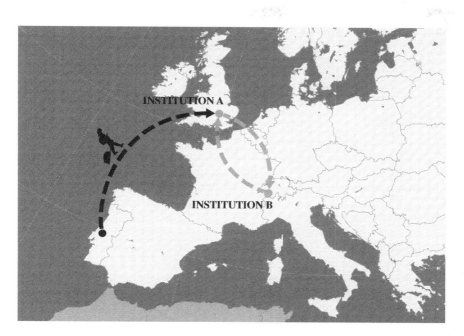

Figure 2.1 Descriptor 5: direction of academic movement. Map source: Wikipedia Commons

I call this movement 'vertical'; when it occurs within, the term 'horizontal' is used. In situations when the movement takes place within and across levels of study, I argue that the term 'diagonal' should be used.

It should be also noted that unlike Wächter (2008, 2014) and Teichler (2009, 2015), when the terms 'horizontal' and 'vertical' are employed in this book no assumption is made on the quality of higher education systems. To elaborate further, according to Wächter and Teichler, horizontal mobility occurs between countries with similar higher education systems, with *Erasmus* being considered such an example. Vertical mobility, in turn, is bound to unbalanced levels of development. Following this classification, the movement of degree-seeking students from the developing world to OECD-type countries is deemed vertical (Wächter, 2008). Notwithstanding the light drawn by Wächter (2008, 2014) and Teichler (2009, 2015) onto the role of higher education systems in predicting mobility patterns, I have opted not to make this distinction. The reason is twofold. First, this classification neglects cross-categorisations. Second, the complex ways student mobility is enacted can go beyond economic imbalances and uneven higher education systems.

To summarise, any attempt to name, describe or classify student mobility by typologies should be grounded in a coherent logic that captures the complexity of this phenomenon and concepts under scrutiny – in our case, the different types

60 Foundations of an interdisciplinary approach

or modalities of physical student mobility. As contended by Larsen (2016), such logic should move from binary categories to a multifaceted, multiscalar analysis aggregating the different facets underpinning the movement of mobile students. And yet, the legitimacy of any taxonomy hinges upon its practical application, and is addressed next.

Applied taxonomies

Much of the existing literature on student mobility assumes mobile students start their studies in one country, move to another and then return home. This obviously ignores the complex ways by which student mobilities are actualised.

To put this linear logic into perspective, this section categorises common types of student mobility in European higher education according to the descriptors previously outlined: (1) academic purpose, (2) nature, (3) duration, (4), level of study. The fifth descriptor (direction) is not addressed here because this category depends both on where the student is standing in the moment of our analysis and where he or she was before (see previous section).

Note that the categorisation into mobility types in this section is by no means exhaustive, but illustrative of some modalities or types of physical student mobility in European higher education. The variety of youth mobility projects in Europe is certainly not confined to the mobility types in Table 2.1. Other modalities, like volunteering, school exchanges, vocational apprenticeships, internships/placements, youth worker mobility, are equally common in Europe. Yet, the particulars of these mobility projects are outside the remit of this book because some of the aforementioned examples do not target higher education nor the pursuit of an academic endeavour. This is not to say that these mobility types are unimportant or do not leverage further mobility opportunities. The contrary is true. School exchanges, for example, may have direct implications to student mobility in tertiary-level education given the ways in which secondary schools may prepare students for international higher education in Europe (Baiutti, 2019) and elsewhere (Rizvi, 2017).

This all the more important given the expected expansion of pupil mobility in the next generation of the *Erasmus+* programme post-2020, and EU efforts towards the realisation of a European Education Area by 2025. Building on the Bologna higher education reform project, a core element of this barrier-free education area (beyond higher education) is the automatic recognition of upper secondary and higher education diplomas and the outcomes of learning periods abroad (see COM, 2018). This will naturally have implications for higher education student mobility as an upper secondary qualification in one member state will be automatically recognised in another.

And yet again, to understand such implications it is crucial to consider the varying types or modalities of student mobility in European higher education. Some of these modalities are categorised in Table 2.1 according to the taxonomy previously outlined, followed by a detailed discussion of each mobility type.

From left to right, Table 2.1 lists the preferred terms used in this book to name frequent types of student mobility in European higher education, followed by other commonly used terminology in Column 2. The types of physical student mobility are listed horizontally and posited against the four aforementioned descriptors (listed vertically).

Of the six modalities of physical student mobility in Table 2.1, degree-seeking is the most widespread in European higher education. According to Teichler et al. (2011 – EURODATA II, Volume I), degree-seeking student mobility is mainly fuelled by students with a non-European nationality. Numerically, they account for 58 per cent of the over 1.5 million foreign students[3] enrolled in the 32 countries surveyed in EURODATA II in 2006/07. Nevertheless, almost two thirds of these students were enrolled in the UK, Germany and France, with one third in the UK alone (Teichler et al., 2011; Wächter, 2014).

Impressive as these figures are, they may not necessarily reflect the real number of international students in Europe Not only do the data definition issues discussed in Chapter 1 blur reliable quantifications, but there is also the fluid and fuzzy nature of cross-border flows. Moreover, different forms of degree-seeking mobility may be considered. Scholars like Cairns (2014, 2017) contend that within degree mobility there are fundamental differences in the educational profile of students. According to Cairns, degree mobility refers to the transnational movement of students who have successfully completed upper secondary education and move abroad for the entire duration of a degree (typically an undergraduate). When this movement takes place after the completion of a tertiary educational qualification, in students' country of residence, Cairns calls this movement 'post-diploma mobility' (typically, students pursuing a Master's or Doctorate abroad).

Despite the large number of degree-seeking students in Europe, studying abroad for academic credits is by no means irrelevant. Strongly incentivised by the EU's regional policy through the *Erasmus* programme, it is of general agreement among the scholarly community that studying for academic credits abroad leveraged regional student mobility in European post-secondary education (see, inter alia, de Wit, 2002; de Wit & Merkx, 2012; Huisman, Adelman, Hsieh, Shams, & Wilkins, 2012; Papatsiba, 2006; Smith, 1996; Teichler, 2009; Wächter, 2008). Hence the use of intra-European mobility as a synonym for credit student mobility (see Table 2.1, Column 2).

Numerically, *Erasmus* students are a relatively small share of the total student enrolment in Europe. According to Teichler et al. (2011), these credit-seeking students represent a share 'of less than 1% on average in the Europe 32 region in 2008/09 on an annual basis' (p. 6). Although numbers are far from meeting the EU's ambitious targets, *Erasmus* remains a strategic vehicle for maximising the community's political, cultural and economic outreach across Member States as the following section will show.

The iterations of *Erasmus* have, de facto, been geared towards streamlining its impact and attracting a greater number of students. For instance, at student level,

62 Foundations of an interdisciplinary approach

under Key Action 1 of *Erasmus+*, those students who wish to do a period of study or traineeship during their degrees can now do it up to a maximum of 12 months per study cycle[4] (see Table 2.1, Column 6). Simply put, students can study or train abroad across all three study cycles provided that the minimum duration for each activity (study or traineeship) and a maximum of 12 months per study cycle is respected. This naturally blurs the divide between short and long-term study abroad. Typically, in Europe credit-seeking student mobility is understood as short-term (e.g., Brooks & Waters, 2011; Cairns, 2014; Teichler et al., 2011; Wächter, 2008), regardless of whether students spend three months or one year abroad. At the same time, degree-seeking student mobility is deemed long-term, even if its duration can also vary.

On the other side of the Atlantic, both the Forum on Education Abroad and the Institute of International Education posit short-term as lasting eight weeks or less at the education abroad site (see Forum on Education Abroad, 2011; Institute of International Education, 2018). Once again, differences in meaning emerge from the approach to interpretation. Hence my decision to refer to duration by its raw measurement units (see Column 5, Table 2.1). Short is not only imprecise due to contextual factors, but also because it is usually set in opposition to long. But what is short- and long-term student mobility in European higher education?

In practice, in the framework of *Erasmus+* credit-seeking students can be mobile for a longer period of time than their degree-seeking counterparts. Let us take the example of international students pursuing a Master's in the UK, which typically lasts one academic year on a full-time basis. Against this backdrop, is it accurate to deem credit-seeking student mobility short-term, irrespective of the length of the stay abroad? And, should all forms of degree-seeking student mobility be considered long-term? After all, not only can credit-bearing student mobility last longer than degree-seeking, but there is also variation in the duration of both. International students studying towards a doctorate will spend at least three academic years abroad, whereas those pursuing a Master's can spend only one. Additionally, a one-year exchange student can spend the exact same time abroad as an international Master's student. And yet, whereas the study abroad period of the former student is categorised short-term, for the latter it is deemed long-term.

But let me elaborate further my previous two questions by raising an overarching one:

> How accurate is it to contrast short and long durations to differentiate between the different types of student mobility?

Due to the dearth of preciseness in using short- and long-term as contrasting scores, examples like the ones pointed out above fall between the cracks.

Another example is the *Erasmus Mundus Joint Master Degrees* (EMJMD). This case is very insightful as it cuts across categories. In addition to helping

Table 2.1 Common types of physical student mobility in European higher education

Preferred term	Common terms	Purpose	Nature	Duration	Level of study[a]
Credit-seeking	• Short-term • Temporary • Horizontal • Intra-European • Organised • Regional • Student exchange	To study or do a traineeship abroad for academic credits	Horizontal	Measured by: month/term/semester/year • 3–12 mos. (for studies)[b] • 2–12 mos. (for traineeship)[b]	UG (MA)[b] (PhD)[b]
Degree-seeking	• Diploma • Long-term • Vertical • Spontaneous • International • Global	To study abroad to obtain a whole degree or certificate abroad	Vertical	Measured by: academic year	UG MA PhD
Joint degree programmes	• Joint programmes • In-build • Joint degrees	To study abroad for academic credit with the end goal of obtaining a joint degree	Diagonal	Measured by: term/semester/academic year • 1 – 2 years[b] • 3 – 4 years[b]	UG MA[b] PhD
Double/multiple degree	• Joint degrees • Dual degrees • Combined degree • Simultaneous degree • Parallel/ simultaneous/ common degrees	To study abroad to obtain a double or multiple degree	Vertical	Measured by: term/semester/academic year	UG MA PhD

(Continued)

Table 2.1 Continued

Preferred term	Common terms	Purpose	Nature	Duration	Level of study[a]
Field work	• Field study programme • Field trip • Field research	To learn experientially abroad, usually to collect data or conduct empirical work	Horizontal	Measured by: weeks, months, term/semester	UG MA PhD
Residence abroad	• Year abroad • Study abroad • Teacher language assistantships • Assistantship placements • Bilateral language assistants programmes	To improve language learning in situ, either for academic or professional purposes	Horizontal	Measured by: academic year	UG

Note. UG = Undergraduate (or Bachelor, BA); MA = Master's; PhD = Doctorate.

Note.[a] Typical levels of study. Exceptions can exist.

Note.[b] Under *Erasmus+*. The use of brackets (MA), (PhD) in Row 1, Column 6 indicates the recent rules of *Erasmus+*, namely the possibility of credit-seeking students being mobile across all three levels of study.

one reassess the degree of shortness that should be called short, this international joint master's programme combines elements of vertical and horizontal student mobility (i.e., what I call diagonal). On the one hand, students in these programmes must spend at least two mobility periods for credit at two higher education institutions of the transnational consortium responsible for delivering the joint programme. On the other hand, the periods abroad should lead to a (joint) degree. To complicate things further, the doctoral strand of *Erasmus Mundus* (in effect until 2017 and targeting non-EU candidates) required students to spend the entire doctoral programme abroad (see Table 2.1, Column 5). This hybridism prompted researchers like Yarosh, Lukic and Santibáñez-Gruber (2018) to deem the Master's strand of *Erasmus Mundus* 'horizontal' and the doctoral 'vertical'. I personally consider the Master's component 'diagonal' given the minimum number of academic credits students should obtain abroad so that a degree is conferred.

Another aspect of these collaborative programmes is the potential overlap between joint and double degrees. Conceptually, whereas a joint degree programme should lead to a single (albeit jointly signed) degree or qualification, a double or multiple degree awards two (double) or more (multiple) degrees (Knight, 2011). In practice, these lines can be easily offset. The careful reading of the *Erasmus+ Programme Guide* explains why:

> The successful completion of the joint EMJMD Master programme must lead to the award of either a joint degree (i.e. one single diploma issued on behalf of at least two HEIs from different Programme Countries) or multiple degrees (i.e. at least two diplomas issued by two higher education institutions from different Programme Countries).
>
> (COM, 2019, p. 89)

Part of the problem derives from national qualification frameworks which do not always contemplate the award of a national educational qualification with a foreign one. Issuing two independent degrees apparently solves the problem but raises another: the overlap between completion requirements for a joint programme degree vs. a double or multiple degree. As Knight (2011, 2012) explains, such intersection can translate into double counting as the award of double degrees should be based on course requirements for two full degrees and differentiated learning outcomes. Unsurprisingly, the term 'joint degree' is commonly used in Europe to address both joint and double/multiple degrees. Possibly, the recent EU work towards the automatic mutual recognition of school and higher diplomas, through the realisation of a European Education Area, may facilitate national impasses in the recognition of foreign educational degrees. However, it is also possible that the automatic recognition of educational diplomas may boost 'double counting' in joint study programmes.

Despite the manifold challenges these programmes raise, the *Trends* (2015) report, by the European University Association (see Chapter 1, Point no. 5

66 Foundations of an interdisciplinary approach

in Box 1.1) showed a burgeoning number of international joint programmes across all three levels of study in Europe, albeit mostly at Master's level. Of the 451 European higher education institutions surveyed, 70 per cent offered joint Master's with partners from other countries (Sursock, 2015). However, it is unclear whether these programmes are joint or double/multiple degrees. The *Trends* (2015) report only differentiates between national, international and online joint programmes without specifying the completion requirements emanating from each.

Two other common types of physical student mobility in European postsecondary education are: 'field work' and 'residence abroad'. Both are embedded into academic curricula within a level of study, but their purposes differ. Moreover, whereas one is discipline-specific the other is not.

In field work, students from any discipline are offered opportunities for experiential learning outside the formal classroom. In Europe, field work usually takes place in the framework of student ongoing studies and does not necessarily involve teacher instruction on site as it is mainly used by students to collect data or conduct practical work in a natural environment. While field work, in some cases, may involve the presence of academic staff and teacher instruction, I would say that in Europe it is not so common to have academics travelling with students because higher education student mobility in the European context is generally perceived as an individual unsupervised experience (de Wit, 2002). By contrast, in the US faculty-led study abroad programmes are common practice.

While field work is not bound to a specific discipline, residence abroad is embedded in foreign language degree programmes to improve future language teachers' second language proficiency in context. As explained by Coleman (1997, 1998), who has written extensively about the topic from a British perspective, residence abroad can take three forms:

1. teaching as a foreign language assistant (initially, in exchange of residence abroad);
2. undertaking a work-based placement (e.g., an internship in a company);
3. studying at a university (or at two different universities for language students learning two foreign languages).

In all three cases, the stay abroad takes place in a country whose language the students are studying. Residence abroad is, for the most part, mandatory in modern language degrees in countries like the UK. Dating back to the dawn of the twentieth century (e.g., the British Council teaching assistantship scheme in 1905), residence abroad is among the earliest forms of education abroad in Europe, pre-dating the *Erasmus* scheme and other forms of mobility. In Germany, for example, the *Foreign Language Assistants Programme* was officially established in 1904–1905, representing until the 1990s the main stated-funded opportunity for German students of modern languages to spend time abroad (Ehrenreich, 2008). In addition to these two country-specific examples, one should also note

Educational foundations   67

the European-wide programme *Lingua*. Established by the EU in 1989, *Lingua* allowed foreign language teachers to do in-service training in a Member State where the language they teach is spoken. Today, assistantships fall under Key Action 1 of *Erasmus+*, namely under 'student mobility for traineeships'.

Notwithstanding the relevance of residence abroad in countries like the UK, Germany and France, it is not the norm in Europe. In many European countries, studying abroad in language degrees is optional, with students specialising in languages using *Erasmus* for the same purposes (I am an example of that).

Residence abroad can be referred to from a variety of labels. Terms like 'teacher language assistantships', 'assistantship placements', 'bilateral language assistantships programmes', 'foreign language assistants', 'teaching for residence abroad' (see Table 2.1, Column 2) refer to the first form of residence abroad. What is perhaps most problematic is that residence abroad, in all three forms, can be also referred to as 'year abroad', 'period abroad' (mostly at the institutional level) or used interchangeably with 'study abroad' (e.g., Coleman, 1998, 2015; Mitchell, Tracy-Ventura, & McManus, 2015; Murphy-Lejeune, 2002). I should therefore clarify that I see residence abroad as one type of education abroad, even if it can be argued that the third form of residence abroad could be also categorised as credit-seeking, given that it forms part of the credit requirements for language degree programmes. However, these requirements are just a mechanism to enable the period of studies abroad. A distinction should, therefore, be made. Whereas residence abroad is discipline-specific and aims to improve language skills as an academic and professional endeavour, in credit-seeking student mobility language learning is not an explicit academic pursuit as this type of student mobility is not bound to language degree programmes.

On a final note before moving to the next section, a reflection about the disciplinary thinking underpinning student mobility types should be made. Let us take as an example the body of research about residence abroad which, as noted earlier, has been predominantly developed from an Anglophone perspective, especially by applied linguists and language professionals (e.g., Alred & Byram, 2002; Byram & Alred, 2002; Coleman, 1996; Parker & Rouxeville, 1995). This includes projects like *Residence Abroad Matters* and, more recently, the *Languages and Social Networks Abroad* project, LANGSNAP, (see Mitchell, Tracy-Ventura, & McManus, 2017).

The extensive body of work developed by applied linguists on residence abroad and study abroad in general led some academics to posit study abroad as a 'sub-field of applied linguistics' (Kinginger, 2009), 'a sub-field of SLA research' (Ferguson, 1995) or a 'domain of inquiry in the field of applied linguistics' (Borghetti & Beaven, 2018). Not disregarding the valuable stock of knowledge generated by these professionals, such assumptions preclude an interdisciplinary approach to student mobility because disciplinary allegiances precede the identification of the variables of interest.

To recap, this section aimed to help the reader to identify common types of student mobility in European higher education beyond binaries, and discuss

68 Foundations of an interdisciplinary approach

existing taxonomies and points of overlap. At the same time, it sought to draw readers' attention to the need to develop a set of agreed-upon definitions that prevents scholars and practitioners from using different terms for the same concept; or, more importantly, from using distinct concepts as if they were a single one. Better put, we should be more concerned about inconsistencies in terminology than using more than one term to name a concept. With this, I am not defending that a surplus of terms is ideal. When various terms exist, it is imperative to understand whether they are all necessary and what rationales underpin them. One way to clarify the use (and therefore the meaning) of certain terms is to analyse them from an historical perspective. This historical approach is narrated next.

Chronological synopsis

Student mobility and other forms of cross-border higher education should not be singled out from the post-secondary enterprise. Understanding the evolution of student mobility requires considering its embedding in this environment and its internationalisation efforts in synchronic and diachronic ways – the typological and chronological synopses, respectively. Building on this complementary, this section offers an historical account of student mobility in European higher education from the dawn of the Second World War to the present day.

In Europe, contemporary student mobility cannot be disassociated from the interplay between the supranational intents of the EU and the intergovernmental objectives of the Bologna Process. Launched in 1999 with the Bologna Declaration and currently implemented across 48 countries,[5] this process aimed to reform European higher education and establish regional convergence across the sector. Naturally, this brought profound implications to the internationalisation of tertiary education and its most visible component: student mobility.

Of major relevance to this reform project has been the creation of a barrier-free European Higher Education Area (EHEA), assumed from the outset as its primary goal (see EHEA, www.ehea.info). This background currently sets the context for student mobility and how it is depicted in European policy agendas – i.e., as a lever for the competitiveness of European knowledge economies and the European higher education system worldwide. This may be one of the reasons why the promotion of student mobility carries a high degree of continuity between earlier and present-day intergovernmental and supranational approaches. For instance, from the initial six action lines (outlined in the Bologna Declaration) to the current ten (since the Berlin Communiqué in 2003), 'more' student mobility has always been posited as an operational objective to facilitate the establishment of the EHEA. Papatsiba clearly stated the problem in 2006: 'increasing student mobility emerges as one of the ultimate reasons for establishing the EHEA, and at the same time, its expected outcome' (2006, p. 97).

The supranational, intergovernmental and national sway surrounding student mobility since the 1990s is a relatively recent practice. In the two preceding decades, higher education policy on student mobility was primarily bolstered by the then-European Economic Community (hereafter referred to as the European Community). During these decades, this predecessor organisation of the EU laid the groundwork for studying abroad for academic credits in European higher education, thus overshadowing the view of student mobility as the movement of elite degree-seeking students that dominated the aftermath of the Second World War (de Wit & Merkx, 2012).

To elaborate further, it was in the 1970s and 1980s that student mobility in European higher education[6] went beyond the ad hoc transnational movement of students studying towards a degree abroad, to incorporate programmatic ways of enabling students to study abroad as part of home degrees. In the two preceding decades (1950s and 1960s), student mobility in Europe was still unorganised and done on an individual basis (Neave, 1992 in de Wit & Merkx, 2012). The concern in Europe in these decades was post-war rebuilding, with the few existing academic exchanges occurring primarily through bilateral and governmental agreements driven by foreign policy rationales. As explained by de Wit and Merkx (2012), at the time the few internationally oriented activities in European higher education referred to: (a) the movement of elite degree-seeking students from developing countries to their colonial superpowers (e.g., the UK, France) or (b) within Central and Eastern Europe under the Soviet Union's intention of political integration of communist countries and, finally, (c) the academic cooperation between the US and Europe.

National foreign policy arguments lost ground in the mid-1970s as the European Community affirmed itself globally and expanded its integration ambitions to education. From this decade onwards the European Community became an active player in forms of cooperation in education, particularly since the implementation of the first action programme for education in 1976. Recognising the central role of education in the development of the Community, this programme identified six areas for priority action including cooperation in higher education (see COM, 1994 for more information).

A major contribution was the launch of the *Joint Study Programme Scheme* and, in particular, the European Community Action Scheme for the Mobility of University Students (*Erasmus*) in 1976 and 1987, respectively. The former laid the foundations for the latter, paving the way for interdepartmental networks of higher education institutions across the then 12 Member States of the Community.

In 1987, when *Erasmus* was established, the European Community set a 10 per cent benchmark of mobile students by 1992. The popularity of *Erasmus* over the years has, *de facto*, made credit student mobility a reality in Europe, even if its ambitious quantitative targets have lagged behind. Despite this, academic student mobility in Europe did acquire a clear supranational dimension through what is today the largest public scheme of credit student mobility in the world. It is no coincidence that the integrated programme for Education, Training, Youth and Sport (*Erasmus+*) builds on the powerful brand of *Erasmus*. This EU

70 Foundations of an interdisciplinary approach

flagship programme had not only the merit of removing legal barriers to student exchange as part of academic degrees, but of also facilitating the financial accessibility of this educational opportunity. It is, therefore, no surprise that both issues remained central concerns in supranational, intergovernmental and national discourses, strongly influencing research agendas, as Chapter 1 demonstrated.

In the last two decades of the twentieth century, the international dimension of European higher education and academic cooperation became more structured. A landmark was the ratification of the Treaty of the EU, in 1993, which formally recognised education as an area of EU competency. Consequently, the project of European integration became high on higher education policy agendas. For scholars like Teichler (1999), the 1990s represent three substantial qualitative leaps in higher education cooperation policies and practices, culminating in an integrated internationalisation of European higher education. For others, like Van der Wende (2001), the 1990s marked the shift from cooperation to competition.

It was also in 1990 that *Erasmus* entered its second phase, with no substantial changes being made to its support actions (Teichler & Maiworm, 1997). Much experience was, nonetheless, gained in the first two phases the programme ran. During this eight-year period (1987–1994) significant developments were made in academic exchanges and cooperation; that is to say: (a) the formal recognition by the European Community of the Network of National Academic Recognition Information Centres (NARIC), in 1989, to facilitate the recognition of diplomas and periods of study abroad across Member States; (b) the introduction of the European Community Course Credit Transfer System (ECTS) in 1988 (initially on a pilot basis) as an instrument of academic recognition for studying abroad; and finally, (c) the monitoring and evaluation of education programmes run by the European Community through regular evaluation meetings and annual reports implemented from 1987/88 onwards (Teichler & Maiworm, 1997). During this period other major education and training programmes were also adopted, including: (a) *Commett*, which supported cooperation between European universities and industry to promote training in advanced technologies and the development of high-level human resources in this area; (b) *Lingua*, focused on encouraging multilingualism and the teaching and learning of foreign languages; and finally, (c) *Petra* and (d) *Force* that targeted vocational training. *Petra* focused on initial training and *Force* on continuing training.

In the middle of the decade, *Erasmus* was formally integrated into the more broadly based *Socrates* (1995–1999) to give greater coherence to the EU's education and training programmes or actions. With regard to learning competencies, the advent of the 'learning society' put forward by the European Commission's 1995 White Paper on Education and Training, *Teaching and Learning Towards the Learning Society*, emphasised the acquisition of new knowledge, learning capacities and language skills in which physical mobility played also a part.

In the first phase of *Socrates*, student mobility continued to be envisioned as a means to produce qualified human resources with experience of economic and social aspects of the Community's Member States, i.e., with the necessary language and citizenship skills to function in European multicultural societies.

Educational foundations 71

These intentions, outlined in the decision establishing *Erasmus* in 1987, remained valid throughout *Socrates* even if organisational and managerial matters were substantially revised (Teichler, 2001). Language skills and citizenship ideals were also strengthened throughout *Socrates*. Two major contributors were: the introduction of the concept of European citizenship (in the Treaty of the EU), and the learning of three European languages (two community languages + mother tongue) as part of this transnational citizenry.

In 2000, when *Socrates* entered its second phase (2000–2006), it further rationalised EU's education and training programmes into three major strands: (1) *Socrates* for education,[7] (2) *Leonardo da Vinci* for vocational training and (3) *eLearning* to promote information and communication technologies in education and training. Once again, historical developments cannot be put aside as these changes were also a result of the EU's recognition of lifelong learning education and training as a lever for employability and growth in the Lisbon Strategy.

During the second phase of *Socrates*, more attention was paid to academic recognition and quality requirements in academic mobility and cooperation. These concerns led to the implementation of the *Erasmus University Charter* (currently, *Erasmus Charter for Higher Education*) outlining the fundamental principles of the programme and requirements for participant tertiary institutions. The charter brought considerable managerial changes by replacing the previous system of networks of cooperating departments (the so-called Interuniversity Cooperation Programmes) and requiring the administration of grants to be decentralised to the national agencies of participant countries. The charter was (and still is) accompanied by a *European Policy Statement* (currently, *Erasmus Policy Statement*), requiring higher education institutions to define their internationalisation strategies, namely the incorporation of a European dimension and implementation of *Erasmus*. Unsurprisingly, these changes occurred at a time when the Bologna Process was already in motion and synergies with EU policy in education and training were actively sought.

It was also during the seven academic years of *Socrates II* that the EU launched *Erasmus Mundus* (in 2004) following a Council directive (2004/114/EC) that established the legal framework from third-country nationals to enter the EU for learning purposes. The launch of this external cooperation programme occurred at a time when the Bologna Process continued to emphasise the global attractiveness of the European Higher Education Area and the EU aimed to promote itself as a worldwide centre of excellence in learning. The programme joined previous external cooperation programmes: *Jean Monnet* (launched in 1989–1990), *Tempus* (1990), *Alfa* (1994) and *Cooperation with Industrialised Countries* (1995).

In 2007, *Socrates II* sub-programmes were incorporated into the umbrella programme *Lifelong Learning* in alignment with EU's Strategic Framework for European Cooperation in Education and Training (ET 2010) and ongoing Bologna reformist intentions. Once again, emphasis was placed on making Europe a leading knowledge economy and European higher education a worldwide reference through lifelong learning. Academic mobility, inter-exchange and cooperation were means to reach such goals.

72 Foundations of an interdisciplinary approach

Quantitative milestones came again into play. A 20 per cent benchmark of mobile graduates in the European Higher Education Area by 2020 was set by the Bologna Process (in the 2009 Leuven Communiqué) and endorsed by the EU. To reach this milestone the *Lifelong Learning Program.* *e* adopted a streamlined organisation into four sectoral sub-programmes, one transversal programme with four key actions and, finally, the *Jean Monnet* programme. Under the *Lifelong Learning Programme, Erasmus* continued to support student and staff mobility in higher education. Unlike in *Socrates II*, vocational education and training in tertiary education fell under *Erasmus* instead of *Leonardo da Vinci*. On that account, *Erasmus* was subdivided into student mobility for studies and for placements, as well as into staff mobility for teaching assignments and for staff training.

The streamlined architecture of the *Lifelong Learning Programme* was maximised in *Erasmus+* (2014–2020) to achieve greater systematic impact and support Europe's 2020 Strategy for smart, sustainable and inclusive growth. To this end, *Erasmus+* brought together seven existing programmes[8] into an integrated programme in the fields of education, training, youth as well as sports (upon recognition of sports as an area of EU competency in the Lisbon Treaty).

Offering opportunities for individuals and organisations alike, *Erasmus+* put a renewed emphasis on learning mobility in formal and non-formal dimensions, with an estimate of four million Europeans studying, training, gaining experience or volunteering abroad by 2020 (COM, http://ec.europa.eu). On that account, the programme allocated the greatest share (at least 63 per cent) of its budget to Key Action 1: 'Learning mobility of individuals'. This simplified architecture also aimed to facilitate cooperation for innovation and exchange of good practices (Key Action 2) and support policy reform (Key Action 3). And yet, if the EU promise is to hold true, credit student mobility needs to go beyond a concept that is politically correct but pedagogically empty (Papatsiba, 2003).

Academic value of student mobility

This section discusses the academic value of student mobility, i.e., the extent to which students are learning academically during the stay abroad. To elaborate further, academic value is here understood as the relative importance of developing discipline-specific skills, knowledge and experiences to obtain proficiency in a given subject matter and underlying curricula (see Chapter 1, Learning domains abroad).

As a type of formal learning, disciplinary learning takes place in structured educational environments (e.g., in a classroom) and leads to validation or certification of achievement. It therefore involves an explicit intention on the part of both those who teach (the teachers) and those who learn (the students).

There is, however, a basic tension between the academic and monetary value of studying abroad, with participant metrics frequently used as primary markers of success by higher education institutions. The number of student enrolments are certainly easy to demonstrate, but these figures do not tell us much about the educational value of studying abroad for individuals and the kind of learning outcomes reaped. This holds true for credit-seeking student mobility in Europe. As discussed in Chapter 1 (see Learning domains abroad), the academic value of this type of student mobility is hardly ever addressed in specialised research or is, at best, equated to student satisfaction (Byram, 2008) or personal maturation. The same can be said about internationalisation processes and the constant refraining from using qualitative outcomes instead of quantitative outputs in evaluating these efforts, as also noted in Chapter 1 (e.g., Aerden, 2015, 2017; de Wit, 2009; Deardorff, 2015; Green, 2012; Hudzik & Stohl, 2009; Jones, 2013). European higher education policy is lagging behind in enacting evaluation and monitoring systems of the impact of internationalisation efforts, particularly in terms of the expected academic learning gains for exchange students. This is a notable gap in policy discourses and its regulatory frameworks, as will be demonstrated later in this section.

The ambiguous framing of the educational nature of credit student mobility in European higher education is evidenced by the two credit-bearing programmes the exchange students in this book participated in: (a) *Erasmus* under the *Lifelong Learning Programme*, and (b) *Campus Europae* (http://campuseuropae.org/). In both cases, there is a misalignment between pedagogical frameworks and evaluation systems, both of which are fundamental to ensure the academic value of student mobility is clear and rewarding.

Whether in *Campus Europae* or in *Erasmus*, supranational and intergovernmental policies have taken centre stage in shaping public perception of the expected value of credit-seeking student mobility in Europe, without necessarily addressing its academic significance. Or, as put by Cairns (2014), without moving away from the idea of *Erasmus* as 'fun' and the all-too-frequently-justified 'Erasmus party animal'. Much of the problem lies with the assessment of students' academic learning and the preferred language of instruction being left to the discretion of higher education institutions. As a result, there are varying institutional practices towards the relative importance of academic learning in credit student mobility and a lack of uniformity in evaluation standards.

One way to discuss the expected academic value of European credit-seeking student mobility is to analyse the objectives of *Erasmus* outlined in policy documents, namely in the decisions establishing the different iterations of the *Erasmus* programme. To this end, Table 2.2 categorises these objectives according to two broad types of impact – (a) system and (b) individual-level impact – here understood as:

> *system:* the effect exerted or fundamental changes caused by *Erasmus* at wider national and supranational levels, including in national, governments, higher education systems and other relevant institutions.
> (Vossensteyn, Lanzendorf, & Souto-Otero, 2008)

> *individual:* the effect exerted or fundamental changes caused by *Erasmus* on the learner and the learning gains reaped through studying abroad (e.g., academic, intercultural and language learning outcomes).

Table 2.2 Objectives of the different iterations of Erasmus

Iteration of Erasmus	Decision	Article	Nature of impact	Type of learning outcome
Erasmus Phase 1 and 2	Decision No. 87/327/EEC	Article 2 (Objectives of the Erasmus Programme)	• System: 2 • Individual: 1 • Both: 2	• Economic and social knowledge • Citizenship (Objectives i, iv and v)
Socrates I	Decision No. 819/95/EC	Article 3 (Objectives)	• System: 4 • Individual: 4 • Both: 1	• Linguistic • Intercultural • Citizenship (Objectives a, b, d, e and f)
Socrates II	Decision No. 253/2000/EC	Article 2 (Objectives of the Programme)	• System: 3 • Individual: 1	• Linguistic • Intercultural (Objective b)
Lifelong learning Programme	Decision No. 1720/2006/EC	Article 1 (Objectives of the Lifelong Learning Programme)	• System: 8 • Individual: 3	• Linguistic • Intercultural • Citizenship • Personal development (Objectives d, e and g)
		Article 27 (Objectives of the Erasmus Programme)	• System: 8 • Individual: 0	Non-applicable
Erasmus+	Regulation (EU) No 1288/2013	Article 5 (Specific objectives of Education and Training)	• System: 4 • Individual: 2	• Linguistic • Intercultural • Professional (Objectives a and e)

Note. Decisions establishing the iterations of Erasmus, available at http://eur-lex.europa.eu

Educational foundations   75

When the impact is at individual level, further examination of the type of learning outcomes is carried out (see Table 2.2, Column 5). By learning outcomes, I mean what learners should know, understand and be able to do as a result of learning (Bingham, 1999) – in our case, as a result of studying abroad.

Despite the 26 years separating the decisions establishing *Erasmus* in 1987 and *Erasmus+* in 2013, the joint analysis of the five regulatory frameworks in Table 2.2 demonstrates that system impact takes precedence over individual impact, even if the two can overlap. Hence the hybrid category 'both' when system and individual impact are represented in the same objective of the decisions establishing *Erasmus* (e.g., in *Socrates* I, Article 3, Objective 2). It can certainly be argued that the system level is addressed to leverage individual agency and that the overemphasis on systematic impact derives from the regulatory nature of the analysed policy instruments.

However, if there is an expected individual impact, should not this impact be specified in terms of the targeted learning outcomes for its participants? While the analysis of the decisions establishing *Erasmus* points to some individual learning outcomes, the macro changes necessary to instil the EU's integration project seem to preside over individual agency and capacity. Added to this, the academic gains and enrichment of discipline-specific knowledge may be overlooked as they are not even mentioned in the objectives of *Erasmus* in these policy frameworks. In fact, the learning outcomes identified in these objectives relate to the following domains: intercultural, linguistic, citizenship, professional, personal, economic and societal (Table 2.2, Column 5).

In the end, for the academic value of any exchange programme to be unambiguous, the learner and expected learning gains (in its underlying soft and hard skills) need to be included in policy enactment. This gap has implications for mobile students' academic learning and their expectations regarding the mobility period (as Part II of this book will demonstrate).

Intercultural outcomes and student mobility

In European higher education the development of intercultural outcomes through education abroad is not just an academic pursuit, but also a socio-political endeavour stemming from the historical, social and political context of Europe.

This section addresses the contextual conditions behind the widening interest in Europe's language and cultural diversity since the 1990s, with an emphasis on the political rationales underpinning the development of intercultural competence in study abroad. This synopsis is accompanied by a summary of the typological features of intercultural competence models.

Politically, the growing interest in Europe's language and cultural heritage has been primarily bolstered by the EU and the Council of Europe. As asserted by Coleman in 1998, these two institutions 'embody both the political will and the practical policies which are fundamental to student mobility in Europe' (p. 168).

76 Foundations of an interdisciplinary approach

Coleman's statement remains valid today, even if intergovernmental steering, via the Bologna Process, comes also into play (as the preceding sections have shown).

Historically, the interest in Europe's language and cultural diversity became high on the EU's agenda in the 1990s. This decade saw the phasing out of internal borders in the EU, with the conclusion of the two Schengen agreements and the establishment of European citizenship through the Treaty of the EU. In terms of the EU's language policy, a key objective was (and still is) that every European citizen masters two other languages in addition to their mother tongue. Hence the role of exchange schemes like *Erasmus* in delivering EU's multilingual ideals (e.g., the promotion of language learning and linguistic diversity has remained a key objective in the iterations of *Erasmus*) and the current expectations that, with the establishment of a European Education Area by 2025, speaking two languages will become the norm.

The Council of Europe has also played a fundamental role in promoting plurilingualism, linguistic diversity and language learning, as well as intercultural and citizenship education across the European continent. This human rights organisation enacted major language policies and pedagogical instruments towards linguistic diversity and plurilingual education across Europe.

In 2001, the Council of Europe published the *Common European Framework of Reference for Languages* (CEFR)[9] along with the *European Language Portfolio*. During the preceding decade, the interculturalists Michael Byram and Geneviève Zarate (1994) coined the phrase 'intercultural speaker', with the CEFR building, to some extent, on the four 'savoirs' purported by this model, (see Byram, 2009 for further information). Since its publication, the CEFR has remained an influential language policy instrument by facilitating transparency and comparability in the provision of language education and qualifications across the Council's Member States.

Intercultural initiatives (e.g., the *European Day of Languages*, the *European Year of Intercultural Dialogue* in 2008), pedagogical platforms or resource centres (e.g., the *Platform of Resources for Plurilingual and Intercultural Education*, the *Pestalozzi Programme*, the *European Wergeland Centre*), campaigns (e.g., *All different – All equal* in 1995, renewed in 2006) and frameworks (e.g., the 2018 *Reference Framework of Competences for Democratic Culture*) are also attributed to the Council of Europe.

The political will for tolerance and integration of Europe's language and cultural diversity transcends policy actions, influencing public perception and research agendas. Multilingualism and multiculturalism, for instance, are not only advocated in the regulatory frameworks of the EU and the Council of Europe but also in research. The combination of conceptual anchors like 'plurilingual' and 'intercultural competence' (e.g., Galisson, 1997) or 'plurilingual' and 'pluricultural' (e.g., Coste, Moore, & Zarate, 1997) or even terms like 'intercomprehension' (e.g., Andrade & Araújo e Sá, 1999) is not fortuitous. Interestingly, these terms are quite prolific in Southern Europe and still actively researched today, both in student and teacher training (e.g., Melo-Pfeifer & Helmchen, 2018).

Other frequently used terms strongly rooted in European policy include: 'intercultural dialogue', 'intercultural understanding', 'European/EU citizenship' and 'European identity'.

As explained by Guilherme (2015) and Byram (2009), the term 'intercultural competence' itself started to be used across European policy and academic circles in the mid-1990s. The introduction of intercultural competence in European academic circuits is strongly related to the acceptance of the communicative approach in second/foreign language education that took place at the time. The work of Bredella (1992) in Germany, Risager (1993) in Denmark and Byram (1997) in the UK are among the early attempts in Europe to incorporate an explicit cultural dimension into second/foreign language teaching. The monograph of Byram (1997) and his model of intercultural communicative competence have been very influential in this regard.

The substantial contribution from language-related disciplines to furthering intercultural competence in the European continent has remained a constant ever since, although the notion of intercultural competence is not consensual among scholars (e.g., Ferri, 2018).

Notwithstanding the lack of consensus, much has been said about the role of intercultural abilities in student mobility, especially from a language-based perspective. For example, many European research efforts towards enhancing the intercultural abilities of mobile students were developed by language educators and applied linguists (see Chapter 1, Learning domains abroad). By contrast, in the US these kinds of study tend to fall under the label 'intercultural communication' and are strongly related to the behavioural sciences, psychology and professional business (Kramsch, 2001). In both cases, there is little cross-referencing, even if intercultural competence is considered a multidisciplinary domain. Hence the calls from various scholars to promote more interdisciplinary dialogue (e.g., Arasaratnam-Smith, 2017), understand the variety of labels used (e.g., Deardorff, 2006; Deardorff & Jones, 2012; Fantini, 2006b) and systematise the conceptualisations produced so far (e.g., Almeida, Simões, & Costa, 2012; Bird, Mendenhall, Stevens, & Oddou, 2010; Spitzberg & Changnon, 2009). The latter aspect in particular has caused a great measure of confusion.

To throw some light on the flurry of intercultural competence models published since the 1990s, Table 2.3 summarises possible conceptual pathways based on the framework by Spitzberg and Changnon (2009). The aim is to offer the reader a working grammar that will help frame the intercultural gains of the 50 sojourners in Part II of this book. The fivefold typology proposed by Spitzberg and Changnon will be described according to key characteristics for each conceptual type along with illustrative models. This listing of models is by no means exhaustive nor does it aim to describe individual models, but rather their typological features.

Of the 5 typologies in Table 2.3, 2 conceptual types and 4 models will be used to analyse the intercultural gains of the 50 sojourners in this book while

78 Foundations of an interdisciplinary approach

Table 2.3 Typological features of intercultural competence models, adapted from Spitzberg and Changnon (2009)

Type	Key characteristics	Illustrative models
Compositional	Identifies components of intercultural competence (e.g., traits, characteristics, skills) without specifying the relation between them	• Pyramid model of intercultural competence (Deardorff, 2006) • Intercultural competence components model (Howard-Hamilton, Richardson, & Shuford, 1998)
Co-orientational	Focuses on interactional processes through communicative mutuality or shared meanings	• Intercultural communicative competence model (Byram, 1997) • Intercultural communicative Competence model (Fantini, 2006a)
Developmental	Describes the stages of progression through which intercultural competence is acquired	• Developmental model of intercultural sensitivity (Bennett 1986, 1993) • Developmental model of intercultural maturity (King & Baxter Magolda, 2005)
Adaptational	Focuses on mutual adjustment processes between interactants from different cultural backgrounds as criteria of competence	• Model of attitudes towads acculturation (Berry, Kim, Power, Young, & Bujaki, 1989) • Relative acculturation extended model (Navas et al., 2005; Navas, Rojas, García, & Pumares, 2007)
Causal path	Postulates specific causal relationships between the components of intercultural competence, often translated into testable propositions	• Process model of intercultural competence (Deardorff, 2006) • Multilevel process change model of intercultural competence (Ting-Toomey, 1999)

demonstrating the need for an interdisciplinary approach in this domain as well. These models are:

- *developmental models:* Bennett's (1986, 1993) developmental model of intercultural sensitivity and King and Baxter Magolda's (2005) developmental model of intercultural maturity;
- *co-orientational models:* Fantini's (2006a) and Byram's (1997) models of intercultural communicative competence.

The first conceptual type is concerned with identifying, describing and articulating the progressive steps in achieving an intercultural developmental threshold over time and through ongoing interaction. Developmental models are usually rooted in developmental psychology but open up to other academic disciplines. The two developmental models used in this book illustrate this eclectic nature. Whereas Bennett's (1986, 1993) model is situated within the late 1980s and early 1990s intercultural communication field, King and Baxter Magolda's (2005) model is more recent and draws on developmental psychology. Naturally, different theories inform these models. The former is informed by constructivist views on culture and grounded-theory approaches. The latter draws on human lifespan theories and is informed by constructivist-developmental pedagogy.

The selection of Bennett's (1986, 1993) and King and Baxter Magolda's (2005) models is based on their added-value in grasping the developmental contours of intercultural development among adult learners. While each conceptual framework derives from different theoretical perspectives, both models attend to the development of cognitive structures.

In contrast with developmental models, co-orientational models are not geared towards a developmental threshold but a common ground of mutual understanding in interaction. This alignment towards a minimal level of reciprocity is seen as a proxy for developing intercultural competence (Spitzberg & Changnon, 2009), although different components of competence can be underscored. The models purported by Fantini (2006a) and Byram (1997), in particular, stress the language–culture nexus (and concomitant abilities) in achieving a threshold of intercultural communicative competence, as will be illustrated in Part II of this book. Both models can be generally situated within theories of second/foreign language education and communicative approach theory. Byram's (1997) model draws on notions of applied and sociolinguistics, theories of social identity and cross-cultural communication, and Bourdieu's (1979) theory of social and cultural capital (see Byram, 1997, 2009). Similarly, Fantini's (2006a) model draws on applied and sociolinguistics, intercultural communication and on cultural anthropology views on culture as analogous to language and communication (see Fantini, 2019 for further information).

The integrated analysis of all four models and the disciplines they draw upon is based on the interdisciplinary assumption behind this book. The aim is to continue fostering a broad dialogue between the disciplines developing research on student mobility and its manifold variables. Intercultural outcomes are one of them.

Summary

Drawing on the conceptual foundations laid out in the previous chapter, Chapter 2 addressed the educational underpinnings of student mobility in European higher education. This component of student mobility was discussed through an interdisciplinary dialogue to bring together disconnected research and/or theories.

The chapter started by painting a broad picture of student mobility within the internationalisation of higher education landscape. The underlying premise is that the ways in which higher education internationalisation is conceptualised can have profound implications for theorising student mobility. Such implications

80   Foundations of an interdisciplinary approach

were brought to light in a typological synopsis that advanced five key descriptors for staking out different types of academic movement: (1) academic purpose, (2) nature, (3) duration, (4) level of study, and (5) direction. And yet, as any taxonomy hinges upon its practical application, the section that followed categorised common types of student mobility in European higher education according to the aforementioned descriptors. The aim was twofold: (a) to systematise knowledge about student mobility types or modalities in European post-secondary education, and (b) to offer a framework that may assist readers in pinning down the features of academic movement.

As other social phenomena, student mobility does not happen in a vacuum but is shaped by historical, social and political circumstances. A historical synopsis of the role of student mobility in European higher education was therefore offered to readers. Attention was brought to how policy discourses can shape public perceptions about student mobility and expected gains. While some of these gains are clearly assumed in these discourses, others seem to be pushed to a subsidiary level. This is the case of the academic value and/or disciplinary-specific learning that study abroad opportunities should lead to. In contrast, intercultural gains seem to be readily assumed by European educational policy, even if the academic community is still at odds in making sense of the array of intercultural competence models available.

Box 2.1 – Reflective questions and/or points of Chapter 2

To help you review critically the content of this chapter, ask yourself the following questions and discuss them with colleagues from other disciplines.

1. To what extent do higher education internationalisation processes affect how student mobility is enacted?
    1.1. Take different definitions of higher education internationalisation, identify the key elements, strengths and weaknesses, and the role of student mobility in it.
2. What policy expectations underpin student mobility in European higher education? How do these expectations impact its linguistic, intercultural and academic value?
3. Does your institutional experience of exchange students' academic learning suggest I am right to argue that the academic value of credit student mobility in Europe needs to be strengthened and acted upon?
4. This chapter has demonstrated the importance of reflecting upon misnomers like 'international', 'foreign' and 'culturally and linguistically diverse' students.
    4.1. Can you think of other controversial or misunderstood terms whose meanings need to be clarified?

5. Take the taxonomy in this chapter and apply its descriptors to the types of student mobility you work with or are involved in (as in Table 2.1).
6. In case your work or role addresses intercultural learning and/or development among mobile students, take the typology in Table 2.3 and select an intercultural construct that fits your needs, then justify why you adopted this construct (and its conceptual type) against the remaining four conceptual types.

Notes

1 Study abroad is used in this book in a broad sense, and synonymously with education abroad, to address study and/or education outside students' home university campuses.
2 The type of institution can complicate things further. For example, how can we classify a British student studying towards a degree in a British branch-campus institution in Singapore? And, what about a Portuguese international student attending a branch American campus in Italy?
3 According to Teichler et al. (2011), with a nationality different from that of the country of study.
4 In European literature the term 'study cycle' was introduced by the Bologna Process and is used synonymously with level of study. The three cycles of study in European higher education refer to: (1) Bachelor or equivalent (EQF level 5); (2) Master's or equivalent (EQF level 7); (3) doctoral level (EQF level 8).
5 The Bologna Process is an intergovernmental cooperation in the higher education of 48 countries (and the European Commission) committed to establishing a comparable and compatible European Higher Education Area (EHEA), initially set by 2010 and currently by 2020 (see www.ehea.info).
6 While it was in the 1970s and mid-1980s that the EU took the lead in the development of large-scale youth mobility programmes in higher education, the Council of Europe is accredited for being the first intergovernmental organisation addressing learning mobility at European level but focusing mainly on non-formal learning. Among early initiatives of the Council of Europe in the youth sector are: the *European Agreement on Young People Travelling with Collective Passports* (1961) and the *European Agreement on 'au pair' Placements* (1969) (see Friesenhahn, Hanjo Schild, Wicke, & Balogh, 2013 for further information).
7 During Socrates II, education programmes encompassed: (a) *Comenius* (School education) ;(b) *Erasmus* (Higher education); (c) *Grundtvig* (Adult education and other education pathways); (d) *Lingua* (Teaching and learning foreign languages); and (e) *Minerva* (Open and distance education and ICT in the field of education).
8 *Erasmus+* integrates the *Lifelong Learning Programme*, the *Youth in Action Programme*, the *Erasmus Mundus Programme*, *Tempus*, *Alfa*, *Edulink* and programmes of cooperation with industrialised countries in the field of higher education.
9 The Common European Framework of Reference for Languages (CEFR) purports six reference proficiency levels: basic (A1; A2), independent (B1; B2), and proficient user (C1; C2) (see www.coe.int). For purposes of clarity, the CEFR can be understood as the European equivalent of the ACTFL Proficiency Guidelines in the US.

References

Aerden, A. (2015). Frameworks for the assessment of internationalization. *ECA Occasional Paper*. Retrieved from www.ecahe.eu

Aerden, A. (2017). The guide to quality in internationalization (2nd ed). *ECA Occasional Paper*. Retrieved from www.ecahe.eu

Almeida, J. (2018). Internationalisation at home: An epistemology of equity. Retrieved from the EAIE blog website www.eaie.org/blog/internationalisation-at-home-an-epistemology-of-equity.html

Almeida, J., Robson, S., Morosini, M., & Baranzeli, C. (2019). Understanding internationalization at home: Perspectives from the global north and south. *European Educational Research Journal, 18*(2), 200–217.

Almeida, J., Simões, A. R., & Costa, N. (2012). Bridging the gap between conceptualisation & assessment of intercultural competence. *Procedia - Social and Behavioral Sciences, 69*, 695–704.

Alred, G., & Byram, M. (2002). Becoming an intercultural mediator: A longitudinal study of residence abroad. *Journal of Multilingual and Multicultural Development, 23*(5), 339–352.

Andrade, A. I., & Araújo e Sá, M. H. (1999). A intercompreensão em línguas românicas: Propostas didácticas no quadro do programa Galatea. In A. Ikor (Ed.), *Plurilinguismo e Ensino* (pp. 147–159). Faro: Faro Editorial, Universidade do Algarve.

Arasaratnam-Smith, L. A. (2017). Intercultural competence: An overview. In D. K. Deardorf & L. A. Arasaratnam (Eds.), *Intercultural competence in higher education: International approaches, assessment and application* (pp. 7–18). London: Routledge.

Baiutti, M. (2019). *Protocollo di valutazione Intercultura*. Pisa: ETS.

Beelen, J., & Jones, E. (2015). Redefining internationalization at home. In A. Curai, L. Matei, R. Pricopie, J. Salmi & P. Scott (Eds.), *The European Higher Education Area: Between critical reflections and future policies* (pp. 59–72). Dordrecht: Springer.

Bennett, M. J. (1986). A developmental approach to training for intercultural sensitivity. *International Journal of Intercultural Relations, 10*(2), 179–196.

Bennett, M. J. (1993). *Towards ethnorelativism: A developmental model of intercultural sensitivity*. Yarmouth, ME: Intercultural Press.

Berry, J. W., Kim, U., Power, S., Young, M., & Bujaki, M. (1989). Acculturation in plural societies. *Applied Psychology: An International Review, 38*, 185–206.

Bingham, R. (1999). *Learning outcomes: A guide*. Sheffield: Learning and Teaching Institute. Sheffield Hallam University.

Bird, A., Mendenhall, M., Stevens, M. J., & Oddou, G. (2010). Defining the content domain of intercultural competence for global leaders. *Journal of Managerial Psychology, 25*(8), 810–828.

Borghetti, C., & Beaven, A. (Eds.). (2018). *Study abroad and interculturality: Perspectives and discourses*. London: Routledge.

Bourdieu, P. (1979). *La distinction: Critique sociale du jugement*. Paris: Les éditions de Minuit.

Bredella, L. (1992). Towards a pedagogy of intercultural understanding. *Amerikastudien, 37*, 559–594.

Brooks, R., & Waters, J. (2011). *Student mobilities, migration and the internationalization of higher education*. Basingstoke: Palgrave Macmillan.

Byram, M. (1997). *Teaching and assessing intercultural communicative competence*. Clevedon: Multilingual Matters.

Byram, M. (2008). The value of student mobility. In M. Byram & F. Dervin (Eds.), *Students, staff and academic mobility in higher education* (pp. 30–45). Newcastle upon Tyne: Cambridge Scholars Publishing.

Byram, M. (2009). The intercultural speaker and the pedagogy of foreign language education. In D. K. Deardorff (Ed.), *The Sage handbook of intercultural competence* (pp. 321–330). Thousand Oaks, CA: Sage.

Byram, M., & Alred, G. (2002). The year abroad: Ten years on. In S. Cormeraie, D. Killick & M. Parry (Eds.), *Revolutions in consciouness: Local identities, global concerns in 'languages and intercultural communication*. Leeds: International Association for Languages and Intercultural Communication.

Byram, M., & Zarate, G. (1994). *Definitions, objectives and assessment of socio-cultural competence* (Vol. CC Lang 94). Strasbourg: Council of Europe.

Cairns, D. (2014). *Youth transitions, international student mobility and spatial reflexivity*. Basingstoke: Palgrave Macmillan.

Cairns, D. (2017). Exploring student mobility and graduate migration: Undergraduate mobility propensities in two economic crisis contexts. *Social & Cultural Geography, 18*(3), 336–353.

Carroll, J. (2015). *Tools for teaching in an educationally mobile world*. London: Routledge.

Coleman, J. A. (1996). *A survey of Bristish and European students*. London: Centre for Information on Language Teaching and Research.

Coleman, J. A. (1997). Residence abroad within language study. *Language Teaching, 30*(1), 1–20.

Coleman, J. A. (1998). Language learning and study abroad: The European perspective. *Frontiers: The Interdisciplinary Journal of Study Abroad, IV*(Fall), l67–203.

Coleman, J. A. (2015). Social circles during residence abroad: What students do and who with? In R. Mitchell, N. Tracy-Ventura & K. McManus (Eds.), *Social interaction, identity and language learning during residence abroad* (pp. 33–51). Amsterdam: European Second Language Association.

COM. (1994). Cooperation in education in the European Union 1976–1994. *Education Traing Youth Studies*. Retrieved from http://bookshop.europa.eu

COM. (2018). Proposal for a council recommendation on promoting automatic mutual recognition of higher education and upper secondary education diplomas and the outcomes of learning periods abroad. Retrieved from https://eur-lex.euro pa.eu/legal-content/EN/TXT/?uri=CELEX:52018DC0270

COM. (2019). Erasmus+. Programme Guide. Retrieved from https://ec.europa.eu/ programmes/erasmus-plus/resources/documents/erasmus-programme-guide-2 019_en

Coste, D., Moore, D., & Zarate, G. (1997). *Compétence plurilingue et pluriculturelle – Vers un cadre européen commun de référence pour l'enseignement et l'apprentissage des langues vivantes: Études préparatoires*. Strasbourg: Council de l'Europe.

de Wit, H. (2002). *Internationalization of higher education in the United States and in Europe: A historical, comparative, and conceptual analysis*. Westport, CT: Greenwood Press.

84 Foundations of an interdisciplinary approach

de Wit, H. (2009). Measuring success in the internationalization of higher education. *EAIE Occasional Paper 22*. Amsterdam: European Association for International Education.

de Wit, H., Hunter, F., Howard, L., & Egron-Polak, E. (2015). Internationalisation of higher education study. *Directorate-General for Internal Policies: Policy Department B: Structural and Cohesion Policies*. Retrieved from http://www.europarl.europa.eu/studies

de Wit, H., & Merkx, G. (2012). The history of internationalization of higher education. In D. K. Deardorff, H. De Wit, J. D. Heyl & T. Adams (Eds.), *The Sage handbook of international higher education* (pp. 43–59). Thousand Oaks, CA: Sage.

Deardorff, D. K. (2006). Identification and assessment of intercultural competence as a student outcome of internationalization. *Journal of Studies in International Education, 10*(3), 241–266.

Deardorff, D. K. (2015). *Desmystifying outcomes assessment for international educators: A practical approach*. Sterling, VA: Stylus Publishing.

Deardorff, D. K., & Jones, E. (2012). Intercultural competence: An emerging focus in international higher education. In D. K. Deardorff, H. de Wit, J. D. Heyl & T. Adams (Eds.), *The Sage handbook of international higher education* (pp. 283–303). Thousand Oaks, CA: Sage.

Egron-Polak, E., & Marmolejo, F. (2017). Higher education internationalization: Adjusting to new landscapes. *The globalization of internationalization: Emerging voices and perspectives*. In H. de Wit, J. Gacel-Ávila, E. Jones & E. Jooste (Eds.), (pp. 7–17). London: Routledge.

Ehrenreich, S. (2008). Teaching for residence abroad: Blending synchronic and diachronic perspectives on the assistant year abroad. In M. Byram & F. Dervin (Eds.), *Students, staff and academic mobility in higher education* (pp. 65–80). Newcastle upon Tyne: Cambridge Scholars Publishing.

Fantini, A. E. (2006a). About intercultural communicative competence: A construct. *Appendix E*. Retrieved from World Learning. SIT Digital Collections website http://digitalcollections.sit.edu/worldlearning_publications/1/

Fantini, A. E. (2006b). A list of alternative terms for ICC. *Appendix D*. Retrieved from World Learning. SIT Digital Collections website http://digitalcollections.sit.edu/worldlearning_publications/1/

Fantini, A. E. (2019). *Intercultural communicative competence in educational exchange: A multinational perspective*. New York, NY: Routledge.

Ferguson, C. (1995). Foreword. In B. Freed (Ed.), *Second language acquisition in a study abroad context* (pp. xi–xv). Amsterdam: John Benjamins.

Ferri, G. (2018). *Intercultural communication: Critical approaches and future challenges*. Basingstoke: Palgrave Macmillan.

Forum on Education Abroad. (2011). Education abroad glossary. Retrieved from https://forumea.org/wp-content/uploads/2014/10/Forum-2011-Glossary-v2.pdf

Friesenhahn, G. J., Hanjo Schild, Wicke, H.-G., & Balogh, J. (2013). Introduction: Learning mobility and non-formal learning. In G. H. Friesenhahn, H. Schild, H.-G. Wicke & J. Balogh (Eds.), *Learning mobility and non-formal learning in European contexts: Policies, approaches and examples* (pp. 5–8). Strasbourg: Council of Europe Publishing.

Galisson, R. (1997). Problématique de l'éducation et de la communication interculturelles en milieu scolaire européen. *Éla. Études de linguistique appliquée*, *106*, 141–160.

Gonzalez, R., Pagan, M., Wendell, L., & Love, C. (2011). *Supporting ELL/culturally and LInguistically diverse students for academic achievement*. Rexford, NY: International Center for Leadership Education.

Green, M. (2012). *Measuring and assessing internationalization*. Washington, DC: NAFSA. Retrieved from www.nafsa.org/epubs

Guilherme, M. (2015). Intercultural communication in Europe. In J. M. Bennett (Ed.), *The Sage encyclopedia of intercultural competence* (pp. 463–467). Thousand Oaks, CA: Sage.

Howard-Hamilton, M. F., Richardson, B. J., & Shuford, B. (1998). Promoting multicultural education education: A holistic approach. *College Student Affairs Journal, 18*(1), 5–17.

Hudzik, J., & Stohl, M. (2009). Modelling assessment of the outcomes and impacts of internationalization In H. de Wit (Ed.), *Measuring success in the internationalization of higher education. EAIE Occasional Paper 22* (pp. 9–21). Amsterdam: European Association for International Education.

Huisman, J., Adelman, C., Hsieh, C.-H., Shams, F., & Wilkins, S. (2012). Europe's Bologna Process and its impact on global higher education. In D. K. Deardorff, H. de Wit, J. D. Heyl & T. Adams (Eds.), *The Sage handbook of international higher education* (pp. 81–100). Thousand Oaks, CA: Sage.

Institute of International Education. (2018). Open doors 2018 "fast facts". Retrieved from https://www.iie.org/Research-and-Insights/Open-Doors/Fact-Sheets-and-Infographics/Fast-Facts

Jones, E. (2013). Internationalization and student learning outcomes. In H. de Wit (Ed.), *An introduction to higher education internationalisation* (pp. 107–116). Milan: Vita e Pensiero.

King, P. M., & Baxter Magolda, M. B. (2005). A developmental model of intercultural maturity. *Journal of College Student Development, 46*(6), 571–592.

King, R., & Raghuram, P. (2013). International student migration: Mapping the field and new research agendas. *Population, Space and Place, 19*(2), 127–137.

Kinginger, C. (2009). *Language learning and study abroad: A critical reading of research*. New York, NY: Palgrave Macmillan.

Knight, J. (1994). *Internationalization: Elements and checkpoints*. (Research monograph no.14). Ottawa: Canadian Bureau for International Education.

Knight, J. (2004). Internationalization remodeled: Definitions, rationales, and approaches *Journal of Studies in International Education, 8*(1), 5–31.

Knight, J. (2011). Doubts and dilemmas with bouble degree programs. *Revista de Universidad y Sociedad del Conocimiento, 8*(2), 297–312.

Knight, J. (2012). Concepts, rationales, and interpretive frameworks in the internationalization of higher education. In D. K. Deardorff, H. de Wit, J. D. Heyl & T. Adams (Eds.), *The Sage handbook of international higher education* (pp. 27–42). Thousand Oaks, CA: Sage.

Kramsch, C. (2001). Intercultural communication. In R. Carter & D. Nunan (Eds.), *The Cambridge guide to teaching English to Speakers of Other Languages* (pp. 201–206). Cambridge: Cambridge University Press.

Larsen, M. A. (2016). *Internationalization of higher education: An analysis through spatial, network and mobilities theories.* New York, NY: Palgrave Macmillan.

Marginson, S., & Sawir, E. (2011). *Ideas for intercultural education.* Basingstoke: Palgrave Macmillan.

Maringe, F. (2010). The meanings of globalisation and internationalization in HE: Findings from a world survey. In F. Maringe & F. Foskett (Eds.), *Globalization and internationalization in higher education: Theoretical, strategic and management perspectives* (pp. 17–34). London: Continuum.

Melo-Pfeifer, S., & Helmchen, C. (Eds.). (2018). *Plurilingual literacy practices at school and in teacher education.* Bern: Peter Lang.

Mitchell, R., Tracy-Ventura, N., & McManus, K. (2017). *Anglophone students abroad: Identity, social relationships, and language learning.* London: Routledge.

Mitchell, R., Tracy-Ventura, N., & McManus, K. (Eds.). (2015). *Social interaction, identity and language learning during residence abroad.* Amsterdam: European Second Language Association.

Murphy-Lejeune, E. (2002). *Student mobility and narrative in Europe: The new strangers.* London: Routledge.

Navas, M., García, M. C., Sánchez, J., Rojas, A. J., Pumares, P., & Fernández, J. S. (2005). Relative acculturation extended model (RAEM): New contributions with regard to the study of acculturation. *International Journal of Intercultural Relations, 29*(1), 21–37.

Navas, M., Rojas, A. J., García, M. C., & Pumares, P. (2007). Acculturation strategies and attitudes according to the relative acculturation extended model (RAEM): The perspectives of natives versus immigrants. *International Journal of Intercultural Relations, 31*(1), 67–86.

Papatsiba, V. (2003). *Des étudiants européens: «Erasmus» et l'aventure de l'altérité.* Berne: Peter Lang.

Papatsiba, V. (2006). Making higher education more European through student mobility? Revisiting EU initiatives in the context of the Bologna Process. *Comparative Education, 42*(1), 93–111.

Parker, G., & Rouxeville, A. (1995). *Preparation, monitoring, evaluation: Current research and development.* London: AFLS in association with CILT.

Raghuram, P. (2013). Theorising the spaces of student migration. *Population, Space and Place, 19*(2), 138–154.

Risager, K. (1993). Buy some petit souvenir aus Dänemark. Viden og bevidsthed om sprogmødet. In K. Risager, A. Holmen & A. Trosborg (Eds.), *Sproglig mangfoldighed: Om sproglig viden og bevidsthed* (pp. 30–42). Roskilde: ADLA.

Rizvi, F. (2017). School internationalization and its implications for higher education. In H. de Wit, J. Gacel-Ávila, E. Jones & N. Jooste (Eds.), *The globalization of internationalization: Emerging voices and perspectives* (pp. 18–26). London: Routledge.

Robson, S., Almeida, J., & Schartner, A. (2018). Internationalization at home: Time for review and development? *European Journal of Higher Education, 8*(1), 19–35.

Smith, A. (1996). Regional cooperation and mobility in a global setting: The examples of the European Community. In P. Blumenthal, C. Goodwin, A. Smith & U. Teichler (Eds.), *Academic mobility in a changing world* (pp. 129–146). London: Jessica Kingsley Publishers.

Spitzberg, B. H., & Changnon, G. (2009). Conceptualizing intercultural competence. In D. K. Deardorff (Ed.), *The Sage handbook of intercultural competence* (pp. 2–52). Thousand Oaks, CA: Sage.

Sursock, A. (2015). Learning and teaching in European Universities. European University Association. Retrieved from http://www.eua.be/publications/

Teichler, U. (1999). Internationalisation as a challenge of higher education in Europe. *Tertiary Education and Management, 5*, 5–23.

Teichler, U. (2001). Changes of Erasmus under the umbrella of Socrates. *Journal of Studies in International Education, 5*(3), 201–227.

Teichler, U. (2009). Internationalisation of higher education: European experiences. *Asia Pacific Education Review, 10*(1), 93–106.

Teichler, U. (2015). The impact of temporary study abroad. In R. Mitchell, N. Tracy-Ventura & K. McManus (Eds.), *Social interaction, identity and language learning during residence abroad* (pp. 16–32). Amsterdam: European Second Language Association.

Teichler, U. (2017). Internationalisation trends in higher education and the changing role of international student mobility. *Journal of International Mobility, 1*(5), 177–216.

Teichler, U., Ferencz, I., & Wächter, B. (2011). *Mapping mobility in European higher education: Overview and trends* (Vol. I). Brussels: A study produced for the Directorate General for Education and Culture (DGEAC), European Commission.

Teichler, U., & Maiworm, F. (1997). The Erasmus students' experience: Major findings of the Erasmus evaluation research project. Retrieved from http://bookshop.europa.eu

Ting-Toomey, S. (1999). *Communicating across cultures.* New York: Guilford Press.

Van der Wende, M. (2001). Internationalisation policies: About new trends and contrasting paradigms. *Higher Education Policy, 14*, 249–259.

Vossensteyn, H., Lanzendorf, U., & Souto-Otero, M. (2008). *The impact of Erasmus on European higher education: Quality, openness and internationalisation.* Final report to the European Commission. Twente: CHEPS.

Wächter, B. (2008). Mobility and internationalisation in the European Higher Education Area. In M. Kelo (Ed.), *Beyond 2010: Priorities and challenges for higher education in the next decade* (pp. 13–42). Bonn: Lemmens.

Wächter, B. (2014). Recent trends in student mobility in Europe. In B. Streitwieser (Ed.), *Internationalisation of higher education and global mobility* (pp. 87–97). Southampton: Symposium Books.

Yarosh, M., Lukic, D., & Santibáñez-Gruber, R. (2018). Intercultural competence for students in international joint master programmes. *International Journal of Intercultural Relations, 66*, 52–72.

Yemini, M. (2015). Internationalisation discourse hits the tipping point. *Perspectives: Policy and Practice in Higher Education, 19*(1), 19–22.

Chapter 3

Methodological foundations

About Chapter 3

Chapters 1 and 2 laid the conceptual and educational foundations to understand student mobility from an interdisciplinary perspective. The third chapter builds on this discussion by focusing on the ways in which research methodologies can expand or confine our understanding of a given phenomenon (student mobility, in our case).

The overarching goal is to lay the operational foundations for approaching student mobility outside the limits of disciplinary thinking, including the types of methodologies and methods it accepts as valid. With this goal in mind, a descriptive overview of commonly used research methodologies and data collection methods to examine student mobility is offered to the reader. This overview is followed by a prescriptive summary of mixed methods and how the combination of quantitative and qualitative approaches provides a better understanding of student mobility than either approach alone. The next section builds on these overviews by contextualising mixed methods and its essential characteristics. One of these characteristics involves deploying multiple methodological perspectives to construct a systematic and comprehensive understanding of complex phenomena. Hence the similar philosophical outlooks shared by mixed methods and interdisciplinary research and the role integration plays in both literatures, discussed in the section that follows.

Finally, a practical application of the ways in which mixed methods were employed in the two empirical studies in Part II of this book is offered to the reader. It is sought, in this way, to lay the operational foundations for applying mixed methods to readers' own studies. Among mixed methods basics are the concepts of integration and multiple validities, both of which are explained in this chapter and illustrated in the second part of the book.

To conclude, a summary of key points is provided. As in previous chapters, a number of reflective questions and/or points (see Box 3.2) are outlined at the end chapter.

Student mobility and research methodology

The avid interest in student mobility brought about a vast repository of literature, but not necessarily sustained discussions about the type of methodologies and

Methodological foundations **89**

methods of data collection used; and even less about how these vary across the different wings of disciplinary knowledge.

Given this backdrop, in the following section I discuss common research methodologies and methods of data collection in student mobility research and scholarship.

Descriptive overview

Methodological discussions about student mobility research and scholarship tend to happen haphazardly and focus on a given methodology and underlying data collection methods in the context of a given discipline or theoretical framework. In fact, the few available overviews are usually conducted within specific lines of inquiry like second language acquisition (e.g., de Costa, Rawal, & Zaykovskaya, 2017; Yang, 2016) and comparative and international education (e.g., Phillips, 2006; Savvides, 2014; Streitwieser, Le, & Rust, 2012). Very seldom do these reviews systematise the type of methodologies employed in general research about student mobility. Such systematisation is, nonetheless, crucial to leverage the procedural knowledge base of student mobility research.

Apart from a couple of systematic efforts from a North American perspective (e.g., Bleistein & Wong, 2015; Engberg & Davinson, 2015; Ogden, 2015; Ogden & Streitwieser, 2017), most reflections on the type of methodologies and methods of data collection employed in student mobility research are done in passing. Stated another way, there is little methodological theorisation in studies of student mobility. When such rare reflections are offered, they do not usually represent an explicit goal or primary outcome of the produced work.

In Europe, the lack of theorisation about the types of methodologies employed in student mobility research and scholarship is striking. The host of new publications every year has not been accompanied by appropriate theorisation at conceptual and methodological levels, possibly because student mobility research in Europe (and elsewhere) is a hybrid research area spanning several disciplines. As Chapters 1 and 2 demonstrated, this eclectic nature often translates into disconnected literatures and conceptual frameworks. The same can be said of the methodological realm. Hence the importance of developing an expanded agenda for theorising student mobility as an area of study, at both conceptual and methodological levels.

In a brief reflection about the type of research methods most frequently used in European student mobility research from the 1990s to the early 2000s, Murphy-Lejeune (2002) argues that two types of study contributed to progress towards a better understanding of this phenomenon. She refers specifically to the plethora of large-scale quantitative studies like the *Erasmus* evaluations (e.g., Teichler & Maiworm, 1997), projects such as the ADMIT (West, 2002) and to a couple of qualitative studies reinstating the student voice within a narrative that tended to focus on the institutional side of studying abroad. While forefronting the dearth of qualitative research, Murphy-Lejeune (2002) contextualised the contribution of her book the field. This offered a qualitative account of the experiences of

90 Foundations of an interdisciplinary approach

strangeness of European student travellers as voiced by the students themselves, something which was still missing in Europe at the time.

A shortage of qualitative studies about the experiences of mobile students in European higher education is seldom the case today, coming, as they do, either in the format of papers or books. The prolific stock of institutional case studies has, nonetheless, remained unchanged. Findings yielded by Streitwieser, Le and Rust's (2012) review of research on study abroad, student mobility and international student exchange, across five leading comparative education journals, corroborate this assertion. According to this review, the types of study reported most frequently were 'case studies with relatively small numbers of students, and relatively often focused on only one institution' (p. 15). The most commonly used methods of data collection were open surveys and interviews.

Additional conclusions can be inferred from the range of studies reviewed in Chapter 1 against the descriptors of our conceptual diagram (see Figure 1.6). With this overview in mind, I underline five major improvements from the state of the art presented by Murphy-Lejeune (2002) and Streitwieser et al. (2012):

1. increasing number of longitudinal studies;
2. diversification of designs, instruments and samples;
3. greater generalisability of findings;
4. increasing number of qualitative studies (even if typically institutionally bound);
5. more frequent use of pre- and post-designs, often employing comparison groups but not always control groups.

With regard to aspect number five, and as explained by Ogden (2015) and Dwyer (2004), it is extremely difficult to randomly assign students who are completely comparable with education-abroad treatment groups due to self-selection issues. To outweigh such limitations, researchers like Rodrigues (2013) recommend controlling for pre-mobility differences between mobile and non-mobile students to tackle problems of unobserved heterogeneity. Two strategies are proposed by Rodrigues (2013): (a) using an instrumental variables approach, and (b) accounting for many individual characteristics as possible (see pp. 3–4).

Some sample studies employing these strategies can be found in the academic literature exploring the professional value of student mobility and the migration nexus (see Chapter 1, Long-term impact of study abroad), but perhaps not as often as one might assume. Both approaches, and strategy (a) in particular, are methodologically laborious and time-consuming, requiring the mastery of sophisticated statistical analyses. As an example, I would highlight the studies by Oosterbeek and Webbink (2011) and Parey and Waldinger (2010), which use the assignment of a scholarship and participation in the *Erasmus* programme, respectively, as instrumental variables for investigating the causal effect of studying abroad on subsequent work migration. Strategy (b) can be commonly found across a wider array of themes within the specialised literature, albeit with varying degrees of robustness.

The introduction of the notion of mobility capital by Murphy-Lejeune (2002) has been instrumental in this regard, namely by bringing attention to mobile students' attribute variables and experiences that may be present before the study abroad experience. Since then, researchers in Europe have more consciously accounted for 'pre-mobility' differences, using qualitative (e.g., Brooks & Waters, 2010) and quantitative methods (e.g., Bryła, 2019; Rodrigues, 2013) alike. Fewer researchers have, nonetheless, done so in an explicit attempt to determine the causal effect of study abroad on the outcomes of interest, and even fewer explicitly integrating quantitative and qualitative methods.

Looking beyond this procedural aside, some methodological issues have, in my opinion, remained largely unchanged since 2002. I am referring specifically to (the):

1. abundance of single-institutional case study accounts of study abroad, often employing narrative approaches;
2. paucity of sound empirical analyses addressing different types of student mobility simultaneously (e.g., credit and degree-seeking);
3. overemphasis on country or world region-specific analyses (e.g., the Anglosphere);
4. poor quality of statistical indicators of cross-border flows;
5. dichotomy between quantitative and qualitative approaches.

Each of these five issues brings about specific challenges. In the order outlined previously, these challenges are: (1) the extent to which institutional contexts can act as confounding variables and the dearth of clarity in operationalising the variables of interest (particularly when narrative approaches are used); (2) the complex influence of student mobility types on study abroad outcomes; (3) induction of geographical biases that may underestimate the role of local and temporal circumstances underpinning student mobility (see Cairns, 2014, 2015 in this regard); (4) the use of proxy indicators as measures of genuine student mobility (see Wächter, 2014 or the EURODATA studies for further information); and, finally, (5) the limitations of quantitative and qualitative methods when used alone (to understand complex phenomena such as student mobility).

Naturally, all research has limitations; the very limitations that make it fundamental to assess the implications of our own methodological choices when examining a given problem. The next section attempts to clarify the implications inherent to issue (5) on the assumption that the combination of the strengths of quantitative and qualitative approaches may offset the weaknesses of either approach alone (Creswell & Plano Clark, 2007, 2011, 2017). It is hoped, in this way, to produce a more integrated account of student mobility (in depth and breadth) by examining its multifarious variables from different methodological standpoints.

92 Foundations of an interdisciplinary approach

Prescriptive overview

The dichotomy between qualitative and quantitative methods alluded to by Murphy-Lejeune in 2002 applies to current European student mobility research, even if methodologically studies have grown increasingly complex. If we visualise a methodological continuum of existing studies, the majority tends to fall either on the quantitative or qualitative end but seldom in the middle.

As Chapter 1 has demonstrated, quantitative studies span the primary literature as well as literature outside traditional academic channels. It is impossible to say in absolute figures whether the majority is subsumed under the primary literature or spread across sources of information that are not published or distributed in the usual academic outlets and may, therefore, be problematic to pin down. I am referring in particular to theses and dissertations, technical reports, working papers, meta-studies and online documents released, for instance, by third-party organisations which are difficult to trace or may have limited distribution (i.e., the grey literature).

Although I do not have a rigorously validated answer to whether quantitative studies can be most commonly found in the primary or grey literature, I would venture to say that in Europe a sheer volume of quantitative research outputs about student mobility (credit-seeking in particular) are coalesced into the grey literature; more specifically, surveys, reports or evaluations related to *Erasmus* exchanges and sponsored by third parties, including the European Commission, its departments and agencies. Take, for instance, the major evaluation studies sponsored by the Commission and surveyed regularly since 1988. Other quantitative studies subsidised by the Commission include, for example: the EURODATA I and II studies by the Academic Cooperation Association, the *Erasmus Impact Study* (Brandenburg, Berghoff, & Taboadela, 2014) and survey-research projects conducted by the Erasmus Student Network (ESN) on student mobility-related issues (see Chapter 1, Global student dynamics and Long-term impact of study abroad). Well-known examples of ESN projects are: the two-edition project *Problems of Recognition in Making Erasmus* (PRIME, ttps://www.esn.org/prime) or the ESN survey about the student exchange experience conducted since 2005 with an average of 14,000 responses per year from *Erasmus* students. In both cases, findings are summarised in downloadable online reports.

Quantitative overviews of cross-border flows of students by national and international data collectors are also available online, often coupled with online ready-to-use indicators. As referred to in Chapter 1, other quantitative studies include reports on the internationalisation of European higher education like the *Trends* reports published by the European University Association since the signing of the Bologna Declaration in 1999. Outside secondary and grey-area publications, one can also find robust quantitative studies in the primary literature. Among the most-easy-to-find examples are studies exploring the professional value of student mobility and the migration nexus. This is possibly because these studies seek to determine the causal effect of studying abroad on professional-migration outcomes.

On the other end of the methodological continuum, one can find qualitative studies addressing the human experience of European student mobility and related outcomes. Take, for instance: Murphy-Lejeune's (2002) qualitative case study of 50 students in the theoretical light of the sociology of the stranger; Papatsiba's (2003) content analysis of 80 texts by *Erasmus* students from the Rhône-Alpes region (France) regarding their representations of Otherness; Montgomery's (2010) ethnographic work on the human and learning experience of seven international students in a UK university. Anquetil's (2006) action research can be also coupled with this set of studies, although we need to be cautious of differences. Situated within language and culture didactics (*'didactologie des langues et cultures'*),[1] this monograph is less empirically oriented than the former three, given its goal of establishing a pedagogical framework for developing the intercultural communicative competence of *Erasmus* students at an Italian university.

Overall, these four qualitative monographs provided a contextualised understanding of European student mobility against the preponderance of quantitative studies in the 1990s and early 2000s. Certainly, many other qualitative studies could have been pointed out. I choose these four sample monographs in particular because they are in-depth empirical studies examining student mobility as a whole rather than some isolated variables of interest. Stated differently, in all four monographs mobile students were not simply selected to shed insight into a given variable or issue. The goal was, instead, to understand student mobility from an evidence-based perspective.

To summarise, the reflection offered in this section draws attention to the divide between quantitative and qualitative studies of student mobility in Europe. Not that empirical studies using both approaches are inexistent (see, for example, Cairns, 2014), but they seldom explicitly integrate quantitative and qualitative data (see Van Mol, 2014 for an exception). Overall, few are the studies making overt use of mixed methodologies other than a couple of isolated initiatives, notably unpublished Doctoral and Master's investigations. The adoption of mixed methods in student mobility research and scholarship can, however, be a springboard to make sense of this phenomenon in more complex and robust ways. This is discussed next.

The need for mixed methods in student mobility research

The multifaceted systems in which student mobility is couched call for an active dialogue between quantitative and qualitative approaches. This procedural dialogism accords with the interdisciplinary approach in this book insofar as it can harness readers' methodological capacity to consider student mobility from different standpoints.

94 Foundations of an interdisciplinary approach

The core premise behind this chapter is that the complexity of student mobility calls for a broad approach at methodological level, in addition to the conceptual (Chapters 1 and 2). To develop this all-encompassing methodological approach, it is fundamental to move beyond past entrenched methodological divides and bring together the strengths of quantitative and qualitative approaches. In the sections that follow I will, thus, explore the meaning of mixed methods and explain how it can open space for an interdisciplinary agenda for theorising student mobility. But before delving into this issue, a few words of contextualisation about this methodology are needed.

On mixed methods

Mixed methods[2] as a distinct methodological orientation is relatively recent, dating back to the 1980s and early 1990s, although its formative antecedents go back further to the 1950s. By the early 1990s, scholars and practitioners from different disciplines and geographical contexts advanced ways to effectively combine quantitative and qualitative data (Creswell & Creswell, 2018; Creswell & Plano Clark, 2011, 2017).

Over the last three decades, important strides have been made in mixed methods research. The current and previous decades in particular witnessed an exponential growth of professional interest in and scientific literature on mixed methods. Specialised books and handbooks were published, peer-reviewed journals launched, professional and/or research associations formed and conferences held.

In 1994, John Creswell pioneered the comparison of qualitative, quantitative and mixed methods research designs in one of the bestselling textbooks in the mixed methods literature, now in its fifth edition (2018). The recognition of mixed methods as a distinct methodological orientation led to the first edition of the *Handbook of Mixed Methods and Behavioral Sciences* in 2003 (see Tashakkori & Teddlie, 2003), reissued in 2010. In 2007, Creswell and Plano Clark published a widely cited textbook for designing and conducting mixed methods research, already in its third edition (2017). It was also in 2007 that the peer-reviewed *Journal of Mixed Methods Research* was launched, later affiliated with the Mixed Methods International Research Association (MMIRA, http://mmira.wildapricot.org/), established in 2013. In addition to this international association, the reader can find interest groups and online platforms dedicated to mixed research. An example is the SAGE online platform *Methods Space* (https://www.methodspace.com/) which includes an interest group on mixed methods.

More recently, in 2015, another handbook of mixed methods (and multimethod research) was released by Oxford University Press (see Hesse-Biber & Johnson, 2015). The number of specialised books about mixed methods has grown exponentially over the current and past decade. Five years after the launch of the *Journal of Mixed Methods Research,* Onwuegbuzie (2012) noted there were more than 30 books published on the topic. In a sense, the list of specialised

Methodological foundations 95

resources devoted to mixed methods is as wide as the range of disciplines showing interest for and actively employing mixed methods; from anthropology, to communication, criminal justice, education, evaluation, nursing, psychology, political science, public administration, public health, sociology, social work, urban studies, to name but a few (Morgan, 2014a).

Given this background, it is unsurprising that mixed methods have been defined according to different foci and standpoints. As a starting point for understanding the meaning of mixed methods I choose the definition proposed by Creswell and Plano Clark in the first edition of their book *Designing and Conducting Mixed Methods Research*:

> Mixed methods research is a research design with philosophical assumptions as well as methods of inquiry. As a methodology, it involves philosophical assumptions that guide the direction of the collection and analysis and the mixture of qualitative and quantitative approaches in many phases of the research process. As a method, it focuses on collecting, analyzing, and mixing both quantitative and qualitative data in a single study or series of studies. Its central premise is that the use of quantitative and qualitative approaches, in combination, provides a better understanding of research problems than either approach alone.
>
> (2007, p. 5)

The reason why I adopted Creswell and Plano Clark's (2007) definition is because it addresses methods, research design and philosophical orientations. In other words, mixed methods research is envisaged in this monograph both as a method and an approach addressing procedural and epistemological realms.

Later, in 2011, Creswell and Plano Clark furthered their definition according to key features or components of mixed research while putting an emphasis on what is required from the researcher to conduct this type of approach to research inquiry. Table 3.1 summarises these features.

Table 3.1 Features of mixed methods research, adapted from Creswell and Plano Clark (2011)

Characteristics	Definition
Form of data collection	Collecting and analysing qualitative and quantitative data in response to the complex research questions or problems
Methods	Using rigorous quantitative and qualitative methods and procedures
Priority	Giving priority to one or both forms of data (in terms of what the research emphasises)
Integration	Combining the two forms of data (either concurrently or sequentially) and integrating data strands as part of specific research designs
Philosophy and worldviews	Framing mixed methods within broader philosophical assumptions (e.g., constructivism) and theoretical lenses (e.g., feminism)

96 Foundations of an interdisciplinary approach

The core characteristics and/or principles of mixed research, and integration in particular, are in line with the rationale for interdisciplinarity. Similar to interdisciplinary approaches, mixed methods research postulates multiple and interconnected perspectives. This is discussed next.

On mixed methods and interdisciplinarity

The pursuit of mixed methods in multiple disciplines derives from a common need – that of providing sustained responses to research problems and/or questions whose complexity cannot be appropriately addressed by a single method or type of data collection. Interdisciplinary research is, likewise, geared towards the incorporation of multiple (disciplinary) perspectives to construct a comprehensive understanding of complex phenomena.

As espoused by Szostak (2015), the two literatures share similar philosophical outlooks because both draw on the advantages of integrating methods and/or disciplines to examine multifaceted problems. As further elaborated by this interdisciplinarian, both are also criticised on the grounds that scholars can only truly master one discipline and one type of method.

The philosophical outlook underpinning interdisciplinary and mixed methods research is in tune with the rationale behind this book and its goal of developing an awareness of the multifarious disciplines and theories informing knowledge of student mobility. This awareness can leverage an expanded agenda for theorising student mobility (in conceptual and methodological realms), through the same 'integrative habit of mind' advocated by interdisciplinary and mixed methods research. That is, a capacity to see and make sense of social phenomena in multiple ways, from diverse disciplinary and methodological standpoints.

Earlier, in Chapter 1, I used different themes and/or variables of interest to set out a conceptual diagram for continued abstracting of the multifarious facets characterising student mobility. Upon identifying the variables of interest, I pointed out sample studies across various disciplinary and theoretical orientations. The process was interactive in a to-and-fro movement between relevant disciplines and variables of interest. These steps are actually among the strategies recommended by interdisciplinarians to ascertain disciplinary insights. According to Repko and Szostak (2017), interdisciplinary strategies include: (a) pinning down relevant disciplines related to the topic under scrutiny and searching within the disciplinary literature for relevant studies and variables, and (b) consulting a list of illustrative phenomena and key variables proposed by Szostak (2004) to determine which might be applicable. Such strategies can be a stepping stone to mutually constructed knowledge (of student mobility) that is not confined to one single discipline and its own favoured variables.

The same logic applies to the methodological realm. When opting for a specific methodology and methods of data collection it is fundamental to be cognisant of the strengths and limitations of our methodological choices (and predispositions), as well as of the paradigmatic assumptions in which they nest. Simply put, it is imperative to recognise how our own methodological positioning can influence knowledge generation. In practice, methodological (and theoretical) choices should be driven by a 'both/and' thinking instead of a 'either/or' approach (Repko & Szostak, 2017; Szostak, 2015). Hence the importance of integration for interdisciplinary and mixed research.

Integration is all the more important if methodological options are to follow from research problems; stated differently, if we are to take research in the directions it calls for rather than those pre-planned. Yet, this is not always the case, since disciplinary preferences regarding methodologies often mirror preferences regarding theory and subject matter (Szostak, 2015). The overviews in this chapter and Chapter 1 have shown that specific research strands tend to adopt specific research methods. The literature exploring the migration nexus in student mobility, for instance, lends itself to statistical analyses. By contrast, second language acquisition (SLA) research on student mobility is more likely supported by qualitative accounts. This qualitative preference became more pronounced after the cultural turn and the emphasis on poststructuralist thinking which brought heightened attention to the contextual conditions in which language learning takes place and the learning pathways of mobile learners. For example, skimming through the methodological sections of the sample studies in Chapter 1 (e.g., Collentine & Freed, 2004; Dufon & Churchill, 2006; Kinginger, 2013; Mitchell, Tracy-Ventura, & McManus, 2017, 2015; Pellegrino Aveni, 2005; Regan, Howard, & Lemée, 2009; Segalowitz et al., 2004), it is clear that qualitative approaches prevail.

The prevalence of quantitative and qualitative approaches in these two strands of research is not problematic in itself, as long as the research problem warrants a mono-method approach. What is problematic is the preference of one approach over the other in light of purist positions pledging allegiance to a particular school of thought. These uncritical loyalties hinder the search for the fullest responses to the research questions and/or problems at hand. Both quantitative and qualitative approaches are important and useful, and both have strengths and limitations. Purist views of disciplines and methodologies set up borders – the very borders mixed methods and interdisciplinary research seek to water down. Crossing these boundaries entails reaching across lines of demarcation through 'border work' that 'moves beyond one-way questions' in theory and praxis (Hesse-Biber, 2015).

Methodological integration arises from this need to see and work from different mental models and lenses. While the concept itself leaves room for much discussion (see Maxwell, Chmiel, & Rogers, 2015 in this regard), it is of general agreement among mixed methodologists that the power of mixed methods research lies in:

> a synergetic methodological approach bridging the quantitative-qualitative divide through an 'integrated craft' that brings together quantitative and

98 Foundations of an interdisciplinary approach

qualitative inferences to produce a comprehensive understanding of complex research problems from different mental models or lenses.

(Bazeley & Kemp, 2011; Bryman, 2007; Creswell & Plano Clark, 2011, 2017; Maxwell et al., 2015)

Despite this realisation, there are no precise guidelines for mixing quantitative and qualitative methods as mixed methods research continues to clarify and parse its understanding of it.

As explained by Creswell and Plano Clark (2017), the practice of integration is not intuitive, because for many years quantitative and qualitative strands were kept separate. Great strides have, nonetheless, been made towards integrating the quantitative and qualitative phases of mixed methods studies, including: (a) *frameworks or terminology* to explain the reasons for mixing methods (e.g., triangulation complementarity, development, initiation, expansion – see the seminal work of Greene, Caracelli and Graham, 1989); (b) *procedural diagrams* to illustrate the research steps and activities of mixed methods designs; (c) *research designs* to plan out mixed methods studies, either according to a typology-based approach whereby a preset design is chosen from a given typology (see Creswell & Plano Clark, 2017, pp. 54–57) or according to an interactive approach to design components (see Maxwell et al., 2015); (d) *data analysis strategies* to integrate quantitative and qualitative data (see Bazeley, 2018; Brannen & O'Connell, 2015); (e) *metaphors* to explain the process of integrating data analyses (see Bazeley & Kemp, 2011); and (f) the integration of paradigms via a dialectical or 'middle-ground stance' whereby competing paradigms are combined under the meta-paradigm of pragmatism (see Johnson, 2012; Morgan, 2014b). Importantly, this dialectical stance accords with the epistemological pluralism of interdisciplinary research.

To summarise, both interdisciplinary and mixed methods research push researchers to think about integration to produce a whole greater than its discrete parts. In methodological terms, and as argued by Fetters and Freshwater (2015) – '1+1=3', i.e., 'qualitative + quantitative = more than the individual components' (p. 116).

On the use of mixed methods in this book

The use of mixed methods agrees with the interdisciplinary approach in this monograph to generate a comprehensive understanding of student mobility. This understanding is the outcome of integration at conceptual and methodological levels, the former of which is described in the two previous chapters.

The current section draws on integration strategies outlined in the previous section to explain the mixing of quantitative and qualitative approaches in the two empirical studies in Part II of this book (Chapters 4 to 6). This was done in four regards, at the level of: (a) design, including its representation through a procedural diagram; (b) data collection; (c) analysis and interpretation of quantitative and qualitative results; and (d) within the programmatic evaluation component of the intercultural intervention in Study 1. All four aspects are explained next.

RESEARCH DESIGN AND DATA COLLECTION

Mixed methodologists like Bryman (2007) and Maxwell et al. (2015) cast doubt on the use of *typology* designs to think about integration on the grounds that a *systemic* or *interactive* concept of design is better able to achieve and capture the mixing of quantitative and qualitative approaches. Others like Creswell and Plano Clark (2011, 2017) maintain that:

> typologies provide the researcher with a range of available options to consider that are well defined, facilitate a solid approach for addressing the research problem, and help the investigator anticipate and resolve challenging issues.
> (Creswell & Plano Clark, 2017, p. 59)

My position is closer to Creswell and Plano Clark's because I consider typological designs useful to ascertain the value of mixed methods to European student mobility research, to help clarifying the methods decisions taken by researchers and facilitate comparison of studies. This argument finds new ground in a recent exploratory study by McKinley (2019) that assessed the quality of 24 mixed methods studies within European student mobility research, showing the need to establish mixed methods frameworks and a shared understanding of this methodological approach in this area of research.

Of the several perspectives on design typologies in the specialised mixed methods literature I adopted the typology proposed by Creswell and Plano Clark in 2011 due to the clarity and range of different models for doing research. The adopted design is a multiphase design which 'combines both sequential and concurrent strands over a period time that the researcher implements within a program of study addressing an overall program objective' (2011, p. 72).

This design was adopted from six designs[3] due to its alignment with my own understanding of mixed methods, the centrality of integration in different research phases and its multidimensional nature. The composite organisation of multiphase designs, into concurrent and sequential quantitative and qualitative data collection, matches triangulation and development rationales of the two empirical studies in Part II of the book, by not only seeking convergence of results but also by using the results of one method to inform the other. Additionally, the multifaceted nature of multiphase designs allowed me to bring together these two studies by coupling different design elements (i.e., mixed methods and case study research).

To elaborate further, the adopted mixed methods design incorporates three case studies across two individual studies (Figure 3.1). Study 1 comprises a group of 19 credit-seeking students as participants in the *Campus Europae* programme (Case Study A), and a mixed group of 3 *Erasmus* students and 9 highly skilled immigrants (Case Study B). The two cases (A and B) in Study 1 are bound by an intercultural intervention that sought to support and enhance the intercultural learning of these 31 sojourners during their stay at a public university in Portugal (see Chapter 6 for a description). The implementation of this intervention in

100 Foundations of an interdisciplinary approach

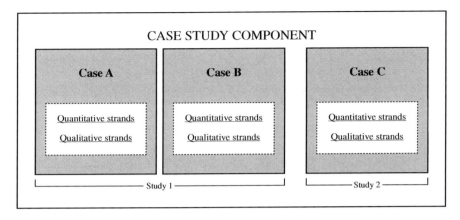

Figure 3.1 Empirical studies: case study component.

two Portuguese language classrooms determined the access to the subgroup of highly skilled immigrants. This was a challenge I decided to embrace, assuming that highly skilled migration could provide additional leverage to understand the particulars of student mobility.

Study 2, in turn, comprises 19 degree-seeking students at 2 universities in the UK (Case Study C). All three sojourner groups were accompanied during one academic year.

To summarise, the experiences of three types of sojourners[4] will be at the heart of the second part of this book: (a) exchange students, (b) international students and (c) highly skilled immigrants. Both (a) and (b) are mobile students but whereas the former group encompasses exchange students at a Portuguese university, the latter comprises international students at two British universities. As noted earlier in Chapter 1, the division of the 50 sojourners into 3 groups aids the comparison of similarities and differences of their cultural immersion experiences. As in cross-cultural psychology research, it is assumed that the identification of the type of sojourn can help in understanding who these sojourners are, why they go abroad and how they respond to in-country experiences.

Implementation of the two studies occurred in two academic years and involved five research phases: three phases in Case A and B (Study 1), and two in Case C (Study 2). To explain individual phases, I will use a procedural diagram (Figure 3.2) in what would otherwise be a long and, most likely, tedious account of the methods decisions I took. While describing this process, I hope to offer readers a useful illustration of key features of procedural diagrams. Before moving forward, a few words of contextualisation are needed on the use of these diagrams in mixed methods research.

These kinds of diagram are graphic representations that convey the complexity of mixed methods designs by illustrating the steps of the research process through the use of geographic shapes and notation systems. As explained by

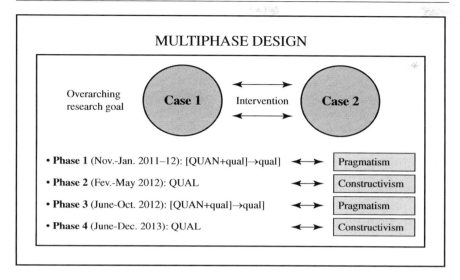

Figure 3.2 Empirical studies: procedural diagram.

Plano Clark and Ivankova (2016), procedural diagrams are essentially flow charts describing the flow of the research process across its quantitative and qualitative components, the underlying research procedures and outcomes. While there is not a preset formula for drawing procedural diagrams, the mixed methods literature offers useful guidelines (see Ivankova, Creswell, & Stick, 2006) and a range of notation systems that can be incorporated into these diagrams (see Creswell & Plano Clark, 2017, p. 66, and Plano Clark & Ivankova, 2016, p. 117, for a summary of notation systems).

The specific notation system used in the procedural diagram I designed (Figure 3.2) is adopted from Morse (1991) and Morse and Niehaus (2009) whereby: uppercase letters (e.g., QUAN) designate the priority of data strands; arrows (→) sequential timing; plus sign (+) concurrent timing; and finally, brackets ([ ]) when a method is embedded in another method – e.g., [QUAN+qual]. But let us look at the procedural diagram before I clutter these pages with excessive technical jargon.

All five phases in the procedural diagram required making sustained decisions about the integration of quantitative and qualitative data strands and the most appropriate instruments of data collection to reach my research goal. Data sets were, therefore, integrated within and across research phases to address the complexity of student mobility and its longitudinal scope.

Quantitative and qualitative data were collected in sequence and concurrently across research phases. For instance, the sequential qualitative data set (→qual) in Phases 1 and 2 in Study 1 (Cases A and B) and Phases 4 and 5 in Study 2 (Case C) depends on the preceding concurrent quantitative and qualitative strands –

102 Foundations of an interdisciplinary approach

[QUAN+qual]. Stated in terms of data collection instruments, the design of the focus groups conducted in Studies 1 and 2 is informed by the results of the pre- and post-test questionnaires assessing the pre- and post-study abroad experience (and hereafter referred to as pre- and post-experience questionnaires). These questionnaires encompassed both closed and open-ended questions and this is why what is primarily a quantitative method embeds a qualitative component – [QUAN+qual]. It should be also noted that the pre- and post-experience questionnaires were the key measurement instruments administered to all three sojourner groups. A period of six to seven months separates the administration of these instruments. The pre-experience questionnaire was administered two months into the sojourn[5], and the post-experience questionnaire six to seven months afterwards.

Overall, the priority given to quantitative and qualitative data varies according to the combination of concurrent and sequential research phases. Whereas Phase 1 and 3 (in Study 1) and Phase 4 and 5 (in Study 2) have a quantitative priority, Phase 2 has a qualitative one (hence the uppercase – QUAL). Note that Phase 2 is specific to Study 1 (Cases A and B), referring to the implementation of an intercultural intervention which included in-class data collection and an interview (in Phase 3) with the Portuguese language teacher who assisted in the intervention. The aim of this interview was to ascertain the intercultural impact of the intervention beyond the participants themselves. A similar interview was not conducted in Study 2 because there was not an intervention.

ABOUT THE SOJOURNERS

As mentioned earlier, the 50 sojourners in this book comprise: (a) 22 exchange students in Portugal, (b) 19 international students in the UK, and (c) 9 highly skilled immigrants in Portugal. Exchange students were participants in the credit-bearing exchange programmes *Erasmus* and *Campus Europae*. No lengthy introduction needs to be made regarding the EU flagship programme *Erasmus*, but a few words of contextualisation are needed about *Campus Europae*, described in Box 3.1 (at the end of this section).

The brief characterisation of sojourner demographics in the next couple of paragraphs aims to help frame participant sojourn experiences, discussed in Part II of the book (Practical applications). When reading the second part of the book, it may be useful for the reader to recall this description and access the list of participants in Appendix 3.1, along with key attributes and sojourn features. The names presented in this appendix, and throughout the second part of the book, are pseudonyms.

Upon administration of the pre-experience questionnaire, sojourners ranged in age from 19 to 56, with an average age of 25.47 years old (SD = 6.87). Age differences stem essentially from the age range of the nine highly skilled immigrants. While highly skilled immigrants were on average 36 years old, mobile students (exchange and international) were 23.

In line with the contemporary higher education landscape, most participants were female. There were 33 female participants (66%) against a minority of 17 male participants (34%). Eighteen nationalities were represented by the 50 sojourners, with 1 immigrant participant having double nationality. Whereas all exchange participants were Europeans, most international students were from outside Europe. The group of the highly skilled immigrants was mixed. Through looking at participant demographics by sojourn type, we can understand better the differences across groups.

Exchange participants represented 7 different nationalities: 1 Austrian (4.5%), 1 French (4.5 %), 2 Lithuanians (9.1%), 2 Latvians (9.1%), 3 Finnish (13.6%), 11 Poles (50.0 %) and 2 Spaniards (9.1 %). International students were from a slightly wider range of nationalities (10 in total), all of which corresponded to their countries of origin. With the exception of Singapore and China that accounted for two (10.5%) and eight international students (42.1%), respectively; all other countries were represented by one student only. These countries included: Angola, Brazil, Czech Republic, India, Kenya, Malaysia, Spain and Thailand. Finally, of the nine immigrant participants, two were Venezuelans, three Russians, three Spanish and one participant was both Venezuelan and Portuguese.

With regard to participant fields of study, the 41 mobile students were engaged in several disciplinary areas. Both the majority of exchange and international students were doing subjects in Science, Technology, Engineering and Mathematics (STEM). In the international student group, this was the case of 12 participants against 7 international students in the Social Sciences and the Humanities. The share for STEM subjects was also greater in the exchange student group. Twelve exchange students attended these kinds of study programme against 10 students in the Social Sciences and the Humanities. A detailed account of student study programmes is provided in Appendix 3.1.

Most mobile students were pursuing a Master's degree. Of the 22 exchange students, 8 (36.4%) were undergraduates and 14 (63.6%) Master's candidates. Of the 19 international students, 10 were pursuing a Master's degree, 8 an Undergraduate and 1 student a Doctorate.

All nine immigrant participants held a higher education degree (Undergraduate, Master's or PhD), and moved to Portugal for family reasons and/or professional added-value (described in greater detail in Chapter 4).

Box 3.1 – On *Campus Europae*

Campus Europae is a credit-bearing mobility programme and a form of cooperation of a university consortium registered as a foundation (the European University Foundation, EUF, http://uni-foundation.eu/) under the patronage of the Government of the Grand Duchy of Luxembourg. Formally established in 2003, the initial consortium was composed of 12 higher education institutions across 11 European countries, including Eastern European countries that were not part of the EU at the time.

The initial project was closely aligned with Bologna reform intents and EU's integration project, placing 'longer and more structured mobility and multilingualism as core rules of the project' (EUF-CE, 2013, p. 7). In practice, students participating in this consortium-based exchange programme could spend one to two academic years at member universities (during their Undergraduate and Master's studies), and were expected to reach an intermediate level of host language proficiency in two foreign languages (B1 according to the Common European Framework of Reference for Languages – Endnote 9 in Chapter 2). Today, the *Campus Europae* programme is a past project of the European University Foundation, with the foundation positing it as 'a laboratory for enhancing European student mobility, pioneering several concepts that have subsequently been integrated in the Erasmus programme' (EUF, http://uni-foundation.eu/).

DATA ANALYSIS

The data analysis procedures employed to examine sojourner experiences consist of *mono* and *multi*-data analyses (Johnson & Christensen, 2017). Mono-analysis refers to the examination of quantitative or qualitative data through one analytical procedure only, specifically, the individual application of statistical and thematic analyses across the three chapters in Part II of the book. Multi-analysis (or mixed analysis) refers to the use of these quantitative and qualitative analytical procedures in tandem (Johnson & Christensen, 2017). Both types of analysis are described next.

Quantitative analysis entails the application of descriptive and inferential statistics to the variables characterising the sojourn of the 50 participants during their stay in Portugal (for Case Study A and B) and the UK (for Case Study C). Frequency distributions were computed for nominal and ordinal variables, and central tendency and dispersion measures for numerical variables and variables measured through rating scales. The aim was to summarise data by analysing the observations of variables in each sojourner cohort. When exploring the relationship between pairs of variables (either numerical or dichotomous), Spearman correlation coefficients were calculated.

To go further into the quantitative data set and make general inferences about the observations of the 50 participants in the 3 case studies, inferential procedures were used at a significance level of .05. Given the small sample size, non-parametric tests were employed. The main test used was the Kruskal–Wallis test which operates on the principle of ranking data to test differences between two or more independent groups (Field, 2013). Given the use of this non-parametric test as a mixed analysis procedure, its application will be described further ahead in the mixed analysis section.

Qualitative analysis concerns the application of thematic analytical procedures to: (a) the open-ended questions in the pre- and post-experience questionnaires, (b) the verbatim text of the focus groups that followed the post-experience questionnaire and (c) the verbatim text of the interview with the Portuguese language teacher who assisted in the intercultural intervention with Case Study A and B, i.e., the exchange students and highly skilled immigrants in Portugal.

Thematic analysis is here understood as a process of systematic pattern recognition whereby themes capturing the richness of the phenomenon of interest become the categories for analysis (Boyatzis, 1998; Fereday & Muir-Chochrane, 2006). A theme is, thus, the basic coding 'that at minimum describes and organizes possible observations and at maximum interprets aspects of the phenomenon' (Boyatzis, 1998, p. 4).

The generation of themes followed inductive and deductive approaches. Inductive themes were generated directly from qualitative raw information and deductive themes from relevant theories reviewed in Chapters 1 and 2 (hence the importance of an interdisciplinary outlook). Comparisons across data sources were also valuable in refining data-driven themes in open-ended questions as will be demonstrated in Chapter 5.

Mixed analysis refers to the integration of findings from the quantitative and qualitative analyses into a coherent whole (Johnson & Christensen, 2017). Two data types (multi-data) and multiple analytical procedures (multi-analysis) are therefore employed, either sequentially or concurrently.

The sequential application of multiple analytical techniques (statistical and thematic) can be found across the three chapters that form the second part of the book. In Chapter 5, in particular, the combination of multiple analytical procedures occurs also concurrently to transform qualitative data into quantitative data. For these purposes, two strategies were employed. The first strategy consisted of representing numerically qualitative themes and analysing these themes statistically through frequency counts. The aim was to clarify the qualitative results through quantitative methods, namely the frequency of categories and/or themes within the qualitative data set.

The second strategy to quantify data combined analytical procedures to integrate quantitative and qualitative data as if they were one single data set. This type of analysis is employed in Chapter 5 insofar as quantitative and qualitative results are associated via the application of the Kruskal–Wallis test. To clarify further, open-ended questions from the pre- and post-experience questionnaires were categorised into one-meaning themes which were then analysed statistically and integrated into a coherent whole (i.e., the meta-inferences drew from both quantitative and qualitative findings).

The concurrent combination of analytical procedures implied a higher level of statistical sophistication than the sequential analysis (Strategy 1), since 'latent effect sizes' were associated to qualitative themes. The aim was to triangulate qualitative and quantitative data by seeking convergence of results between the two methods. The potential corroboration of results would then enhance the validity of findings and bring about the concept of multiple validities through the combination of quantitative and qualitative significance indices (Onwuegbuzie & Leech, 2004). This requirement is known in mixed research as multiple validities legitimation.

Summary

This chapter expanded the conceptual discussion in Chapters 1 and 2 to raise readers' awareness of how methodological decisions can shape the lenses through which we look at student mobility and interpret it. As posited by Repko and Szostak (2017), disciplinary views on reality entail several defining elements, including the studied phenomenon, philosophical outlook, assumptions, concepts, theories and methods.

The ways disciplines and their preferred theories relate to research methodology, the methods they favour to collect and analyse data and how they process these data have implications for the testing of theories and the type and quality of knowledge produced. The 'integrative habit of mind' advocated by this book is essential for those seeking to produce a systematic and comprehensive understanding of student mobility at conceptual and methodological levels alike. The subject matter of this chapter was the latter in an attempt to heighten readers' awareness of how methodological options within the disciplines examining student mobility can shape knowledge production about it. Two types of overview were developed: a descriptive overview of research methodologies and methods used to investigate student mobility across disciplines; a prescriptive overview of the role of mixed methods in providing fuller responses to student mobility.

Some of the sample studies in Chapter 1 were reviewed according to their methodological options. Conclusions were drawn regarding five major methodological challenges and five improvements of European student mobility research from the 1990s to the present day. An ongoing methodological challenge is precisely the lack of integration (not just combination) between quantitative and qualitative data.

To tackle this challenge and provide more sustained responses to research inquiries about student mobility, a mixed methods approach was suggested. Particular attention was paid to the role of integration through mixed methods typological designs. Methodological integration is not confined to a specific design, but a typology approach to design offers a range of tangible options that can enable a sound approach to mixed methods and integration practices, especially for those new to mixed methods research. The practical application of a multiphase design to the two empirical studies at the heart of Part II of this book was explained to the reader. This explanation included a discussion about integration at different levels, of: (a) design, (b) data collection and (c) analysis of quantitative and qualitative results. Ultimately, it is in this sort of integrative process where the explanatory power of a mixed approach lies.

Box 3.2 – Reflective questions and/or points of Chapter 3

To help you review critically the content of this chapter, ask yourself the following questions and discuss them with colleagues from other disciplines.

1. Consider methodological discussions elsewhere; what other challenges and improvements can you identify in European student mobility research from the 1990s to the present?
2. To what extent is research on student mobility driven by the need to validate disciplinary theories and their favoured methods?
   2.1. And, to what extent can this hinder the impact of research on education abroad practice?
3. What might the methodological pluralism of mixed methods add to your knowledge of student mobility?
4. In what ways are mixed methods and interdisciplinarity related?
5. In case you are currently conducting research on student mobility, can your topic be addressed by either quantitative or qualitative methods?
   5.1. For each one, describe the strengths and weaknesses and explain if their integrated use can lead to a more comprehensive understanding of your topic.
6. Since there are no precise guidelines for mixing data, how would you integrate the quantitative and qualitative data sets in your study?
7. What explanatory systems would you use for the mixing of data? Would you use a procedural diagram as in my case? (Please recall Figure 3.2).
   7.1. If so, read the guidelines by Ivankova, Creswell and Stick (2006) and choose a notation system (see Creswell, 2017, p. 66 for a summary), then draw your procedural diagram and explain it according to the selected notation.
   7.2. While designing your procedural diagram, think of the main reason for mixing in your study. You can always use the seminal framework by Green et al. (1989) to help you identify the primary rationale for mixing: Was it *triangulation, complementarity, development, initiation* or *expansion*?

108 Foundations of an interdisciplinary approach

Appendix 3.1

No	Pseudonym	Gender	Level of study	Study programme[a]	Nationality	Sojourn type
1.	Saskia	Female	UG	Biology	Finish	Exchange
2.	Greta	Female	UG	Languages and Psychology	Latvian	Exchange
3.	Maja	Female	UG	Education and Training	Polish	Exchange
4.	Milosz	Female	MA	Electronic Engineering	Polish	Exchange
5.	Gabija	Female	UG	Education and Training	Lithuanian	Exchange
6.	Karol	Female	MA	Tourism	Polish	Exchange
7.	Jeane	Male	UG	Biology	Finish	Exchange
8.	Bartek	Male	MA	Tourism	Polish	Exchange
9.	Jürgen	Female	MA	Electronic Engineering	Polish	Exchange
10.	Agnë	Female	UG	Electronic Engineering	Lithuanian	Exchange
11.	Jan	Male	MA	Electronic Engineering	Polish	Exchange
12.	Łukasz	Female	MA	Electronic Engineering	Polish	Exchange
13.	Martyna	Female	MA	Tourism	Polish	Exchange
14.	Tanja	Female	MA	Languages and Education	Polish	Exchange
15.	Nikola	Female	MA	Economics	Polish	Exchange
16.	Jonas	Male	UG	Biology	Finish	Exchange
17.	Aija	Male	UG	Education and Training	Latvian	Exchange
18.	Andresz	Male	MA	Electronic Engineering	Polish	Exchange
19.	Kinga	Female	MA	Tourism	Polish	Exchange
20.	Gaëlle	Female	MA	Chemical Engineering	French	Exchange
21.	Juan	Male	MA	Electronic Engineering	Spanish	Exchange
22.	Borja	Male	MA	Civil Engineering	Spanish	Exchange
23.	Felix	Male	UG	Urban Planning	Singaporean	International
24.	Ying	Female	MA	Education and Training	Chinese	International
25.	Yuwei	Female	MA	Accounting and Finance	Chinese	International
26.	Feng	Female	PhD	Civil Engineering	Chinese	International
27.	Elinah	Female	UG	Civil Engineering	Kenyan	International
28.	Anette	Female	UG	Accounting and Finance	Chinese	International

(Continued)

No	Pseudonym	Gender	Level of study	Study programme[a]	Nationality	Sojourn type
29.	Adrian	Male	UG	Computer Science	Malaysian	International
30.	Jane	Female	UG	Speech Therapy	Thai	International
31.	Lin	Female	MA	Transport Planning	Chinese	International
32.	Mantas	Male	MA	Linguistics	Czech	International
33.	João	Male	MA	Civil Engineering	Angolan	International
34.	Zhi Ruo	Female	UG	Business and Management Studies	Singaporean	International
35.	Tao	Male	MA	Transport Planning	Chinese	International
36.	Cristina	Female	MA	International Development and Education	Brazilian	International
37.	Regina	Female	MA	International Development and Education	Spanish	International
38.	Krisha	Female	MA	International Development and Education	Indian	International
39.	Dong	Male	UG	Accounting and Finance	Chinese	International
40.	Chao	Male	UG	Law	Chinese	International
41.	Fei	Female	MA	TESOL	Chinese	International
42.	Lucia	Female	UG*	Journalism	Venezuelan	Immigrant
43.	Belén	Female	UG*	Unknown	Spanish	Immigrant
44.	Paula	Female	UG*	Marketing	Venezuelan	Immigrant
45.	Elena	Female	UG*	Media Studies	Spanish	Immigrant
46.	Alexei	Male	PhD*	Physics	Russian	Immigrant
47.	Liliya	Female	MA*	Psychology	Russian	Immigrant
48.	Mercedes	Female	MA*	Business and Management	Venezuelan	Immigrant
49.	Anfisa	Female	UG*	Unknown	Russian	Immigrant
50.	Jimena	Female	PhD	Chemistry	Spanish	Immigrant

Note. [a]Study programmes were roughly categorised according to the subject areas in *Times Higher Education* rankings; *Completed level of study; UG = Undergraduate, MA = Master's, PhD = Doctorate.

Notes

1 The discipline of language and culture didactics emerged in the 1980s focusing on the teaching-and-learning processes and methods to assist future language teachers and, by implication, their learners. This disciplinary field is prolific in southern European countries like Portugal, Spain and France (see Galisson, 2002 for further information).

2 Mixed methodologists like Johnson (2012) prefer the label 'mixed research' or 'mixed methods research' to 'mixed methods', as the latter term emphasises methods rather than a methodological orientation. While agreeing with Johnson (2012), for ease of reference I have used both terms in this book.

3 The typology by Creswell and Plano Clark has evolved through the years, from the first edition of their book (2007), to the second (2011) and the current edition (2017). In the latter, the authors propose three core designs – explanatory sequential, exploratory sequential and convergent – to reflect their most parsimonious statement of designs according to three major intents: to explain, explore, converge. Yet, in this monograph I kept the 2011 typology and the multiphase design in particular because I believe this design captures better the question of timing and sequence in designs involving a number of interrelated phases (concurrent or sequential).

4 Typically, sojourners refer to voluntary, temporary acculturating groups who move abroad for a limited period of time with a particular goal, returning to their home countries when this goal is met (Safdar & Berno, 2016). Accordingly, the three most significant sojourner groups are: (a) expatriates, (b) international students, (c) tourists. Although by definition, highly skilled immigrants are not considered sojourners, for the purposes of this book I refer to them as sojourners. The underlying reason is that in highly skilled migration there is a fine line between permanent and temporary migration. This type of migrants tend to have an international mindset which is often bound to the pursuit of international career opportunities in a foreign country during a fixed period of time to, then, return home.

5 With the exception of the nine highly skilled immigrants.

References

Anquetil, M. (2006). *Mobilité Erasmus et communication interculturelle: Une recherche action pour un parcours de formation*. Berne: Peter Lang.

Bazeley, P. (2018). *Integrating analyses in mixed methods research*. Thousand Oaks, CA: Sage.

Bazeley, P., & Kemp, L. (2011). Mosaics, triangles, and DNA: Metaphors for integrated analysis in mixed methods research. *Journal of Mixed Methods Research*, *6*(1), 55–72.

Bleistein, T., & Wong, M. S. (2015). Using qualitative research methods to assess education abroad: The value of qualitative methods in education abroad. In V. Savicki & E. Brewer (Eds.), *Assessing study abroad: Theory, tools, and practice* (pp. 103–121). Sterling, VA: Stylus Publishing.

Boyatzis, R. E. (1998). *Thematic analysis and code development: Transforming qualitative information*. Thousand Oaks, CA: Sage.

Brandenburg, U., Berghoff, S., & Taboadela, O. (2014). Erasmus impact study: Effects of mobility on the skills and employability of students and the internationalisation of higher education institutions. Retrieved from http://ec.europa.eu/dgs/educat ion_culture/repository/education/library/study/2014/erasmus-impact_en.pdf

Brannen, J., & O'Connell, R. (2015). Data analysis I: Overview of data analysis strategies. In S. Hesse-Biber & B. Johnson (Eds.), *The Oxford handbook of multimethod and mixed methods research inquiry* (pp. 257–274). New York, NY: Oxford University Press.

Brooks, R., & Waters, J. (2010). Social networks and educational mobility: The experiences of UK students. *Globalisation, Societies and Education, 8*(1), 143–157.

Bryła, P. (2019). International student mobility and subsequent migration: The case of Poland. *Studies in Higher Education, 44*(8), 1386–1399.

Bryman, A. (2007). Barriers to integrating quantitative and qualitative research. *Journal of Mixed Methods Research, 1*(1), 8–22.

Cairns, D. (2014). *Youth transitions, international student mobility and spatial reflexivity*. Basingstoke: Palgrave Macmillan.

Cairns, D. C. (2015). Mapping the youth mobility field. In A. Lange, C. Steiner, S. Schutter & H. Reiter (Eds.), *Handbuch Kindheits- und Jugendsoziologie* (pp. 1–16). Wiesbaden: Springer Fachmedien Wiesbaden.

Collentine, J., & Freed, B. (2004). Learning context and its effects in second langauge acquisition. *Studies in Second Language Acquisition, 26*(2), 153–171.

Creswell, J. W. (1994). *Research design: Qualitative and quantitative approaches.* Thousand Oaks, CA: Sage.

Creswell, J. W., & Creswell, J. D. (2018). *Research design: Qualitative, quantitative, and mixed methods approaches.* Thousand Oaks, CA: Sage.

Creswell, J. W., & Plano Clark, V. L. (2007). *Designing and conducting mixed methods research* (1st ed.). Thousand Oaks, CA: Sage.

Creswell, J. W., & Plano Clark, V. L. (2011). *Designing and conducting mixed methods research* (2nd ed.). Thousand Oaks, CA: Sage.

Creswell, J. W., & Plano Clark, V. L. (2017). *Designing and conducting mixed methods research* (3rd ed.). Thousand Oaks, CA: Sage.

de Costa, P. I., Rawal, H., & Zaykovskaya, I. (2017). Special issue: Study abroad in contemporary times: Toward greater methodological diversity and innovation. *System, 71*, 1–126.

Dufon, M. A., & Churchill, E. (Eds.). (2006). *Language learners in study abroad contexts*. Clevedon: Multilingual Matters.

Dwyer, M. M. (2004). More Is better: The impact of study abroad program duration. *Frontiers: The Interdisciplinary Journal of Study Abroad, 10*(Fall), 151–163.

Engberg, M. E., & Davinson, L. (2015). Quantitative approaches to srudy abroad assessment. In V. Savicki & E. Brewer (Eds.), *Assessing study abroad: Theory, tools, and practice* (pp. 122–144). Sterling, VA: Stylus Publishing.

EUF, C. E. (2013). *Campus Europae: A laboratory for mobility*, C. Ehmann (Ed.). Retrieved from https://issuu.com/euf-ce/docs/ce-10-years

Fereday, J., & Muir-Chochrane, E. (2006). Demonstrating rigor using thematic analysis: A hybrid approach of inductive and deductive coding theme development. *International Journal of Qualitative Methods, 5*(1), 80–92.

Fetters, M. D., & Freshwater, D. (2015). The 1 + 1 = 3 integration challenge. *Journal of Mixed Methods Research, 9*(2), 115–117.

Field, A. (2013). *Discovering statistics using SPSS* (4th ed.). London: Sage.

112   Foundations of an interdisciplinary approach

Galisson, R. (2002). Didactologie: de l'éducation aux langues-cultures à l'éducation par les langues-cultures. *Éla. Etudes de linguistique appliquée, 128*(4), 497–510.

Greene, J. C., Caracelli, V. J., & Graham, W. F. (1989). Toward a conceptual framework for mixed-method evaluation designs. *Educational Evaluation and Policy Analysis, 11*(3), 255–274.

Hesse-Biber, S. (2015). Introduction: Navigating a turbulent research landscape: Working the boundaries, tensions, diversity and contradictions of multimethod and mixed methods inquiry. In S. Hesse-Biber & R. B. Johnson (Eds.), *The Oxford handbook of multimethod and mixed methods research inquiry* (pp. xxiii–liii). New York, NY: Oxford University Press.

Hesse-Biber, S., & Johnson, R. B. (Eds.). (2015). *The Oxford handbook of multimethod and mixed methods research inquiry.* New York, NY: Oxford University Press.

Ivankova, N. V., Creswell, J. W., & Stick, S. L. (2006). Using mixed-methods sequential explanatory design: From theory to practice. *Field Methods, 18*(1), 3–20.

Johnson, B., & Christensen, L. B. (2017). *Educational research: Quantitative, qualitative, and mixed approaches* (6th ed.). Thousand Oaks, CA: Sage.

Johnson, R. B. (2012). Dialectical pluralism and mixed research. *Journal of Mixed Methods Research, 56*(6), 751–754.

Kinginger, C. (2013). *Social and cultural aspects of language learning in study abroad.* Amsterdam: John Benjamins.

Maxwell, J., Chmiel, M., & Rogers, S. (2015). Designing integration in multimethods and mixed methods research. In S. Hesse-Biber & R. B. Johnson (Eds.), *The Oxford handbook of multimethod and mixed methods research inquiry.* New York, NY: Oxford University Press.

McKinley, K. M. (2019). Assessing mixed methods research quality in the European student mobility literature. *Research in Comparative and International Education, 14*(4), 433–449.

Mitchell, R., Tracy-Ventura, N., & McManus, K. (Eds.). (2015). *Social interaction, identity and language learning during residence abroad.* Amsterdam: European Second Language Association.

Mitchell, R., Tracy-Ventura, N., & McManus, K. (2017). *Anglophone students abroad: Identity, social relationships, and language learning.* London: Routledge.

Montgomery, C. (2010). *Understanding the international student experience.* Basingstoke: Palgrave Macmillan.

Morgan, D. L. (2014a). *Integrating qualitative and quantitative methods: A pragmatic approach.* Thousand Oaks, CA: Sage.

Morgan, D. L. (2014b). Pragmatism as a paradigm for social research. *Qualitative Inquiry, 20*(8), 1045–1053.

Morse, J. M. (1991). Approaches to quantitative-qualitative methodological triangulation. *Nursing Research, 40*(2), 120–123.

Morse, J. M., & Niehaus, L. (2009). *Mixing methods design: Principles and procedures.* Walnut Creek, CA: Left Coast Press.

Murphy-Lejeune, E. (2002). *Student mobility and narrative in Europe: The new strangers.* London: Routledge.

Ogden, A. (2015). Toward a research agenda for U.S. education abroad. In E. Brewer (Ed.), *AIEA research agendas for the internationalization of higher educational and psychological measurement.* Retrieved from http://www.aieaworld.org/assets/doc s/research_agenda/ogden_2015.pdf

Ogden, A., & Streitwieser, B. (2017). Research on US education abroad: A concise overview. In D. M. Velliaris & D. Coleman-George (Eds.), *Handbook of research on study abroad programs and outbound* (pp. 1–39). Adelaide: IGI Global Press.

Onwuegbuzie, A. J. (2012). Introduction: Putting the MIXED back into quantitative and qualitative research in educational research and beyond: Moving toward the radical middle. *International Journal of Multiple Research Approaches, 6*(3), 192–219.

Onwuegbuzie, A. J., & Leech, N. L. (2004). Enhancing the interpretation of "significant" findings: The role of mixed methods research. *The Qualitative Report, 9*(4), 770–792.

Oosterbeek, H., & Webbink, D. (2011). Does studying abroad induce a brain drain? *Economica, 78*(310), 347–366.

Papatsiba, V. (2003). *Des étudiants européens: «Erasmus» et l'aventure de l'altérité*. Berne: Peter Lang.

Parey, M., & Waldinger, F. (2010). Studying abroad and the effect on international labour market mobility: Evidence from the introduction of ERASMUS. *The Economic Journal, 121*(551), 194–222.

Pellegrino Aveni, V. A. (2005). *Study abroad and second language use: Constructing the self*. Cambridge: Cambridge University Press.

Phillips, D. (2006). Research in comparative and international education. *Comparative Education: Method, 1*(4), 304–319.

Plano Clark, V., & Ivankova, N. V. (2016). *Mixed methods research: A guide to the field*. Thousand Oaks, CA: Sage.

Regan, V., Howard, M., & Lemée, M. (2009). *The acquisition of sociolinguistic competence in a study abroad context*. Bristol: Multilingual Matters.

Repko, A., & Szostak, R. (2017). *Interdisciplinary research: Process and theory* (3rd ed.). Thousand Oaks, CA: Sage.

Rodrigues, M. (2013). Does student mobility during higher education pay? Evidence from 16 European countries. *European Commission Joint Research Centre: Scientific and Technical Reports*. Retrieved from http://www.jrc.ec.europa.eu/

Safdar, S., & Berno, T. (2016). Sojourners. In D. L. Sam & J. W. Berry (Eds.), *The Cambridge handbook of acculturation psychology* (2nd ed., pp. 173–195). Cambridge: Cambridge University Press

Savvides, N. (2014). Methodological issues in intercultural, international and comparative education. *Research in Comparative and International Education, 9*(4), 370–374.

Segalowitz, N., Freed, B., Collentine, J., Lafford, B., Lazar, N., & Diaz-Campos, M. (2004). A comparison of Spanish second language acquisition in two different learning contexts: Study abroad and the domestic classroom. *Frontiers: The Interdisciplinary Journal of Study Abroad, 10*(Fall), 1–18.

Streitwieser, B. T., Le, E., & Rust, V. (2012). Research on study abroad, mobility, and student exchange in comparative education scholarship. *Research in Comparative and International Education, 7*(1), 5–19.

Szostak, R. (2004). *Classifying science: Phenomena, data, theory, method, practice*. Dordrecht: The Netherlands: Springer.

Szostak, R. (2015). Interdisciplinary and transdisciplinary: Multimethod and mixed methods research. In S. Hesse-Biber & R. B. Johnson (Eds.), *The Oxford handbook of multimethod and mixed methods research Inquiry* (pp. 128–143). New York, NY: Oxford University Press.

Tashakkori, A., & Teddlie, C. (Eds.). (2003). *Handbook of mixed methods in social and behavioral research*. Thousand Oaks, CA: Sage.

Teichler, U., & Maiworm, F. (1997). The Erasmus students' experience: Major findings of the Erasmus evaluation research project. Retrieved from http://bookshop.europa.eu

Van Mol, C. (2014). *Intra-European student mobility in higher education systems: Europe on the move*. Basingstoke: Palgrave Macmillan.

Wächter, B. (2014). Recent trends in student mobility in Europe. In B. Streitwieser (Ed.), *Internationalisation of higher education and global mobility* (pp. 87–97). Southampton: Symposium Books.

West, A. (2002). Higher education admissions and student mobility: The ADMIT research project. *European Educational Research Journal, 1*(1), 151–172.

Yang, J.-S. (2016). The effectiveness of study-abroad on second language learning: A meta-analysis. *The Canadian Modern Language Review, 72*(1), 66–94.

Part II

Applications of an interdisciplinary approach

Chapter 4

Pre-departure

About Chapter 4

Part I laid the foundational substructure within which the use of an interdisciplinary approach to student mobility is housed. Chapter 1 set the conceptual foundations, and Chapters 2 and 3, the educational and methodological, respectively.

The current chapter introduces the second part of this interdisciplinary approach – its practical applications. It does so by drawing on the previous foundational work to illustrate how different theories can be interspersed to construct a more comprehensive understanding of student mobility. At the heart of the chapter are the prior experiences and tools sojourners bring in their 'battered suitcases', as well as the motivations and expectations towards the journey they once faced ahead of them. Praxis and theory are brought together in a narrative that builds on quantitative and qualitative data yielded by pre- and post-experience questionnaires and focus groups. All three sojourner groups will be investigated against the same variables to obtain a comparative understanding of their sojourn.

Presentation of data follows the chronological sequence of the study abroad experience. The current chapter addresses pre-departure variables, Chapter 5 adaptation to the host culture and, finally, Chapter 6 the outcomes of living and studying in another country. Analytical procedures include descriptive and inferential statistics for quantitative data and thematic analysis for qualitative data, as explained earlier in Chapter 3. Specific statistical models are restated within the text of the three chronological instances of the study abroad experience which are, in turn, subdivided into overarching themes – Language biography, Motivations, Mobility capital and Steps into mobility in the case of the current chapter. The specification of overarching themes aids the integration of theories and data while framing findings according to the relationship between variables and corresponding groupings. In those cases, wherein one type of data reaches its full explanatory power, the second data source is not used.

Integration of theories and data analyses reflects the gist of an interdisciplinary approach. A common ground between different disciplinary insights and methods is created to construct a relational understanding of student mobility. To this end, disciplinary insights and data strands are combined within each of the four general themes (i.e., the variable groupings) in this chapter.

To conclude, a summary of key points is provided. As in previous chapters, a number of reflective questions and/or points (see Box 4.1) are presented at the end of the chapter.

The road is life

In Kerouac's famous novel *On the Road* we are reminded that the transformative power of travelling can be actively sought. In the same vein, study abroad can start well before arriving in the host country. However, if, for some, studying abroad may be a long-awaited journey, for others it may be an entirely new step.

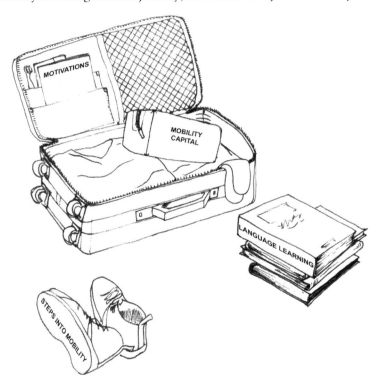

The period preceding the actual move and the accumulated capital mobile students (and migrants) bring with them is crucial to understand how the sojourn unfolds. For this reason, this chapter depicts pre-departure variables which add important information to the demographic profile in Chapter 3. Pre-departure variables such as language biography, motivations to study abroad and choose a specific country, mobility capital and steps into mobility can influence the experience of studying abroad and its outcomes. The aim of this chapter is to account for these pre-departure variables in the immersion experience of the 50 sojourners in this book.

Three sojourner groups will be depicted: (a) exchange students, (b) international students and (c) highly skilled immigrants. The main organising principle for the analysis is this threefold division of sojourners. However, in cases where variables may influence the impact of the intercultural intervention implemented with the exchange students and highly skilled immigrants in Portugal, the original case study analysis is kept. This is because the intervention was only administered to Case Studies A and B. That is, the *Campus Europae* students and the mixed group of *Erasmus* students and highly skilled immigrants in Portugal (please recall Chapter 3).

To consider the experiences, predispositions and tools the 50 sojourners bring in their 'suitcases' the sections of the pre-experience questionnaire (Sections I, II and III in Appendix 4.1) which correspond to the four aforementioned variable groupings will be analysed. In the fourth variable grouping (Steps into mobility), the qualitative themes from the corresponding questions in the focus groups that followed the post-experience questionnaire will be analysed.

Language biography

Of the three types of sojourners, the group of exchange students, stands out as the most plurilingual. These students mastered on average three foreign languages in addition to their mother tongue before their sojourn in Portugal. The minimum number of foreign languages learnt per exchange student was two, and the maximum five.

International students, in turn, learnt a smaller range of foreign languages before studying abroad (from none to three) and mastered on average one foreign language. Highly skilled immigrants mastered two languages, with a maximum of three foreign languages learnt per immigrant before the stay abroad. Interestingly, international students were the group mastering the smallest range of foreign languages before the stay abroad. This is because most international students had only learnt English before the sojourn.

Overall, the group with the richest language biography is the exchange student group, with international students and highly skilled immigrants having learnt fewer foreign languages per person. Figure 4.1 illustrates the range of foreign language learnt across the three sojourner groups before the immersion experience.

Exchange students were the group learning the widest range of foreign languages. Whereas exchange students learnt across nine different foreign languages before the sojourn, in the group of international students this number was six and for the highly skilled immigrants it was four.

English is the most commonly studied foreign language, with all sojourners having learnt it before their stay abroad. The second most frequently learnt language is French (n = 14; 28%), followed closely by German (n = 13; 26%). Portuguese ranks fourth because four highly skilled immigrants and four

120 Applications of an interdisciplinary approach

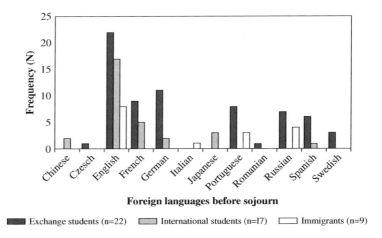

Figure 4.1 All sojourners: foreign languages learnt before the sojourn.

exchange students had learnt the language before their sojourn in Portugal. Since Portuguese was the main language of instruction of the intercultural intervention implemented with the two sojourner cohorts in Portugal (Case Studies A and B), it is paramount to probe further into the data by case study. Whereas in Case Study A (*Campus Europae* students) only a minority of five students (26.3%) studied Portuguese before the sojourn, this number represented the majority of students in Case Study B (n = 7; 58.3%).

Unlike Case A, the mixed case study of *Erasmus* and highly skilled immigrants had actual intermediate proficiency in Portuguese. The underlying reason is not only their previous knowledge of Portuguese and the longer immersion of immigrants, but also because this particular group included: (a) six speakers of other Romance languages, (b) three Luso-descendant speakers and (c) one speaker who had lived in a Portuguese-speaking country for six months. None of the 19 *Campus Europae* students were in similar circumstances, but they were offered pre-departure and in-country courses of Portuguese before the start of the academic year. These language courses aimed to equip *Campus Europae* students with two beginners' proficiency levels – A1 and A2 (see Endnote 9 in Chapter 2) – as required by the *Campus Europae* programme. However, because only 3 of the 19 *Campus Europae* students took the pre-departure online course beforehand, the intensive summer course at the host institution ended up becoming the first approach to the beginners' level, A1. This gap had a snowball effect, since the first semester of Portuguese as a foreign language targeted A1 and A2 levels simultaneously. As will be discussed later in Chapter 6, this came to influence students' motivation to learn Portuguese and the impact of the intervention.

Moving beyond this parenthetical aside, the learning of the host language is not simply a key learning domain of studying abroad, but also a mediating variable of sojourner adjustment to the host society as widely discussed in the second language acquisition literature (see Chapter 1, Learning domains abroad). Furthermore, the account of pre-departure language learning variables can provide valuable insights into the motivational aspects of study abroad, discussed next.

Motivations

Study abroad is mediated by personal and socio-cultural variables, including the varying motivations with which students embark on this experience.

In European studies of student mobility, motivation is not always included as an explanatory variable and, when used, it is frequently not expected to yield crucial information (Krzaklewska, 2008). Yet, examining the motivations sojourners hold prior to and after the immersion in the host culture can help in understanding the determinants for studying abroad as well as the produced outcomes compared to initial expectations.

More empirical investigations delving into the motivational realm of studying abroad as an explicit variable of interest are needed. The work of Krzaklewska (2008, 2013), in particular, explores the motivations of *Erasmus* students to study abroad in light of migration and youth developmental theories. Survey research like *Erasmus* evaluation (e.g., Maiworm & Teichler, 2002) and impact studies (e.g., Brandenburg, Berghoff, & Taboadela, 2014), and annual surveys by the Erasmus Student Network (e.g., Alfranseder, Fellinger, & Taivere, 2011; Krzaklewska & Krupnik, 2007) do include variables accounting for motivation. The depth of the conceptual analyses is, nonetheless, restricted by the descriptive nature of these reports and the wide range of variables measured. The *Erasmus* student questionnaire in Maiworm and Teichler (2002), for example, comprised 50 questions and more than 450 variables.

Added to this shortcoming, different understandings and constructs may be at stake as evidenced by the plethora of terms used: reasons, motivations, motives, determinants, forces, drivers, expectations, incentives. To give a practical example, whereas Maiworm and Teichler (2002) use motivations and reasons interchangeably, the EURODATA II study alternates between motivations, incentives and obstacles (see Rumbley, 2011). Survey research often measures the choice of the action of studying abroad (hence terms like reasons, motives, incentives) without necessarily ascertaining behavioural and psychosocial implications. The latter implications tend to be addressed by psychology and its subdisciplines investigating acculturating groups (see Chapter 1).

Measuring variables accounting for motivation in study abroad contexts can vary according to the methods of inquiry used, targeted disciplines and their own favoured theories. In contrast with study abroad survey research, which is often stripped of conceptual anchors and focuses on large sojourner groups, qualitative research tends to investigate motivation across individual sojourners following specific disciplinary frameworks. Murphy Lejeune's (2002) monograph, for instance, examined sojourner motivation through a narrative approach framed in the sociology of the stranger. Hence the foci of her categorisation into: (a) 'speaking foreignness', (b) 'living foreignness' and (c) 'international openness' (see pp. 82–96).

Studies of motivation in second language acquisition (SLA) have, in turn, posited motivation against language use while depicting the sojourner as a language learner. Common categorisations of motivation in SLA reflect a strong influence of psychological and socio-cultural theories through the identification of motivational orientations: integrative, instrumental, resultative, intrinsic versus extrinsic (see Dörnyei & Ushioda, 2011; Isabelli-García, 2006 for further information).

Another strand of research investigating sojourner motivation is sociology and migration theory in particular. In this case, motivation is commonly equated to push-and-pull factors, especially for migrants and degree-seeking students (e.g., Brooks & Waters, 2011). In psychology, one is more likely to find studies addressing psychosocial development, including identity formation processes in determining the main motivations to study abroad (e.g., Severino, Messina, & Llorent, 2014).

Remarkably, little research has compared the motivations of credit to degree-seeking students, something which this section also sheds insight into. To identify the types of motivation influencing sojourner decisions to study abroad, different variables were assembled from: (a) a literature review of studies of student mobility targeting or including motivation as a variable and (b) a pilot study with 31 incoming exchange students in Portugal. As a guiding measurement principle, the four motivational areas posited by Krzaklewska (2008) were taken into account. Twelve variables were identified and listed as preset categories in the pre-experience questionnaire along with the open-ended category 'Other' (through which 'Good weather' was added to the pre-questionnaire administered to exchange students in Portugal, see Appendix 4.1). These variables are listed below following the fourfold organisation by Krzaklewska (2008):

1. *academic*: 'field-specific knowledge', 'academic quality of host institution', 'international career prospects', 'improving marks easily';
2. linguistic: 'learning a foreign language';
3. cultural: 'knowing another culture', 'broadening European identity';
4. *personal*: 'personal development', 'having new experiences', 'having fun', 'doing tourism', 'meeting new people'.

All categories are illustrated in Figure 4.2 by frequency.

The comparison of the motivations of exchange and international students discloses similarities and differences. Starting with the similarities, both student groups selected the possibility of having new experiences among the top four motivations to study abroad. Yet, its relative importance appears to differ, emerging in first place for international students (n = 14; 87.5%), and second for

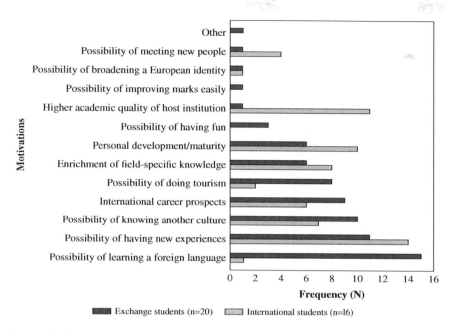

Figure 4.2 Mobile students: motivations to study abroad.

exchange (n = 11; 55%). In fact, for the latter group, 'learning a foreign language' was the category assembling the highest number of responses, with 15 exchange students selecting it. By contrast, language learning scored quite low for international students as it was chosen by one participant only. For the group of international students, the 'yearn for novelty' came first, followed by academic drivers like the possibility of studying at a post-secondary institution with high academic prestige (n = 11; 68.8%) and enriching their field-specific knowledge (n = 8; 50.0%). While the academic realm was not disregarded by exchange students, the drivers were not exactly the same. Whereas international students emphasised academic learning, exchange students forefronted the international career opportunities an exchange experience can enable (n = 9; 45%).

Overall, results indicate that various motivations can trigger students' decision to study abroad. The most common motivation among those doing an exchange was language learning, thus confirming previous research examining the motivation of this type of mobile students (e.g., Alfranseder et al., 2011; Krzaklewska & Krupnik, 2007; Maiworm & Teichler, 2002; Murphy-Lejeune, 2002). International students, in turn, rated this category quite poorly, with only one student choosing the possibility of learning foreign languages. Although the motivations of exchange and international students diverge in some regards, they are also similar in others. In both student groups, personal motivations and the 'yearn for novelty' in particular had high frequency rates for exchange and international students. This finding supports Krzaklewska's (2008, 2013) assertion that student motivations to study abroad can echo the values of today's youth.

As posited by youth developmental theories, today's youth transition into adulthood is characterised by experimentation in different spheres of life and postponement of entry into adulthood (Arnett, 2015). This transition is epitomised by the two mobile student groups, since their longing for new experiences and personal development is accompanied by competition for a space in a global labour market where lifelong jobs are increasingly scarce.

Unsurprisingly, the motives of the nine highly skilled immigrants were quite different.[1] Three key reasons led them to migrate: (a) family reasons, (b) professional reasons and (c) better living conditions. Five of them migrated to Portugal for family reasons due to direct or indirect kinship ties that prompted them to look for work in the country. These five immigrants were descendants by lineage or married to or partners of a Portuguese person. The remaining immigrants refer to two individuals who moved to Portugal strictly for work.

The reasons prompting these nine immigrants to migrate remind us that the decisions to move to another country (whether to study or work) are interwoven in a complex mix of personal and social circumstances where home and destination countries have a role to play. With this premise in mind, the remainder of this section examines the reasons that led mobile students (exchange and international) to choose Portugal and the UK, respectively.

Before delving into these reasons, it is important to emphasise that mobility levels differ dramatically between individual European countries (Teichler, Ferencz, & Wächter, 2011). In addition to these differences, the depth of available information about student mobility varies substantially across individual countries. Portugal, for example, is seldom selected as a case study in European-wide analyses of student mobility flows and the internationalisation of higher education, produced for the European Commission or other third-party organisations. Little is known about mobile students' personal motivations for choosing Portugal as a destination country. The same cannot be said about the UK.

As a major receiving country of degree-seeking students (see Chapter 3), student mobility in the UK is depicted in the sheer number of studies and reports. In addition to differences in mobility levels, the profile of the 2 countries hosting the 50 sojourners in this book is also distinct. While Portugal has, in recent years,[2] emerged as a net importer of credit-seeking students (even if not compared numerically with major European net importers of this type of student mobility), the UK has a long tradition in recruiting degree student mobility.

Interestingly, both countries are linked by neo-colonial logics aimed at attracting international students from their former colonies. In Portugal, despite the increase of degree-seeking students from Lusophone countries, their recruitment is yet to become a major source of revenue for the Portuguese higher education system given the only recent introduction of full-cost tuition fees for this student population.[3] Conversely, international students in the UK are key to the financial stability of the British higher education system, with an estimation of 14 per cent of the total university income in 2014/15 attributed to the higher tuition fees paid by these students (Universities UK, 2017).

Another interesting difference is that for Portugal two political discourses coexist based on its geopolitical alliances. The recruitment of degree-seeking students, on the one hand, is rooted in Portugal's desire to continue upholding its influence over its former colonies through shared cultural and language heritage. On the other hand, the attraction of credit-seeking students responds to the European Commission's integration project and to the pressure to boost internationalisation levels in the European Higher Education Area. In the British case, European supranational pressure never really had the same impact nor influence in the set-up of administrative structures to internationalise higher education as in the Portuguese case.

However important student mobility policies and the individual profiles of hosting and sending countries may be, it is in itself an insufficient condition to understand the reasons leading students to study abroad. Their perceptions need to be born in mind as well. For this reason, Figure 4.3 analyses student perceptions of destination choices, i.e., the personal reasons prompting the 22 exchange students and the 19 international students to choose Portugal and the UK, respectively.

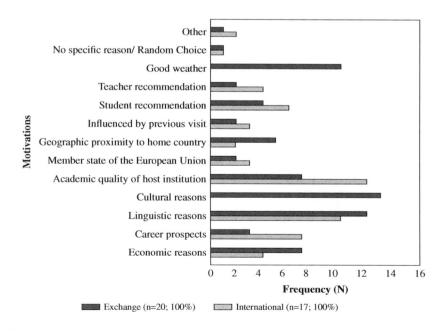

Figure 4.3 Mobile students: motivations to study in the host country.

126 Applications of an interdisciplinary approach

According to exchange students, Portuguese culture is the most frequent attracting factor for studying in Portugal (n = 13; 65%). The second top motivation was linguistic, with 12 exchange students having selected this category. The good weather conditions in Portugal were also among the top motivations, representing the choice of ten respondents. Finally, the low costs of living in Portugal and the academic quality of the Portuguese host institution were also attraction factors. The two categories were on a par (with seven responses each).

For international students, the academic quality of the host British institution was the most frequent motivation to choose the UK as their study abroad destination, gathering 12 responses (58.8%). Linguistic reasons and career prospects offered by the host country followed closely with ten and seven responses, respectively. Student recommendation also influenced destination choices, with six students selecting this category.

When comparing the motivations of exchange and international students, the academic realm of studying in another country is more commonly selected by international students. Exchange students, in turn, emphasised intangible conditions like culture and good weather. Linguistic reasons were among the top motivations for both mobile students to choose the destination country. However, there might be considerable differences in how the two groups perceive language learning. If we relate these data to data yielded by the previous question (Figure 4.2), it may be fair to assume that the language motivations of international students are more instrumental given the role English as a lingua franca may play in enhancing student academic and career prospects. Exchange students, on the other hand, seem to be more naturally open to learning a wider range of foreign languages. One cannot forget that all 22 exchange students were citizens of EU countries, whereas in the international student group this was only the case for 2 students. Thus, the openness of exchange students to learn less widely learnt and taught languages might mirror EU's multilingual policies in instilling foreign language mastery in European citizens to better appreciate the values of a culturally diverse Europe and, in this way, improve European youth employability prospects in the continent.

Finally, whether the sojourn is part of an educational journey or migration flows searching for better living conditions, there is an individual narrative that begins well before the stay abroad. It is this narrative and the accumulated capital sojourners bring with them that is examined next.

Mobility capital

Mobile students and highly skilled immigrants, as social agents, have their own personal history, accumulated knowledge and stock of skills, i.e., a particular human capital termed 'mobility capital' in Murphy-Lejeune's (2002) monograph. Her definition builds on the notion of cultural capital by the French sociologist Pierre Bourdieu (1979) and applies it to student mobility as 'a subcomponent of human capital, enabling individuals to enhance their skills because of the richness of the international experience gained by living abroad' (2002, p. 51). This capital is, according to Murphy-Lejeune, what distinguishes mobile students from their peers, and is composed of four main constituent pre-departure elements: 'family and personal history, previous experience of mobility including language competence, the first experience of adaptation which serves as an initiation, and finally the personality features of the potential wanderer' (p. 52).

The seven variables in this section operationalise Murphy-Lejeune's four constituent elements (Table 4.1). The fourth element ('Personality features') is not measured because it is outside the remit of this book and my own skills.

Before delving into the analysis of mobility-capital variables, it should be noted that my method and working hypothesis is different from Murphy-Lejeune's (2002). Whereas her narrative analysis explores mobility-capital variables as antecedents of European student mobility, the proposition undergirding my analysis is non-directional and seeks to examine the extent to which mobility-capital variables influence the intercultural development of the 50 sojourners while abroad. To elaborate further, the aim is to examine the extent to which these background variables are associated with sojourners' intercultural development in the post-experience questionnaire (see Question 13 in Appendix 5.1). To test the association between the variables in Table 4.1 Spearman's non-parametric coefficient is used.

Reliability analyses were conducted to ascertain if the intercultural competence scale (Question 13 in Appendixes 4.1 and 5.1) was consistently measuring the targeted construct (i.e., the four intercultural competence areas). To this end, the scale reliability was assessed by calculating Cronbach's alpha (α) which is the most common reliability index for instruments using rating scales (DeVellis, 2012). To assess the scale's quality, this reliability coefficient was calculated for each of the four component variables. The 'comfort ranges' followed were the

Table 4.1 Operationalisation of mobility capital

Constituent elements	Variables	Question	Instrument
I. Family and personal history	Multicultural family background	Q1	Pre-test
	No. of languages studied	Q2.	Pre-test
II. Previous experience of mobility	Previous experience of living abroad	Q3.	Pre-test
	No. of countries visited before the stay abroad	Q4.	Pre-test
	Previous participation in study abroad	Q6.	Pre-test
III. Experience of (cross-cultural) adaptation[1]	Foreign relationships abroad before the stay abroad	Q4.2.	Pre-test
	Foreign relationships in home country before the stay abroad	Q5.	Pre-test
IV. Personality features			

Note [1] The third constituent element refers in this book to experiences of cross-cultural adaption abroad and in sojourners' home countries, and not necessarily to the first experience of adaptation as in Murphy-Lejeune's (2002) work.

128 Applications of an interdisciplinary approach

ones suggested by DeVellis (2012) following a cut-off point of 0.60 whereby alphas below this value are unacceptable.

Table 4.2 lists the results yielded by each component variable in the post-experience questionnaire.

All component variables yielded alphas above the .60 lower reliability bound, thus making correlation analyses reliable.

To assess the strength of correlation coefficients between mobility-capital variables and intercultural attainment in the post-experience questionnaire, Cohen's effect ranges will be used, as suggested by Field (2013, p. 82):

- small effect: $\rho = [.10, .30]$
- medium effect: $\rho = [.30, .50]$
- large effect: $\rho = [.50, 1]$

Correlations will be analysed against these intervals and not focusing on statistical significance which is highly dependent on sample size.

Table 4.3 displays the correlation coefficients yielded by the paired variables for the three sojourner groups (separately). That is, the seven mobility-capital variables and the four dimensions of intercultural competence – Attitudes, Skills, Knowledge and Awareness – as per Fantini's (2006) intercultural communicative competence model.

The first mobility-capital variable ('Multicultural family background') is only measured for international students and immigrants because all exchange students answered negatively to this question. The same applies to the mobility-capital variable 'Previous study abroad' but with regard to immigrant participants.

Another relevant aspect of this analysis concerns the third constituent element proposed by Murphy Lejeune (2002), 'The first experience of adaptation', which is here operationalised as 'Experiences of cross-cultural adaption'. The aim is not to ascertain sojourners' very first experience of adaption per se whose chronological linearity is far from water-tight. Rather, it is to explore the association between cross-cultural encounters (abroad and in sojourners' home countries) to intercultural development. Notwithstanding the conceptual line drawn by Murphy-Lejeune (2002) between experiences of adaptation abroad and at home (see p. 60), there is not a clear-cut operationalisation of the corresponding variables. The variables 'Foreign relationships abroad' and 'Foreign relationships in home country' (Tables 4.1 and 4.3) are, thus, meant to shed empirical insight into this

Table 4.2 Post-experience questionnaire: reliability of the intercultural competence scale

	Attitudes (n = 49)	Skills (n = 47)	Knowledge (n = 50)	Awareness (n = 47)
No. of items	4	5	4	5
Cronbach's alpha	.63	.83	.77	.87

Table 4.3 Mobility capital correlation matrix (Spearman rank correlation – ρ)

Mobility capital	Attitudes			Skills			Knowledge			Awareness		
	Exch.	Int.	Immi.	Exch.	Int.	Immi.	Exch.	Int.	Immi.	Exch.	Int.	Immi.
Multicultural family life	–	.391	.135	–	.389	.617	–	.379	.826**	–	.391	.894**
No. of languages studied	.166	.196	–.209	.196	–.229	–.217	.216	–.024	–.197	.511*	–.262	–.671
Previous experience of living abroad	.297	.143	.173	.199	–.361	–.058	.550**	–.412	–.113	.413	–.044	–.291
No. of countries visited	–.110	.398	.000	–.171	–.089	–.300	.006	–.122	–.273	.372	.146	–.750
Previous study abroad	.306	.022	–	.033	–.339	–	–.052	–.183	–	.222	–.220	–
Foreign relations abroad	.417	.422	.429	–.060	–.054	.000	.017	.211	–.069	.192	–.018	–.423
Foreign relations in home country	–.016	.132	–.162	–.171	.230	.000	–.087	.218	.000	–.036	.000	–.258

Note. Exch. = exchange; Int. = international; Immi. = immigrants
Sample size: Exch. n = 19–22; Int. n = 13–19; Immi. n = 7–9
*Correlation is significant at .05, 2-tailed
**Correlation is significant at .01, 2-tailed

130 Applications of an interdisciplinary approach

distinction by measuring how cross-cultural experiences (with and without an element of national border crossing) relate to the realisation of a mobility capital, which is not only cultural but also social.

Correlation coefficients demonstrate that intercultural development unfolds differently across the four intercultural competence dimensions. These dimensions appear to behave differently across mobility-capital variables with different situations triggering varying domains in participant intercultural development; or conversely, distinct dimensions of intercultural development leading sojourners to embrace the seven situations differently. Likewise, the three types of sojourners seem to activate different areas of intercultural development across mobility-capital variables, showing that similar experiences can produce different results. Hence the dissimilar correlations (in nature and strength) yielded by the same paired variables.

Whereas for exchange students the number of foreign languages is positively and strongly correlated (ρ = .511) with awareness, for international and immigrant participants this relationship is negative with correlation coefficients of $-.262$ and $-.671$, respectively. These results indicate that intercultural development and the number of foreign languages learnt before the stay abroad move in opposite directions for sojourners. For exchange students, the higher the number of foreign languages learnt, the higher their awareness levels (and vice versa). For international students and highly skilled immigrants, the higher the number of foreign languages learnt, the lower their awareness levels. This suggests that awareness may be less dependent on foreign language learning for the latter two groups, something which is in line with participant language biographies. In fact, of the three sojourner groups, exchange students were the sojourners learning a greater number of foreign languages before the stay abroad (three on average). By contrast, international students and the highly skilled immigrants learnt on average one and two foreign languages, respectively.

Note, however, as Field (2013) points out, that 'correlation coefficients say nothing about which variable causes the other to change' because in correlational research we observe co-occurrence of variables (p. 270). Moreover, there may be other measured or unmeasured variables affecting the results. Even if intuitively it might be appealing to conclude that background socio-cultural variables like mobility-capital variables trigger intercultural development, one can only assume that these variables may influence this type of development (but not necessarily as triggers): statistically, because correlation coefficients do not say in which order the association operates; conceptually, because it would be naive to assume that sojourners initiate international living experiences as a blank slate, that is, without any prior degree of intercultural development. Intercultural competence can unfold into varying levels of development as supported by intercultural developmental models (see Chapter 2, Table 2.3). Also, in terms of Bourdieusian theory, symbolic capital follows both a logic of accumulation and exercise. Thus, the sojourn experience may be more than an opportunity arising from a previously held capital. It may also be an opportunity of return on such capital by furthering it via the abroad experience as will be voiced by the sojourners themselves in the following section (Steps into mobility).

As in the number of foreign languages learnt, previous experiences of living abroad[4] reproduce similar patterns of intercultural development among international and immigrant participants. The only exception is the attitudinal realm wherein living abroad prior to the sojourn is positively correlated among all three sojourner groups, all of which yield small correlation coefficients (between .173 and .297). In the remaining three intercultural dimensions, this relationship is negative for international students and immigrants alike. For exchange students, this relationship is always positive, given the moderate and large correlation with awareness ($\rho = .413$) and knowledge ($\rho = .550$).

Another interesting similarity between international and immigrant participants is that in both there is a positive correlation between being raised in a family of mixed origin and all four intercultural domains. Interestingly, none of the 22 exchange students had been brought up in a family of mixed origin, a finding which contrasts with Murphy-Lejeune's (2002) results, since 8 (53.3%) of the 15 *Erasmus* students in her sample were from families of mixed origin. And yet, as asserted by the researcher herself, the 'taste for living abroad' may not be simply fed on family history because other personal factors may also come into play.

But coming back to the group of international and immigrant participants, the association between multicultural family background and intercultural development is especially pronounced for immigrants. The strength of this correlation is moderate (for attitudes and skills) and large (for awareness and knowledge). The hybrid families of immigrant participants come as no surprise due to their experiences of foreignness via direct blood lineage, mixed marriages or relationships and stories of migration within the family compound (see previous section). What is perhaps most surprising is the strong correlation between immigrant multicultural family history and two specific areas of intercultural development – Awareness ($\rho = .894$) and Knowledge ($\rho = .826$). This finding may be also related to the impact of the intervention on these two specific areas of intercultural competence, explained later in Chapter 6.

The fourth variable in Table 4.3 informing mobility capital is the number of countries visited by sojourners prior to studying or working abroad. In contrast with previous variables where results were relatively alike for international and immigrant participants, the association between this mobility-capital variable and intercultural development is more similar among the two mobile student groups. Both positive and negative correlations are obtained. Specifically, there is a positive correlation between the number of countries visited and awareness for exchange and international students alike, albeit the varying strengths – moderate ($\rho = .372$) and small ($\rho = .146$), respectively. In the case of international students, there is also a moderate positive ($\rho = .398$) association in the attitudinal realm. For immigrants, the association is essentially negative.

Within foreign relationships developed abroad and in sojourner home countries, relationships abroad are more often positively correlated to intercultural

132 Applications of an interdisciplinary approach

development than relationships in participant home countries. For the latter case, there is only a positive small association in the attitudes, skills and knowledge dimensions for international students. This result may lay, in part, on the small sample size and the dichotomous nature of the measured variables.

Despite possible limitaions in calculations, results propel one to question which social contacts influence more intercultural development.

> Are foreign relationships developed in one's country of origin as impactful? Or, do foreign relationships developed outside one's country of origin promote higher levels of intercultural development? Does not 'true' adaptation take place in a different cultural *milieu* where one is not simply confronted with difference on an occasional basis but lives it daily?

These questions offer food for thought regarding the overall negative association between foreign relationships in one's home country and intercultural development, and the moderate association between relationships abroad and the attitudinal dimension of intercultural development (with correlation coefficients of .417, .422 and .429 for exchange, international and immigrant participants, respectively). If we bear in mind that participant intercultural development was measured essentially with regard to the host culture, the association between foreign relationships abroad and intercultural attitudes may gain a different light. Framed as a question: Can foreign relationships developed abroad foster positive attitudes towards the host culture, but hinder sojourner performative and awareness skills towards hosts?

As will be discussed in the following chapters, sojourners tend to form tightly knit social networks with their international peers (whether other immigrants or mobile students). These networks, while protecting against feelings of isolation and disorientation, may also fence in sojourners from seeking actual adaptation and socialisation with hosts.

Steps into mobility

The budding capital previously discussed is etched in certain steps prompting students to study abroad. Yet, the stock of dispositions, skills and social habits embodied in this mobility capital may be also furthered during the stay abroad.

This section examines the four steps into mobility by Murphy-Lejeune (2002) for our two groups of mobile students from a non-linear chronological perspective, admitting that this set of variables may be also enhanced during the sojourn. These steps include: (1) Urge to travel ('travel bug'), (2) Language jump, (3) Self-sufficiency, and (4) No constraining responsibilities. To these four steps, inspired by the work of Murphy-Lejeune, two are added: (5) Personal attributes other than self-sufficiency and (6) Shared lifestyle (see Table 4.4). All six steps are analysed based on data from the post-experience questionnaire and the follow-up focus groups with the two student groups, and all but step five were contemplated in the interview protocol. Examination of data is done thematically, with each step corresponding to

Pre-departure 133

Table 4.4 Steps into mobility

	Themes	Definition
1.	Urge to travel	The urge or strong desire to travel
2.	Language jump	Condition of not being afraid to learn or speak a new foreign language
3.	Self-sufficiency	Condition or attribute of being autonomous
4.	No constraining responsibilities	Condition of not being constrained by personal or family responsibilities
5.	Other personal attributes	Personal attributes other than self-sufficiency
6.	Shared lifestyle	Condition or willingness to share a communal way of living

one theme. Data analysis procedures are inductive and deductive in that the analysis explores unexpected viewpoints, but is also guided by prior theoretical assumptions which gave some direction to the analysis of the focus group interviews.

All themes are defined in Table 4.4 and illustrated by verbatim excerpts relevant to understanding participant viewpoints about the steps that may have prompted them to study abroad, for academic credits (exchange students) or to obtain a degree (international students). These excerpts are listed in Table 4.5 by theme. The only exception is Theme 6 (Shared lifestyle) which will be analysed separately given its prominence in the focus group session with exchange students. Note that individual focus sessions with exchange and international students are based roughly on the same interview protocol. Another important point is that the focus group session with exchange students was conducted with *Campus Europae* students only.

Both exchange and international students concur on the steps prompting them to study abroad but not necessarily on a temporal continuity with their past personal history. The urge to travel (Step 1), for instance, can either be a long-term orientation in students' lives, as forefronted by the exchange student Bartek and the international student Cristina, or something triggered during the sojourn. The latter is the case of Jan (exchange) and Ying (international) for whom studying abroad did not feed into their travelling capital but was a lever activated abroad. For Ying living abroad met a concrete purpose – that of obtaining an educational qualification abroad, asserted as a clear individual choice.

The willingness to take the language jump (Step 2) is deemed a necessary condition (Ying) to study abroad which when missed out can make the experience unbearable (Jan) or at least harder (Kinga). Self-sufficiency (Step 3), is perceived as an ability more than a personal attribute or mental disposition before departure. As noted by Karol and Jürgen, taking on the challenge of studying abroad is about gaining abilities students did not know they had before living in the host country. Free from constraining responsibilities (Step 4), their youth allows

134   Applications of an interdisciplinary approach

Table 4.5 Mobile students: perceptions about steps into mobility

Themes	Students		Excerpts
(1) Urge to travel	Exch.	Bartek	I travel since I remember. So, for me Portugal and Aveiro was a good base to travel even more. Even this year, I visited three countries.
	Exch.	Jan	For me, actually it's different because before coming here I wasn't such a big fan of travels. Maybe because here I have more free time and I think it's easier.
	Int.	Cristina	I don't think you need it that but I definitely had that before coming here.
	Int.	Ying	I didn't think about travelling. It's just for this purpose, to study here and get a degree.
(2) Language jump	Exch.	Jan	You have to know the language, because if you don't know the language that's impossible to go.
	Exch.	Andrzej	If you don't know the language it's harder.
	Int.	Ying	Yes, it is necessary!
(3) Self-sufficiency	Exch.	Karol	I agree in part that we have self-sufficiency before coming. But on the other hand, usually we don't have it before going. When we come here we develop it. Before coming here, we don't know what's going to happen. I was always afraid of missing my family and everything, but when I came here I got to know that I can live like this. I became autonomous here not before.
(4) No constraining responsibilities	Exch.	Kinga	At 30 no *Erasmus*!
	Int.	Dong	Even if I had children, maybe I would still like to choose to go abroad.
	Int.	Ying	Even if I had children, maybe I would still take my child to the UK because the public school here is free.
(5) Other personal attributes	Exch.	Jürgen	You have to be open-minded just as curious.
	Exch.	Kinga	Curiosity, open-mindedness.

Note. Exch. = exchange; Int. = international

them to enjoy a privileged freedom and take full advantage of a new social life as pointed out by the exchange student Kinga. International students seem to have a different viewpoint. Ying and Dong, for example, would still consider studying abroad if they had children. But for all of them, the study abroad experience and the new social life attached to it requires one to be as curious as one is open-minded (Step 5).

This new social life seems to be intimately related to a lifestyle shared by mobile students, emerging as a crucial part of their group identity during the sojourn. And yet, this shared lifestyle may not be exactly the same for exchange and international students, even if both form a 'social bubble' based on assumed similarity with their peers. This assumed similarity may not necessarily mean that the social lives of exchange and international students cross much. Each group seems to form its own social networks, mostly with other exchange and international students, respectively. For exchange students this group identity reflects a 'double life' in which having fun may be as (or even more) important as studying, a finding supported by Tsoukalas (2008). Other scholars like Cairns, Krzaklewska, Cuzzocrea and Allaste (2018) term this feature of the *Erasmus* experience 'conviviality'. For international students the sheer intensity of the social experience abroad seems to be balanced out by the academic demands of obtaining a British degree.

To better understand the group life of the two mobile student groups, interviewee viewpoints of Step 6 – Shared lifestyle – are given next. The opinions of exchange students come first, followed by those of international students. Note that in the focus group interviewees defined their lifestyle (exchange and international) on an individual card, followed by a discussion with their colleagues.

Andrzej: 'I think the most common experience was that every time I met an *Erasmus* student it was this shared atmosphere of having fun, partying, and having a great time. I think it was the most common thing. The rest, like travelling, not all *Erasmus* were travelling. Not all *Erasmus* are learning culture, not all came here for learning their field of study. So, I think the most common interest is this atmosphere of having a great time.'

Karol: 'I have points. It's like: Travelling, living on your own, partying, relaxing, meeting new people.'

Jan: '*Erasmus* lifestyle is basically about enjoying, enjoying your time, enjoying your life. And then, I also wrote some points like parties, for example, just for having fun. The people, like making some friendships, talking to people, getting to know some other cultures. And also, travelling, seeing other places, widening your horizons.'

Kinga: 'My *Erasmus* lifestyle means less stress, less rush, more time for friends, more sleep and more time for everything which I love but I didn't have a chance to develop before. But [laughing], after I wrote this I just noticed that I think that one year of *Erasmus* is like five years less of life, generally.'

Jürgen: 'I defined a lifestyle, overall, as a basic way of living, spending time, deciding what you'd like to do and where to spend your money too, and in addition to what Kinga said, for me it's like trying to combine the sleeping, the working, the studying, the partying. It's hard to combine it.'

Bartek: 'I have six points about *Erasmus* lifestyle. It's travelling, meeting people, partying and waking up late. Going to *pastelaria*[1] to have breakfast or

136 Applications of an interdisciplinary approach

something like that, doing some activities (sports, beach), and I forgot about studies in the end.'

> *Note.* ¹*Pastelaria (s)* are shops in Portugal where baked goods are sold, and an important place for socialising.

> (Excerpts from the focus group with exchange students)

As the comments illustrate, the shared lifestyle bringing exchange students together is deeply rooted in the experiential side of the exchange experience. It is a physically and emotionally intense way of living wherein traveling, partying and meeting people emerge as core social activities in view of a less demanding academic workload. This way of living allows a rupture with past everyday routines and obligations attached to the home environment, as noted by Kinga. The intensity of the experience is, nonetheless, physically strenuous and that is why 'one year of *Erasmus* is like five years less of life' (Kinga). Above all, this urge to spend a great time is highlighted by all six interviewees as part of a communal life which makes exchange students a distinctive group with a clear-cut social identity. Interestingly, while describing their social identities none of the interviewees pointed out *Campus Europae* as a category of self-identification, emphasising instead their membership in a wider *Erasmus* community. This finding is line with Tsoukalas' (2008) ethnographic inquiry into the life of *Erasmus* students (in Stockholm and Athens) to whom the self-identification as 'exchange students' was not nearly as salient as 'Erasmus students'. Also worth noting is the alignment between this specific finding and one of my points in Chapter 1 (see Variables informing study abroad), where I argued that the delivery and assessment of programmatic study abroad in European higher education is very seldom (if at all) an object of inquiry, linking my argument to the findings in the form of a question:

> To what extent can a given exchange programme be considered distinctive when it does not emerge as a category of self-identification among its participants?

Moving beyond this parenthetical aside, the strong group identity based on intra-student bonding seems to also characterise international students. Yet, the sheer intensity of the social life seems to be less prominent. But let us frame this discussion in their own words.

Ying: 'International students can make friends with each other easily … I thought about the parties of Chinese students with other international students, it seems different because, for example, most Chinese students do not dare to speak English with hosts, but it seems that with other international students who have English as their second language they like to express their ideas not only in public occasions, like in the classroom, but also outside the classroom. They are less comfortable talking to hosts in English because they are embarrassed of their language mistakes, grammar or vocabulary errors. International students also like to buy food from their home countries. They travel with friends, not alone!'

Tao: 'Most international students maintain the living style from their home countries, although they may adapt a little bit. For example, they may go to pubs more often. One thing I noticed is that international students travel differently from local students because, you know, you are only here for one year. So, we won't buy a car or something. But local students they have a car, and can travel differently. But we travel more than them. International students have more constraints than local students which encourages us to travel more.'

Cristina: 'International students like to stick together because they have no prior social network in the host country. So, international students are usually together. They spend holidays in the UK because sometimes it's hard to go back to the home country. They cook a lot because most of them do not like British food, but they have higher levels of emotional distress because they have to adapt to a whole new culture. They walk a lot around town because most of them live in student accommodations that are not very well located, and they take advantage of discounts whenever possible.'

Dong: 'International students like to contrast the British culture with the reality, questioning their minds by seeing and experiencing: "Wow, is it actually like this?!" … So, it's a verifying experience. All international students are learning to have a positive attitude towards adopting the local culture, and socialising habits based on entertainment.'

(Excerpts from the focus group with international students)

Quite a few aspects of international students' lifestyle seem to be shared by their exchange counterparts: the frequent travelling, the close bonds with their peers, the language strain (even if with a different intensity), the strong need to adapt and socialise especially because they do 'not have prior social networks in the host country' (Cristina). The strength of student bonding makes international students discover the host culture together. Together, they learn to adopt a positive attitude towards this new culture, 'questioning their minds' and previously held assumptions as noted by Dong.

Like exchange students, travelling is key to this shared lifestyle but for some international students, like Ying, this 'travel bug' was not a spontaneous development from a prior travelling capital. Unlike European exchange students, international students stay in the host country during holidays (Cristina) because being from more distant lands they cannot return home. This may give them a valuable opportunity to know the host culture closer than exchange students as highlighted by Tao and Dong when probed further into this specific issue:

Tao: 'I have around six or seven French students in my class. They are Erasmus and whenever it's holidays they go back to their home countries. They just don't spend this socialising period here.'

Dong: 'Maybe they can travel to the UK very easily. Or they have already done it before when they were young. For us, it's very hard to have a living experience here. So, we'll cherish it! Even at Christmas, spring festival we would like to stay here. That's our motivation.'

As explained by Dong, the fact that exchange students are Europeans allows them to visit the host country prior to studying abroad. For many international students, especially non-Europeans, study abroad may be the only chance to know the host country and this is why they will cherish this opportunity.

Finally, although partying with peers also characterises international students' lifestyle, this aspect did not emerge as strongly as in the exchange student focus group. Interestingly, their social lives do not seem to cross much as emphasised by Cristina:

Cristina: 'For me, not interacting with *Erasmus* students had more to do with the fact that they were undergraduate. So, the social life didn't cross much. They had exams and they were doing other stuff, they had a different workload as well, and they were so much younger too. For example, the three *Erasmus* girls that I met, I met because I went to a social activity by the Student Union which is generally attended by undergraduates. So, I had to get into their circle to meet those girls. I think postgraduate do other stuff, they are older.'

Despite some differences in the lifestyle of exchange and international students, the strong group identity in both cohorts is based on assumed similarity with their peers. This assumed similarity may have implications in the time and effort invested by students in socialising with hosts.

Social structures and individual agency come into play in study abroad. In this sense, sociological theories and Bourdieusian theory, in particular, come to remind us that privileging agency over structure or vice versa – 'constructivism structuralism' or 'structuralism constructivism' (Bourdieu, 1990) – may influence how we read the sojourn experience. Hence the attempt in this section to explore the budding capital of mobile students in their own words, according to their cognitive schemes of perception and action (*habitus*) from a non-linear chronological perspective. Not wanting to minimise the challenges in tackling the agency-structure conundrum, with this section I hope to have shed some light on the overemphasis in Murphy-Lejeune's (2002) work on individual agency over social structures (of the host culture) and how the latter may also affect how mobile students live the study abroad experience. This overemphasis stems, in part, from the methodological approach adopted by Murphy-Lejeune in that pre-departure variables were not actively analysed against the outcomes of the experience. After all, and as discussed in Chapter 3, methodologies do also determine what data are considered relevant and how theories are tested.

Most importantly, the current and previous sections demonstrate that the subjective construction of the study abroad experience is also mediated by social structures. These social structures and sojourner adaption to the host culture are narrated in the next chapter.

Summary

Chapter 4, like the next two chapters of Part II, addressed a threefold purpose: (1) to illustrate the practical applications of an interdisciplinary approach in student mobility, (2) to understand the sojourn experience and life stories of the 50 sojourners in this book and (3) to test some of the theoretical (in Chapters 1 and 2) and methodological perspectives (in Chapter 3) against empirical data.

Four pre-departure variable groupings were analysed in this chapter to examine the experiences, predispositions and tools the 50 sojourners brought in their suitcases; more specifically, (1) Language biography, (2) Motivations, (3) Mobility capital and (4) Steps into mobility. Different theories were interspersed across these variable groupings to construct a more systematic and comprehensive understanding of student mobility. Within the motivations that led sojourners to study (mobile students) or work abroad (immigrants), a review of relevant literature was carried out to show how research foci, jargon and categories of analysis can vary across disciplines. In the latter case, examples were provided to illustrate how disciplinary and theoretical allegiances can shape categories of analysis. While this intertwinement is not problematic in itself, it requires the reader to be aware of how theories may thread through the sort of results produced.

With regard to our sojourners, results have shown that the purpose of the stay abroad, and the different social roles of mobile and immigrant participants, may influence the motivations and expectations towards their experiences abroad. Moreover, the accumulated knowledge and skills epitomised by the notion of mobility capital by Murphy-Lejeune (2002) may also have a bearing on the ways the experience abroad is lived. And yet, this budding capital should not be considered a static component of individuals' capital, since some of its variables may be also furthered during the stay abroad. When relating these findings to social theory and Bourdieusian theory in particular, mobility-capital variables and the notion of *habitus* come to remind us that the sojourn experience is mediated by social structures and sojourner cognitive schemes of perception and action, both as individuals and groups. The collective aspect translates into the strong group identity underpinning the social life of mobile students which may affect how they adapt to the host culture, discussed in the next chapter.

140 Applications of an interdisciplinary approach

> **Box 4.1 – Reflective questions and/or points of Chapter 4**
>
> To help you review critically the content of this chapter, ask yourself the following questions and discuss them with colleagues from other disciplines.
>
> 1. In what ways can an interdisciplinary approach help you pin down the multifarious variables of the study abroad experience?
> 2. This chapter has identified pre-departure variables that may mediate the experience of studying and living abroad, including *language learning*, *motivations to study abroad* and to *choose the host country*, *mobility capital* and *steps into mobility*.
>   2.1. What other variables can you think of?
> 3. Understanding different disciplinary theories will enable you to approach student mobility with greater sophistication. Borrowing a single theory can, at times, bias our categories of analysis (as in the motivations to study abroad).
>   3.1. To counteract this, I have used different theories to consider sojourner motivations to study abroad. Can you identify three theories relevant to your topic or variables of interest, and compare and contrast their views?
>   3.2. Having completed the previous step, how would you operationalise your variables according to the selected theories? (e.g., to test the concept of mobility capital by Murphy-Lejeune, 2002, I operationalised it into relevant variables).
> 4. As findings in this chapter have shown, exchange students in the *Campus Europae* programme identified themselves as *Erasmus*.
>   4.1. According to your experience, what makes (or should make) a study abroad programme distinctive?
>   4.2. Does your experience suggest I am right to assert that the delivery and assessment of programmatic study abroad is seldom an object of inquiry in European higher education?
> 5. What relative importance do you assign to *individual agency* and *social structures* in study abroad? Does this relative importance influence how you look at and interpret student mobility?

Pre-departure 141

Appendix 4.1

This questionnaire is part of a research project developed by Dr. Joana Almeida and aims to understand international students' opinion about studying abroad. Your participation is very important to me. Please, answer individually, honestly and remember that there are no right or wrong answers.

Thank you in advance for your participation. **Confidentiality** of each survey is guaranteed. Your name at the top of this survey is for clarification purposes as I will be the only person who will have access to the **identification number** attributed to each survey.

0. Profile

Name: _____ Age: _____

Gender: ☐ Male ☐ Female **Nationality**: _____

Mother tongue(s): _____ **Current Level of study**: ☐ UG ☐ PGT ☐ PGR

Current Study Programme: _____

Date of arrival in Portugal/the UK: ___ / ___ / ___ (Day/Month/Year)

I. Language biography

1. Were you brought up in a multicultural family life (family members from different cultural backgrounds)? ☐ Yes   ☐ No   ☐ I don't know

    1.1. Did your home life make you **more open** to differences across languages and cultures? Please circle the number that best represents your opinion:

    ⓿ (No) ❶ (Very little) ❷ (Somewhat) ❸ (Much) ❹ (To a great extent)

2. How many foreign languages have you studied before studying abroad?

    _____

    2.1. Can you please specify these languages? _____
    2.2. Do you think these languages made you **more open** to differences across languages and cultures? Please circle the number that best represents your opinion:

    ⓿ (No) ❶ (Very little) ❷ (Somewhat) ❸ (Much) ❹ (To a great extent)

142 Applications of an interdisciplinary approach

II. Life path

3. Have you ever lived abroad for **more than 3 months** previously to studying abroad?

    ☐ Yes   ☐ No (If you answered NO, go to Question 4)

    3.1. Has living abroad made you **more open** to differences across languages and cultures? Please circle the number that best represents your opinion:

    ❶ (No) ❶ (Very little) ❷ (Somewhat) ❸ (Much) ❹ (To a great extent)

4. How many different countries have you visited **before studying abroad?**

    _____

    4.1. Did those journeys make you **more open** to differences across languages and cultures? Please circle the number that best represents your opinion:

    ❶ (No) ❶ (Very little) ❷ (Somewhat) ❸ (Much) ❹ (To a great extent)

    4.2. Did you develop any relationships with people from other cultures during these journeys? ☐ Yes   ☐ No (If you answered NO, go to Question 5)

    4.3. Did those relationships make you **more open** to differences across languages and cultures? Please circle the number that best represents your opinion:

    ❶ (No) ❶ (Very little) ❷ (Somewhat) ❸ (Much) ❹ (To a great extent)

5. Do you usually develop relationships with people from other cultures in your home country? ☐ Yes   ☐ No (If you answered NO, go to Question 6)

    5.1. Do you think those relationships made you **more open** to differences across languages and cultures? Please circle the number that best represents your opinion:

    ❶ (No) ❶ (Very little) ❷ (Somewhat) ❸ (Much) ❹ (To a great extent)

III. Studying abroad

6. Have you ever participated in a study abroad programme before studying abroad in Portugal/the UK? ☐ Yes (Specify: the programme: _____ the length: _____)

    ☐ No (If you answered NO, go to Question 7)

    6.1. Did this experience make you more open to differences across languages and cultures? Please circle the number that best represents your opinion:

    ❶ (No) ❶ (Very little) ❷ (Somewhat) ❸ (Much) ❹ (To a great extent)

Pre-departure 143

7. What were your motivations to study abroad? Please **tick (✓)** the **4 most important** motivations:

_____ Enrichment of my field-specific knowledge
_____ Possibility of doing tourism

_____ Higher academic quality of host institution
_____ Personal development/maturity

_____ International career prospects
_____ Possibility of having new experiences

_____ Possibility of improving my marks easily
_____ Possibility of having fun

_____ Possibility of learning a new foreign language
_____ Possibility of meeting new people

_____ Possibility of getting to know another culture
_____ Other (Specify: _____ _____)

_____ Possibility of broadening my European identity

8. Why did you choose Portugal[1]/the UK[2] in particular? Please **tick (✓)** the **4 most important** reasons.

_____ Economic reasons [1](lower costs of living); [2](lower tuition fees than other English-speaking countries)
_____ Influenced by a previous visit to Portugal/the UK

_____ Career prospects
_____ Student recommendation

_____ Linguistic reasons
_____ Teacher recommendation

_____ Cultural reasons
_____ Good weather (for situation[1] only)

_____ Academic quality of host university
_____ No specific reason/Random Choice

_____ Member state of the European Union
_____ Other (Specify: _____ _____)

_____ Geographic proximity to home country

IV. Language courses

9. Did you take any Portuguese[1]/English[2] language course before studying abroad?

☐ Yes (Specify: _____)
☐ No (If you answered NO, go to Question 10)

9.1. Which level did you do? ☐ Beginners ☐ Intermediate ☐ Advanced

144 Applications of an interdisciplinary approach

10. Did you take any Portuguese/English language exam to be admitted to your host institution? ☐ Yes ☐ No

    10.1. What exam did you take? _____

    10.2. What was your final score? _____

11. What is your Portuguese/English language proficiency **now?**

    ☐ Beginners   ☐ Intermediate   ☐ Advanced

V.[1] Intercultural competence

12. Can you think of any situation where you felt culturally frustrated in the process of adapting to the Portuguese[1]/English[2] culture? ☐ Yes ☐ No (If you answered NO, go to Question 13)

    12.1. Can you briefly describe that situation? _____

_____

_____

13. While in Portugal/the UK you often experience different situations. Using a scale of **0 (no competence)** to **5 (very high competence),** rate yourself in each of the sentences by circling the level of competence that best suits you.

No ⓿————┼————┼————┼————┼————→ ❺ Very high
competence   competence

Awareness

While in Portugal/the UK I became aware of ...

differences between my own language and the Portuguese[1]/English[2] language	⓿ ❶ ❷ ❸ ❹ ❺
differences between my own culture and the Portuguese[1]/English[2] culture	⓿ ❶ ❷ ❸ ❹ ❺
my stereotypes to these differences	⓿ ❶ ❷ ❸ ❹ ❺
how I behave differently according to the Portuguese[1]/English[2] culture	⓿ ❶ ❷ ❸ ❹ ❺
how Portuguese[1]/English[2] people see me (their opinion about me)	⓿ ❶ ❷ ❸ ❹ ❺

---

1 Question 13 is an adaptation of the Assessment of Intercultural Competence Questionnaire (YOGA format) developed by the Federation of Experiment in International Living (FEIL). Available at www.worldlearning.org

Attitudes

While in Portugal/the UK I ...

can make friends among Portuguese[1]/English[2] people easily and find opportunities to meet them
⓪ ❶ ❷ ❸ ❹ ❺

use the Portuguese[1]/English[2] language in my daily life (on and off campus), even with other co-nationals (friends who speak your language)
⓪ ❶ ❷ ❸ ❹ ❺

follow the rules and standard behaviours of the Portuguese[1]/English[2] culture (e.g.,[1] I greet everyone with two kisses); (e.g.,[2] I greet everyone with a handshake)
⓪ ❶ ❷ ❸ ❹ ❺

can deal with the frustrations caused by the different habits of Portuguese[1]/English[2] people (e.g.,[1] Many Portuguese people have a specific sense of punctuality); (e.g,[2] English people can express themselves in an apologetic or less straightforward manner)
⓪ ❶ ❷ ❸ ❹ ❺

Skills

While in Portugal/the UK I ...

in situations of misunderstanding, I can identify if the misunderstanding is personal or cultural when I don't understand Portuguese[1]/English[2] people
⓪ ❶ ❷ ❸ ❹ ❺

can think about the Portuguese/English cultural perspective to help me in situations in which I seem to offend a Portuguese[1]/English[2] person or have done something wrong
⓪ ❶ ❷ ❸ ❹ ❺

am able to relate and contrast the Portuguese[1]/English[2] culture with my own
⓪ ❶ ❷ ❸ ❹ ❺

use specific strategies which facilitate my adaptation and help me not feel out of place (e.g., I try to find someone to talk to about my cultural experience)
⓪ ❶ ❷ ❸ ❹ ❺

use specific strategies to learn the Portuguese[1]/English[2] language and culture (e.g., I am doing a language exchange/tandem with a(n) Portuguese[1]/English[2] student)
⓪ ❶ ❷ ❸ ❹ ❺

Knowledge

While in Portugal/the UK I ...

can understand what culture means and identify its components ⓪ ❶ ❷ ❸ ❹ ❺

can compare important historical and socio-political aspects of my culture with the Portuguese[1]/English[2] culture ⓪ ❶ ❷ ❸ ❹ ❺

recognise some of the essential norms and taboos of the Portuguese[1]/English[2] culture (greetings, dress, behaviour, etc) ⓪ ❶ ❷ ❸ ❹ ❺

recognise signs of feeling out of place in the Portuguese/English culture and know strategies for overcoming them ⓪ ❶ ❷ ❸ ❹ ❺

know some techniques to maximise my learning of the Portuguese[1]/English[2] language and culture ⓪ ❶ ❷ ❸ ❹ ❺

14. Do you know what intercultural competence is? ☐ Yes ☐ No (If you answered NO, the questionnaire ends here)

   14.1. What is intercultural competence for you? _____

   _____

   14.2. Have you ever developed intercultural competence **before studying abroad?**

   ☐ Yes   ☐ No   ☐ I don't know

   14.3. In which context did you develop this competence? _____

Thank you for your collaboration!
Dr. Joana Filipa Almeida

Note to readers: For conciseness the questionnaire administered to exchange and international students in Portugal and the UK is presented here jointly. Where examples or situations differed, these cases were marked with [1] and [2], respectively.

Notes

1 An open-ended question ascertained the motives of the nine highly skilled immigrants to migrate to Portugal.
2 According to EURODATA II, Portugal went through a profile change between 1998/99 and 2008/09 – i.e., from net exporter to net importer of credit-seeking students while witnessing one of the largest growth rates of credit-seeking student inflows for the aforementioned 11-year period (Teichler et al., 2011, pp. 86–96).
3 In 2014, The XIX Portuguese Democratic Government introduced an International Student Status which fixed a full-cost tuition regime for international students, who are non-EU nationals and without a permanent address in Portugal, to access undergraduate and integrated Master's studies in Portuguese public higher education institutions.
4 The 'experience of living abroad' is understood in this book as the experience of having lived in a country other than one's country of origin for more than three months.

References

Alfranseder, E., Fellinger, J., & Taivere, M. (2011). *E-Value-ate your exchange: Research report of the ESN survey 2010*. Brussels: Erasmus Student Network AISBL.

Arnett, J. J. (2015). *Emerging adulthood: The winding road from the late teens through the twenties* (2nd ed.). New York, NY: Oxford University Press.

Bourdieu, P. (1990). Social space and symbolic power (M. Adamson, Trans.). In P. Bourdieu (Ed.), *In other words: Essays towards a reflexive sciology* (pp. 125–139). Stanford, CA: Stanford University Press.

Brandenburg, U., Berghoff, S., & Taboadela, O. (2014). Erasmus impact study: Effects of mobility on the skills and employability of students and the internationalisation of higher education institutions. Retrieved from http://ec.europa.eu/dgs/educat ion_culture/repository/education/library/study/2014/erasmus-impact_en.pdf

Brooks, R., & Waters, J. (2011). *Student mobilities, migration and the internationalization of higher education*. Basingstoke: Palgrave Macmillan.

DeVellis, R. F. (2012). *Scale development: Theory and applications* (3rd ed.). Thousand Oaks, CA: Sage.

Dörnyei, Z., & Ushioda, E. (2011). *Teaching and researching motivation* (2nd ed.). London: Routledge.

Fantini, A. E. (2006). About intercultural communicative competence: A construct. *Appendix E*. Retrieved from World Learning. SIT Digital Collections website http://digitalcollections.sit.edu/worldlearning_publications/1/

Isabelli-García, C. (2006). Study abroad social networks, motivation and attitudes: Implications for second language acquisition. In M. A. Dufon & E. Churchill (Eds.), *Language learning in study abroad contexts* (pp. 237–258). Clevedon: Multilingual Matters.

Krzaklewska, E. (2008). Why study abroad? An analysis of Erasmus students' motivations. In M. Byram & F. Dervin (Eds.), *Students, staff and academic mobility* (pp. 82–98). Newcastle upon Tyne: Cambridge Scholars Publishing.

Krzaklewska, E. (2013). Students between youth and adulthood: Analysis of the biographical experience. In B. Feyen & E. Krzaklewska (Eds.), *The Erasmus*

148 Applications of an interdisciplinary approach

phenomenon - Symbol of a new European generation? (pp. 79–96). Frankfurt: Peter Lang.

Krzaklewska, E., & Krupnik, S. (2007). *Exchange students' rights: Research report of the Erasmus Student Network survey 2006.* Brussels: Erasmus Student Network.

Maiworm, F., & Teichler, U. (2002). The students' experience. In U. Teichler (Ed.), *Erasmus in the Socrates programme* (pp. 83–116). Bonn: Lemmens.

Murphy-Lejeune, E. (2002). *Student mobility and narrative in Europe: The new strangers.* London: Routledge.

Rumbley, L. E. (2011). Review of the existing literature on mobility obstacles and incentives. In U. Teichler, I. Ferencz & B. Wächter (Eds.), *Mapping mobility in European higher education: Overview and trends* (Vol. I, pp. 190–205). Brussels: A study produced for the Directorate General for Education and Culture (DGEAC), European Commission.

Severino, S., Messina, R., & Llorent, V. J. (2014). International student mobility: An identity development task? *International Journal of Humanities and Social Science,* 4(3), 89–103.

Teichler, U., Ferencz, I., & Wächter, B. (2011). *Mapping mobility in European higher education: Overview and trends* (Vol. I). Brussels: A study produced for the Directorate General for Education and Culture (DGEAC), European Commission.

Tsoukalas, J. (2008). The double life of Erasmus students. In M. Byram & F. Dervin (Eds.), *Students, staff and academic mobility in higher education* (pp. 131–152). Newcastle upon Tyne: Cambridge Scholars Publishing.

Universities UK. (2017). *The economic impact of international students.* London: Universities UK.

Chapter 5
Adaptation

About Chapter 5

As in the previous chapter, Chapter 5 addresses the practical applications of an interdisciplinary approach to construct a more systematic and comprehensive understanding of student mobility in European higher education. To this end, the chapter explores the experiences of adaptation of the 50 sojourners in this book by interspersing different theories and methods.

Cultural adaptation is subtle and multifaceted, often placing individuals at the crossroads of homelessness and shelter, of exclusion and inclusion. Understanding sojourners' entry into any host culture is highly complex, depending, among other factors, on the relative importance sojourners assign to integration in the host society. Do mobile students feel, for instance, the urge to integrate when their passage is temporary and when the international student community provides a support they can lean on? Conversely, what is the degree of receptivity of host members towards mobile students? And, what about immigrant participants? Is their urge to integrate more pressing given that their stay may not be temporary?

150 Applications of an interdisciplinary approach

Providing responses to these questions implies understanding how the three sojourner groups engaged in the multifarious facets of the new socialisation process. The four facets explored in this chapter concern: (1) Living conditions, (2) Social networks and social support (3) Social activities and host culture facilities, including activities organised by two volunteer organisations in Portugal and the UK and (4) Integration in the local community. These facets correspond to sections I, II and III of the post-experience questionnaire (see Appendix 5.1) and will be analysed through quantitative and qualitative data yielded by closed and open-ended questions.

Presentation of data follows the same organising principle as Chapter 4. That is, data are primarily organised according to the chronological sequence of the stay abroad and subdivided into the four aforementioned facets or variable groupings. Considered together, the facets examined in this chapter demonstrate that the experience abroad (whatever purpose it may have) is embedded in an intricate socio-cultural fabric.

To conclude, a summary of the main key points is provided. As in previous chapters, a number of reflective questions and/or points (see Box 5.1) is outlined at the end of the chapter.

Living conditions

Accommodation choices and building typology can offer valuable clues to sojourners' social participation in the host environment, their social networks, lifestyle and impact on the urban spaces and local communities they navigate within. The issue of accommodation can, nonetheless, be problematic not only for the students themselves but also for local residents and broader urban processes.

In the case of the mobile students in this book, students benefitted from two types of support: support offered by academic services which addresses primarily university accommodation options; and support given by volunteer organisations and centred on private rental accommodation. The incoming exchange group in Portugal benefited from the assistance of a local branch of the European student association Erasmus Student Network (ESN – see Endnote 1 in Chapter 1) located in the city of Aveiro, a medium-sized city in the central coastal region of Portugal. The support offered by ESN Aveiro included a buddy scheme common to many other European ESN branches. These kinds of scheme aim to facilitate the search for accommodation by pairing a domestic student ('the buddy') with a mobile student. The mobile student benefits from the host student's knowledge of local renting practices while having the opportunity to develop relationships, and perhaps make new friends.

Despite this guidance, most exchange students in Portugal lived together with their peers, usually in a privately rented apartment. None lived in university residence halls. All of them lived with other exchange or international student peers in different-sized apartments (from two to four bedrooms) with communal facilities. Of the 22 exchange students, only 4 shared accommodation with both mobile and local students.

By contrast, most international students in the British cohort (n = 10; 52.6%) lived in university student accommodation in Newcastle upon Tyne, the most populous city in the northeast of England housing the two universities attended by the 19 international students. Nine students lived in shared properties of private rental, which in England are typically houses of multiple occupation and, more recently, purpose-built student accommodation.[1] The latter is a fast-expanding property sector in Newcastle and many other university towns in England where university accommodation has not met the demand for student room rental (Hubbard, 2009). This type of accommodation is often inhabited by international students only, facilitating the formation of 'student ghettos' and urban gentrification as discussed in the studentification literature (see Chapter 1, Long-term impact of study abroad).

Interestingly, the UK-centred definition of studentification (see Endnote 7 in Chapter 1) in the form of houses of multiple occupancy and purpose-built student accommodation, does not adequately capture student concentrations in Portuguese urban spaces (Malet Calvo, 2018). In Aveiro, for example, mobile student concentrations are closer to the Spanish concept of 'vertical studentification' (Garmendia, Coronado, & Ureña, 2012), since students tend to cluster in apartment blocks, lessening the impact on the neighbourhood or, at least, making it less perceptible. In larger Portuguese conurbations like Lisbon, urban impact is harder to trace because exchange students tend to inhabit mixed building typologies, i.e., houses and apartments of multiple occupancy (Malet Calvo, 2018).

University accommodation can also facilitate segregation patterns, although the odds of forming 'international student ghettos' are perhaps lower. For instance, in our small student group in Newcastle of the ten students who lived in university accommodation, two lived with other international students, another two with local students, and the remaining six with both international and local students.

Living together in university accommodation does not mean that international students mix and mingle more than their exchange counterparts in Portugal. In fact, when comparing the accommodation choices of international and exchange students, while the former are more inclusive of local students their preferred friendship groups are also other mobile students (as the next section will show in greater detail). But before moving forward, it is important to look at housing preferences of immigrant participants, all of which opted to live in privately rented accommodation. Seven of the highly skilled immigrants lived with their families, while two lived on their own.

Housing options echo the different social roles of mobile and immigrant participants, with the latter seeking independence or time with their relatives. And yet, in both cases the preferred building typology – family household or independent housing – reflects absence of, or casual, interactions with locals and tight social networks closed to other sojourners or family members. This issue is examined next.

152 Applications of an interdisciplinary approach

Social networks and social support

The social networks sojourners form while abroad may provide insights into the relative importance assigned to integration in the host culture and local communities.

This section, thus, explores the social networks formed by the three sojourner groups during their stays in Portugal and the UK. It looks at the following aspects: (1) the type of social contacts sojourners spent more their time with, (2) the number of peer and local friends, (3) the level of difficulty in making local friends, (4) friendship groups and (5) the type of social support provided.

To start with, the type of social contacts sojourners spent more time with during their time abroad is explored.

As discussed earlier in Chapter 1, the development of friendships among exchange and international students is widely documented in the primary academic literature.

The literature comparing friendship patterns across these two student groups is, however, rather thin or non-existent. Typically, international students form social ties with three distinct groups: co-nationals, host nationals and other international students (Bochner, McLeod, & Lin, 1977). Exchange students develop similar friendships, but there is a widely disregarded difference between these two mobile student groups. Whereas peers for international students mean essentially other internationals, for exchange students these are other credit-seeking students. After all, as noted in Chapter 4 by Cristina, an international student in the UK, their 'social life doesn't cross much'.

Results yielded by the exchange student group show that the vast majority spent most of their time with peers, specifically 19 (86.4%) of the 22 exchange students. By contrast, only three students (13.6%) spent most of their time with both their mobile and local student peers. None selected Portuguese students only. Other contacts in their social circles included: their buddy partners, foreign people other than exchange and international peers, Portuguese people other than local students, and 'tandem partners'. The 'tandem partner' refers to mobile students' colleagues in a non-formal language learning activity and/or method taking the form of pairs of language learners who want to learn each other's language.

Like the exchange student group, the social life of international students in the UK was primarily shared with their peers, with all but one student selecting this category. Of the 18 students who chose mobile student peers, 6 selected simultaneously mobile and domestic students.

Results from the two mobile student groups are illustrated by Figure 5.1. Note that each category accounts for 100 per cent with frequencies reflecting the number of positive ('yes') responses.

Adaptation 153

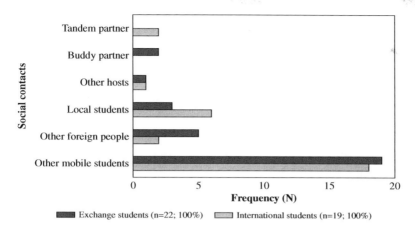

Figure 5.1 Mobile students: social contacts.

Table 5.1 Immigrants: social contacts

Social contacts	N
Co-workers (n = 9; 100%)	3
Other immigrants (n = 9; 100%)	3
Portuguese people (n = 9; 100%)	3
Classroom colleagues of Portuguese (n = 9; 100%)	2
Family (n = 9; 100%)	2

Because the categories given to immigrant participants are not completely comparable, the distribution of their preferred social contacts is presented separately in Table 5.1.

Comparison of results across all three sojourner groups indicate that while mobile students' social networks are confined to other sojourners, immigrant networks are minimally extended to hosts. Among the social contacts with whom immigrants spent more time are their colleagues at work, a finding which reinforces their socio-professional roles as a differentiating variable. Naturally, family members also emerge among categories selected by immigrants.

To probe further into results, it is insightful to compare the number of peer and host friends made during the stay abroad for all three groups. To this end, the data yielded by the two mobile student groups are compared in Table 5.2.

Results in Table 5.2 show that the viewpoints of exchange and international students do not differ much. While the mean and maximum number of host friends is greater for international than exchange students, these differences seem to be residual. Overall, the two groups of mobile students have considerably more sojourner than host friends. In both cases, the average number of peer and host friends is far apart. Exchange students, for example, made

154 Applications of an interdisciplinary approach

Table 5.2 Mobile students: number of sojourner and hosts friends

Friends	Exchange students (n = 20)					International students (n = 18)				
	Mo	M	SD	Min	Max	Mo	M	SD	Min	Max
Other sojourners	40	25.75	16.60	4	60	10	29.94	38.75	3	151
Host friends	10	5.00	3.84	0	10	5	15.33	21.92	0	80

on average 26 peer friends and only 5 Portuguese friends. Similarly, international students made around 30 peer and 15 British[2] friends. Furthermore, in both cases there were students who left the host countries (Portugal and the UK) without making any local friend, as evidenced by the minimum value 0. These results contrast sharply with those yielded by 'sojourners friends'. In the exchange student group, only one student had made fewer than five sojourner friends, i.e., other exchange or international students. A similar number was reproduced by international students as only one student had made fewer than four international peer friends.

The experiences of the nine highly skilled immigrants do not stand that much apart from those of mobile students, even if immigrant social circles were minimally extended to hosts. To elaborate further, immigrant participants had on average eight sojourner friends against three host friends. Whereas the range of peer friends (i.e., other immigrants) was between 2 and 15, this range was between 1 and 5 for host friends. Moreover, while the two ranges are smaller for immigrants than for mobile students (based perhaps on a more stringent evaluation of what a friend is), the shelter of the familiarity of an 'immigrant bubble' may equate to the 'foreign student bubble' sought by mobile students.

Based on results, it is unsurprising that most sojourners across all three groups considered peers their friendship group. In the case of exchange students, all but one student chose exchange and/or international peers as their friendship group. This is because one exchange participant selected mobile and domestic students simultaneously. International students gave similar responses, with 17 students deeming mobile student peers their favoured friendship group. Only one student selected domestic students, and another both domestic and mobile.

As such, the following questions arise:

> Are mobile and domestic students two worlds apart? And why is it so? Is it simply because of cultural differences? In any case, the mobile student network is a multinational and multicultural network whereby cultural differences can work as a unifying element. So, can lack of interaction between both groups be just a cultural thing?

The same questions can be asked for highly skilled immigrants since most of them deemed other immigrants their friendship group. While four immigrant

Adaptation 155

participants considered their immigrant peers their only friendship group, there were three immigrants who did not make this choice and another two who intertwined it with other social relationships.[3] Of these five immigrants: (a) two considered co-workers to be their closest friends, (b) one deemed them to be his/her own family, (c) another considered them both his/her family and immigrant peers and, finally, (d) one immigrant pointed out both immigrants and hosts.

Filling in the gap, between temporary and semi-permanent migration, the extent to which highly skilled immigrants immerse themselves in host communities may, to some degree, be hampered by similar hurdles to those of mobile students. These hurdles are reflected in sojourner level of difficulty in making friends with hosts (Table 5.3).

The greatest share of sojourners assigned some level of difficulty to the friendship-making process with hosts. Only three international students and two immigrant participants considering it to be nil. Overall, sojourners seem to concur on the relative difficulty in making friends with hosts; that is, Portuguese people, in the case of exchange and immigrants, and British people for international students. For most exchange students, making friends with hosts was moderately difficult, whereas for most international students the difficulty was large.

Notwithstanding the similar ratings, the underlying reasons for the difficulty felt by the 50 sojourners may not necessarily be the same. In fact, the analysis of their justifications generated five distinct reasons. These reasons stem from participant responses that fell between Level 2 ('To a moderate extent') and Level 4 ('To a great extent') on the measurement scale (Table 5.3).

From the 30 valid responses, five themes emerged: (a) Closeness of hosts, (b) Language barriers, (c) Cultural barriers, (d) Classroom make-up and (e) Personal circumstances. Verbatim excerpts from all five themes are provided to illustrate sojourner perceptions of the friendship-making process with hosts and the type of difficulties felt. Excerpts were selected based on their relevance and because, considered together, they display enough range and diversity of sojourner experiences in making friends with hosts.

Table 5.3 All sojourners: level of difficulty in making friends with hosts

Difficulty	Exchange		International		Immigrants	
	N	%	N	%	N	%
(0) To no extent	–	–	3	16.7	2	22.2
(1) To a small extent	5	22.7	4	22.2	2	22.2
(2) To a moderate extent	**9**	**40.9**	5	27.8	**4**	**44.4**
(3) To a large extent	7	31.8	**6**	**33.3**	1	11.2
(4) To a great extent	1	4.6	–	–	–	–
Total	22	100.0	18	100.0	9	100.0

Note. Highest frequencies are given in bold.

156 Applications of an interdisciplinary approach

Theme A – Closeness of hosts – addresses sojourner perceived lack of receptivity and/or openness on the part of hosts which may be associated to constraints of varying nature. Six excerpts are provided to offer a window into the raw data set while allowing readers to construct their meanings.

Maja: 'First, I was spending time more with foreign students. Sometimes, I felt Portuguese were a little closed and sceptic and sometimes it was difficult to contact with them.'

Nikola: 'Usually, it's not a problem to make friends with Portuguese people, but at university students stick strongly to some small groups and don't socialise with foreigners.'

Karol: 'There are some people who already had international relationships and friends or speak well English – they are open. But the Portuguese people who don't speak English are either shy or not so outgoing'

Jane: 'British students can be quite closed in their friendship group and not open to other cultures. It takes a bit of time for them to feel comfortable with us.'

Mercedes: 'Portuguese people don't have time for friendships. Portuguese people have always many things to do and they don't interact with other people. Going out and sharing is not part of their lives.'

Felix: 'British people aren't used to interacting with international students.'

While the six sojourners attribute the difficulties in making host friends to their lack of openness, they differ in their understandings. Mercedes, Karol and Jane (an immigrant, an exchange student and an international student, respectively) relate the paucity of host openness to personal traits or individual dispositions, disclosing somehow unfavourable views towards out-group interactions.

Mercedes considers that 'going out and sharing is not part of [hosts'] lives'. Karol, an exchange student in Portugal, even makes the distinction between those who, like her peer group, are open because they have international relationships and speak English and those who, lacking these experiences, are considered closed. Also interesting to note in Karol's comment is the depiction of exchange students as proficient speakers of English (a clear symbol of status in her eyes), while speaking the host language (Portuguese in this case) is not even contemplated. For Jane, an international student in the UK, the issue of 'double proficiency' is not applicable as English is both the language of instruction and of communication. Yet this does not invalidate a common perception to Karol – that of holding low expectations towards making friends with hosts. To Jane, this can be a matter of hosts getting used to the presence of international students.

Maja and Nikola, both exchange students in Portugal, seem to hold a more nuanced understanding of their experiences by acknowledging that friendships also involve their own personal affinities (with other foreign students) and group dynamics in the host environment.

Despite assembling the opinion of most sojourners (n = 14; 46.7%) social distance is not the only factor holding sojourners back from developing friendships with hosts. Language barriers (Theme B) may also come into play, with eight sojourners (26.7%) attributing the difficulties felt to the language realm.

Anfisa: 'Problems with the Portuguese language. Sometimes I'm afraid to speak, because people don't understand me.'

Yuwei: 'I am unable to communicate in English in depth because of language restrictions.'

Kinga: 'Portuguese people are very open, but when we first came to Portugal we didn't speak Portuguese. That's why the contact was limited, and we had more contact with *Erasmus* students.'

The communication strain can be experienced after one academic year of cultural immersion; or more in the case of immigrant participants like Anfisa. Language can block mutual understanding and cause frustration or psychological distress as expressed by both exchange (Kinga) and international (Yuwei) students. Language learning may also mirror sojourner social interactions, as evident in Kinga's testimony.

Language barriers go hand in glove with peer self-identification, thus hindering entry into host social circles and, by implication, constant practice of the host language. Yet, these constraints are not specific to the 50 sojourners in this book, as documented in the vast second language acquisition literature focusing on the social-cultural side of language learning in study abroad contexts. As noted earlier in Chapter 1, socio-cultural variables, like contact with hosts (e.g., Freed, Segalowitz, & Dewey, 2004), social circles (e.g., Coleman, 2015) and type of social networks (e.g., Isabelli-García, 2006), can influence (both negatively and positively) sojourner language gains.

In the case of international students in the UK, the socio-cultural obstacles to making friends with hosts can be heightened by the specific make-up of the academic classroom (Theme D; n = 2; 6.7%). It is not uncommon to find classrooms in British universities composed of a majority of international students and a minority of local students. Ying, an international student in the UK, forefronts this aspect: 'I don't have many British classmates, most of them are international students'.

While Cultural barriers (Theme C) correspond to the opinion of only three sojourners (10.0%) it is also deemed an obstacle to developing friendships with hosts. And yet again, this assumed cultural frontier may, at times, hinge upon self-identification with peers and the tightly knit social networks sojourners tend to form.

Elinah: 'There's so much of a cultural difference and behaviour. We don't do the same things.'

Finally, another three sojourners considered that Personal circumstances (Theme E) hampered the development of relationships with hosts.

Elena: 'I think my personal circumstances didn't help. Most of the time I had to take care of my baby.'

Julija: 'I was spending almost all the time with exchange students and I think I didn't have a big motivation to make friends with Portuguese people.'

Personal circumstances can refer to family responsibilities, in the case of immigrants like Elena, or simply lack of motivation to extend social relationships beyond peers. Consistent with studies showing that effort (or lack thereof) to approach different Others is key to developing intercultural interactions or friendships (Kudo, Volet, & Whitsed, 2019), Julija, an exchange student in Portugal, acknowledges she lacked the motivation to develop friendships with hosts.

Once again, dearth of interaction with hosts comes to the fore since peer networks may hold sojourners back from investing effort in socialising with hosts. This aspect will be discussed in the next paragraphs against social support theory, widely studied across the behavioural and medical sciences.

Employing this theoretical framework is paramount to better appreciate the role of social relationships in study abroad. Both sources of social support, i.e., the members in sojourner social networks (e.g., family, co-workers, foreign peers), and types or functions of perceived social support (e.g., emotional, instrumental, companionship) need to be taken into account. By type of social support, I mean:

> an individuals' perception of general support or specific supportive behaviors (available or acted upon) from people in their social network, which enhances their function or may buffer them from adverse outcomes.
>
> (Malecki & Demaray, 2005, p. 232)

Building on this definition, the remaining paragraphs of this section explore how specific members in sojourner social networks (i.e., the sources of social support) may be bound to specific types of social support. My aim is twofold: to provide insight into sojourner social ties; and to demonstrate the significance of selecting the theories (and methods) that shed more light on one's research question, regardless of disciplinary allegiances.

The use of social support theory, in our case, allows the filling of a notable gap in the European study abroad literature which tends to investigate the structure of sojourner social networks without necessarily looking at how different sources and types of social support intersect. To elaborate further, friendship patterns in European study abroad literature are often posited against outcomes of disciplinary interest (e.g., the relationship between social networks and language outcomes in second language acquisition) without necessarily discussing how specific functions of social support may relate to certain social relationships and sojourn outcomes (other than the outcome of primary research interest). This triangulation is paramount because multiple sources and multiple types of social support should be considered when investigating social support (Malecki & Demaray, 2005).

Several types of social support have been defined and reviewed in the specialised social support literature (e.g., Cohen & Wills, 1985; Malecki & Demaray, 2005; Wills, 1991). As explained by Wills (1991), despite fluctuations in terminology categorisations of types of social support converge in proposing at least four different types of functions through interpersonal relationships. Relationships providing a source of emotional support (acceptance, intimacy, empathy and affection) can be termed 'emotional support', 'confident support', 'intimate interaction', to name but a few terms. The type of support giving someone information or guidance is usually termed 'informational support', 'advice' or 'cognitive guidance'. When the support offered is geared towards tangible assistance (including financial resources, goods or services) it can be designated 'instrumental support', 'tangible assistance or aid', 'task-oriented support', among others. Finally, the type of social support giving one a sense of social belonging, usually by participating in common social activities, can be labelled 'companionship support or belonging' (Wills, 1991, p. 273).

To analyse sojourners' perceived social support I use the social support type categorisation developed by Cohen and Wills (1985) and reviewed by Wills (1991), namely: (1) emotional, (2) informational, (3) instrumental and (4) social companionship support. Sojourner justifications to the preferred friendship group in an open-ended question in the post-experience questionnaire are discussed following this fourfold categorisation. From 37 valid responses, 2 distinct functions of social support emerged: companionship and instrumental support.

Companionship support was the most highly reported type of support provided to sojourners by their peers. Gathering a total of 32 responses (86.5%), this type or function of social support facilitates a sense of belonging, often through common social activities which cement self-identification with foreign peers; that is, exchange and international students (in the case of mobile students) and migrants (in the case of immigrant participants). Six verbatim quotations are provided to establish a clear link with the raw data set while giving readers the chance to construct alternative meanings.

Andresz: 'We are "riding mostly the same shopping car". All of us struggle with new challenges: new place, new accommodation. In extreme groups, you are on your own.'

Agnë: 'Because we are like the same family. We are here for more or less the same reasons. And we are more open-minded and also it is easier to talk with exchange students.'

Lin: 'Easier to understand each other and we are all new here and need new friends.'

Regina: 'To be honest it was difficult to choose between these two groups. But probably I did more activities with my international group.'

Belén: 'We went to Portuguese language classes together, studied together, had lunch together or a coffee.'

Alexei: 'There are many people from my nationality at the university.'

Sojourner responses suggest that in companionship support the provision of social support goes hand in hand with a strong sense of identification with the friendship group. That is, other sojourners who, just like these six participants, lived in a foreign country, shared similar cultural adjustment challenges, social activities (leisure and academic) or even lifestyle and needed to make friends. This shared understanding of a life-altering experience appears to promote well-being and uncertainty reduction in view of adjustment challenges as noted by Andresz and Agnë (two exchange students in Portugal). Or, possibly, and as explained by Lin, the provision of support by similar Others is just easier given their readiness to offer a type of protection commonly sought by sojourners. Regina, who like Lin is an international student in the UK, highlights common social activities as a differentiating variable when choosing the preferred friendship group. The time spent socialising with other international peers is paramount to a sense of belonging to a wider community or 'family,' in Agnë's words. Support from peers can buffer adaptation challenges by enhancing sojourner coping strategies and well-being.

By contrast, Instrumental support is not bound to a sense of belonging to a wider social group. This theme gathers the opinion of five sojourners (13.5%), namely immigrant participants whose sources of support included: (a) co-workers, (b) family members, (c) family and peers and (d) peers and hosts. For those immigrant participants whose source of support were their co-workers the compatibility of schedules and professional interests brought them closer to those they work with.

Elena: 'Work colleagues, because our schedules are compatible. We still don't have many friends.'

Jimena: 'I feel closer to my work colleagues who are mostly Portuguese and some are Brazilian.'

The powerful role of the family household should not be overlooked as shown by two sojourners who considered their family a source of social support.

Lucia: 'My friends in Portugal are my family.'

Paula: 'Friends at the moment are immigrants and the remaining friends belong to my husband.'

For these sojourners, the type of social support provided by the aforementioned sources appears to be utilitarian and related to tangible resources like spending time with co-workers given that their working schedules are compatible. There is not necessarily a sense of belonging to a wider social group, contrasting with Companionship support which was highly reported by those sojourners whose source of social support was peers. Feelings of belonging to a wider international community and assumed similarity are pivotal in making friends with peers.

To summarise, the variable groupings discussed in this section – (1) Social contacts, (2) Number of peer and local friends, (3) Difficulty in making friends with hosts, (4) Friendship groups and (5) Sources and types of social support – indicate that cultural adaption is far from linear and involves multiple adjustments. Adaptation to the host environment follows closely socialisation, language acquisition and socio-cultural adjustment processes. While adapting to a new cultural setting sojourners go through multiple transitions (linguistic, cultural, social, professional or other), relying primarily on the companionship support of their peer group. This support can be of differential importance to higher levels of psychosocial well-being as demonstrated by cross-cultural psychology studies (e.g., Kashima & Loh, 2006; Smith & Khawaja, 2011; Ward, Bochner, & Furnham, 2001).

As a final note on the interdisciplinary use of themes derived from social support theory, it is imperative to understand how this theoretical framework brought attention to sources and types of social support, as well as their bearing on sojourn outcomes. Although my analysis is far from the methodological sophistication of pure social support studies,[4] it breaks down into three questions the specialised study abroad literature should be asking more clearly:

What types of social support are primarily provided to sojourners? By what sources of support? And how do they relate to specific sojourn outcomes (other than the outcomes of disciplinary interest)?

Results suggest that sojourner perceived sources of social support are primarily their peers, with whom they construe a sense of belonging. Personal friends of sojourners were rarely among hosts as they could easily lean on peer communities. These communities, while offering a protection against feelings of isolation and disorientation, may also fence in sojourners from seeking actual adaptation and socialisation with hosts. Close friendship ties developed in peer communities are furthered by living and interacting in the same cultural *milieu* while away from home.

Social activities and host culture facilities

Living in a different cultural *milieu* is a multidimensional experience. Socio-cultural choices like preferred social activities and host culture facilities are an integral part of the sojourn and its outcomes.

Engaging in social activities while abroad can be a double-edged sword, depending on sojourners' interpersonal relationships and functions of social support (as previously discussed). On the one hand, recreational and leisure activities can facilitate integration in the host culture by giving sojourners opportunities for socialising with hosts. On the other hand, they can heighten the closely knit social networks mobile students form with their peers.

While these tight social networks may preclude mobile students from taking full advantage of what the host environment affords, they may, as well, represent a source of positive intercultural learning and sharing. In this way, these student communities may, as asserted by Montgomery (201ᴜ), resemble the concept of 'communities of practice', given the positive learnings occurring among mobile student groups in higher education. But before elaborating this idea further, I should clarify what I mean by 'communities of practice' and why this notion renders itself useful in study abroad contexts.

The concept of 'communities of practice' was coined by the anthropologist Jean Lave and the social learning theorist Etienne Wenger, in the 1990s, while examining learning through social co-participation, namely by studying apprenticeship as a learning model. Their main premise was that social engagement could be the locus of learning (Lave & Wenger, 1991). Learning is, therefore, situated because 'it is an integral part of generative social practice in the lived-in world' (p. 34).

Sojourner communities are a good example of how engagement in social practice entails learning beyond mental schemata and conceptual structures. As a group of people sharing a living experience and, by implication, similar stimuli and challenges, mobile students may resemble a specific community of practice sustained by the social networks they form and underlying group identity, lifestyle and social activities. Like other communities of practice, mobile students' social engagement, as an interacting group, provides a context for positive learning. As espoused by Wenger, McDermott and Snyder (2002):

> Communities of practice are groups of people who share a concern, a set of problems, or a passion about a topic, and who deepen their knowledge, and expertise in this area by interacting on an ongoing basis (p. 4).

Whatever domain these interacting groups share, their sustained interaction renders socially constructed forms of learning through co-participation in common social practices. To consider this aspect among our sojourners, the activities organised by two volunteer organisations and the host culture facilities sojourners used to familiarise themselves with the Portuguese and British cultures will be analysed. As mentioned earlier, the two volunteer organisations refer to a Portuguese branch (in Aveiro) of the European student association Erasmus Student Network (ESN), and the Globe International Student Café, a local organisation in Newcastle organised by Friends International. Note that these activities concern the exchange and international student groups respectively.

Having had the opportunity to follow closely these two volunteer organisations, it was clear to me from the outset their pivotal role in the 'international student life', notably as a unifying element bringing mobile students together. Interestingly, despite differences in nature and vision, both associations offered activities harnessing constructive learning experiences among the mobile student community. Nonetheless, very rarely were these activities attended by local students other than the volunteers themselves. Table 5.4 summarises some of these activities, particularly those with a socio-cultural component.

Adaptation 163

Table 5.4 Mobile students: social activities offered by volunteer organisations

Activities	Country	Description
Buddy programme	PT	Programme facilitating the search for accommodation by pairing a domestic and a mobile student
Celebration of 'Magusto'	PT	Celebration of a popular Portuguese fall festivity by inviting mobile and local students to celebrate it together with roasted chestnuts and a traditional Portuguese wine liqueur
Christmas with Portuguese families	PT	Celebration of Christmas with a Portuguese family
Easter with Portuguese families	PT	Celebration of Easter with a Portuguese family
Language learning activities	PT & UK	Activities promoting non-formal language support, either though conversion groups, language classes or tandems (pairs of language learners)
Movie nights	PT	Organised movie nights celebrating the Portuguese cinema
Trips	PT & UK	Organised trips mainly throughout Portugal and England
Cultural nights/International dinners	PT & UK	Organised dinners or nights dedicated to a particular country, usually with traditional courses and/or sweets from mobile students' home countries
Weekly dinners	UK	Weekly dinners for a symbolic fee
Leisure activities	UK	Recreational activities of varying nature (e.g., watching rugby and football matches, playing on trampolines, British tea etc.)

Of the listed activities, there are clear favourites. Figure 5.2 illustrates mobile students' participation in all ten activities. Note that each category accounts for 100 per cent, with frequencies reflecting the number of positive ('yes') responses (students could engage in more than one activity).

While not all activities cut across the two mobile student groups, those common to the Portuguese and British volunteer organisations are among the most popular activities for both student groups. This is the case of Cultural nights/ International dinners and trips. Of the activities specific to the Portuguese and British volunteer organisations, the most well attended were: movie nights and the Portuguese traditional festivity 'Magusto' (both of which had 10 responses) in the case of the Portuguese association, and Weekly dinners (with 17 responses) in the British association.

Given mobile students 'mobility capital' and 'taste for living abroad' (Murphy-Lejeune, 2002), it is unsurprising that planned trips across host countries were highly attended by both student groups. As findings from Chapter 2 (see Steps into mobility) have also demonstrated, the urge to travel can be furthered during

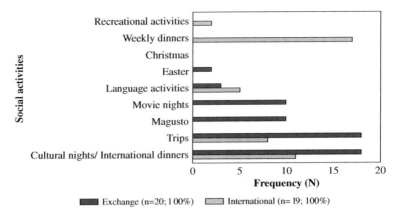

Figure 5.2 Mobile students: social activities.

the stay abroad. This finding accords with sojourners' preferred facilities for immersion in the host culture, as will be discussed later in this section.

Cultural nights and/or International dinners were also well attended by both student groups. Offering opportunities for intercultural sharing with peers, students could learn from social practice even if the social situation determined a participation frame confined to other mobile students. As a result, these types of activities can be a mixed blessing. On the one hand, they may enable positive intercultural learnings and a sense of development about oneself and 'culturally different' Others through co-participation in joint social practices. On the other hand, these activities may reinforce sojourners' closely knit communities by precluding them from actively engaging with hosts and seeking opportunities for culture-specific learning, including learning the host language. That is why I argue that Montgomery's (2010) premise that 'international student communities of practice' can foster positive learning needs further development. There is a dual condition in intercultural learning through social co-participation in study abroad contexts, depending on sojourner sources and types of social support. In this sense, communities of practice can function both as: (a) a 'shelter' against feelings of isolation and a source of culture-general learning and (b) a 'fence' hampering actual socialisation with hosts and culture-specific learning. The latter function is evident in the exchange student group in Portugal because the use of English (as the means of communication with peers) may have hindered exchange students' host language proficiency (Portuguese).

Thus, while 'international communities of practice' can harness positive learning experiences (Montgomery, 2010), or even compensate for the loss of familiar support systems and lack of contact with hosts (Schartner, 2015), they may as well mitigate culture-specific development. The lack of clarity regarding this dual role stems possibly from the Anglophone context of Montgomery's (2010) research and other UK-based studies (e.g., Schartner, 2015; Young, Sercombe,

Sachdev, Naeb, & Schartner, 2013), wherein international students do not experience issues of 'dual proficiency'; that is, the learning of two languages, since the host language and the lingua franca are the same.

The additional language barriers faced by the exchange student group in Portugal did not invalidate interest in symbolic customs and events of the Portuguese culture. Exchange students turn-out rates in the Portuguese autumn festivity 'Magusto' and in Portuguese movie nights show otherwise. This does not, however, mean that their participation in such activities instigated contact with local students. In fact, many activities offered by international student associations and organisations of the kind are most likely to be attended only by sojourners. There are some exceptions, though, as is the case of the two ESN activities enabling the exchange student group to spend Christmas and Easter with Portuguese families. The transformative potential of these two activities is huge, with the low attendance rates not necessarily reflecting their popularity nor impact. My observation can be better understood if the reader takes into account that the 22 exchange student group is comprised of Europeans who normally return home for Christmas. Those mobile students in Aveiro who usually participate in the ESN Christmas activity tend to be from more distant lands, usually non-European countries (see Almeida, Fantini, Simões, & Costa, 2016 for further information). The same does not happen at Easter because while some exchange students go back to their home countries, others stay. And as one of them states, the Easter activity gives them the rare opportunity to enter the local community inner circles and see things anew.

Kinga: 'Yes, yes, I participated in Easter, and I must say that this was one of the best experiences. It was a different perspective because here in Portugal we were rather in our *Erasmus* family or also our peers of Portuguese people, but not seeing all the families in majority. And then, all of the sudden we saw the normal, regular families, who are living in the city. It was something really enriching.'

Finally, non-formal language support was sought by both exchange and international students either through language tandems (in the case of the exchange student group) or conversational groups and English classes for the international student group. Offering advantages for mobile and domestic students alike, the language tandem method paired students up according to their language learning interests. For the group of exchange students in Portugal, additional opportunities to practice Portuguese can be priceless because their in-group (but also out-group) language code is English. Non-formal language support is also important for the international student cohort in the UK, even if the language of instruction and communication is the same. In fact, 5 of the 19 international students resorted to the language provision offered by the British volunteer organisation, either by participating in the weekly 'conversation groups' run by a British volunteer or by attending non-formal English classes with an instructor and/or trainer.

Despite active participation in the social activities offered by the two volunteer organisations in Portugal and the UK, the socio-cultural practices of mobile

166 Applications of an interdisciplinary approach

students are certainly not confined to these activities. Socialisation and entry processes into the host culture can be also inferred from the facilities sojourners use to 'enter' the host culture. Depending on the preferred facilities and underlying social ties, host culture facilities can reproduce feelings both of social distance and of proximity to the local community. Figure 5.3 illustrates the host culture facilities selected by all three sojourner groups for familiarisation with Portuguese and British cultures.

Results reveal points of convergence and divergence between the top choices of the three sojourner groups, with the preferences of the highly skilled immigrant group standing somehow apart from those of mobile students. Both exchange and international students concurred on the three top facilities for immersion in the host culture. More specifically: (a) Travelling, (b) Cafés (in Portugal) and pubs[5] (in the UK), and, finally, (c) Street markets.

Whereas mobile students chose essentially facilities enabling active experimentation and interaction, the nine highly skilled immigrants chose facilities related to gastronomy, knowledge development and aesthetic appreciation, specifically, restaurants, print and broadcast media.

Naturally, the choices of mobile students and immigrants do not simply mirror different ways of approaching the host culture, but also their different agendas and age ranges. Whereas the exchange and international students in this book are

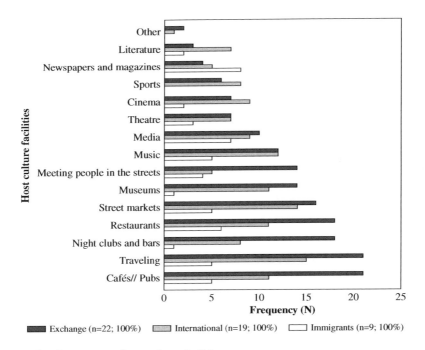

Figure 5.3 All sojourners: host culture facilities.

young and marked by an agenda of active experimentation, immigrants may have other interests as well as professional and family responsibilities.

In summary, sojourners' preferred host culture facilities and social activities echo both personal preferences and the routes taken to enter the local community. The type of socio-cultural activities chosen by participants and whom they share them with may be symptomatic of the extent to which sojourners integrate in the local community, discussed next.

Integration in the local community

Discovering the host culture during a sojourn takes many forms, including the discovery of the host city and its local communities.

This section explores the extent to which sojourners felt at home in the cities they inhabited based on data from a closed question and an open-ended question in the post-experience questionnaire (Appendix 5.1). The closed question ascertained the extent to which sojourners felt at home on a five-point rating scale wherein 0 ('To no extent') represented the lowest score, and 4 ('To a great extent') the highest. The open-ended question elicited justifications for the attributed ratings.

Figure 5.4 illustrates the ratings attributed by the three sojourner groups.

Results show that the ratings of mobile students are more alike than those of immigrant participants, although differences are not substantial. Most participants across the three sojourner groups felt at home in the local community to a moderate or great extent. Only one international student stated he/she did not feel at home. In the immigrant group, all sojourners assigned positive ratings (from moderate to great).

Overall, the three sojourner groups felt at home in the cities they lived in as evidenced by average means of 2.59 (SD = 0.91) for exchange students,

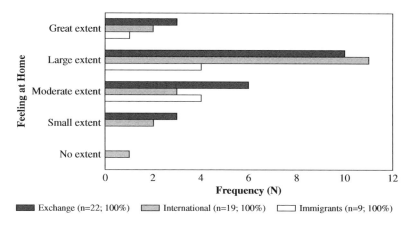

Figure 5.4 All sojourners: extent sojourners felt at home in the local community.

168 Applications of an interdisciplinary approach

2.58 (SD = 1.02) for international students and 2.67 (SD = 0.71) for highly skilled immigrants. Yet, this does not mean that appropriation processes of the 'new home' are equal across sojourner groups. In fact, the thematic analysis of participant justifications of their quantitative scores discloses points of overlap and polarisation.

Three key themes emerge from the analysis of 41 valid responses: (a) Uprootedness and/or homesickness (b) Cityness, (c) Rootedness to the local community through Others (Rootedness through Others in short).

Theme A – Uprootedness and/or homesickness – encompasses those participants who felt uprooted from their host cities and local communities by reporting lack of social and physical connectedness. This theme captures feelings of displacement (e.g., strangeness, non-adaptation and homesickness) arising from lack of physical and social proximity to the local community. Five illustrative excerpts (in range and relevance) are given.

Gaëlle: 'I don't really feel at home in the local community because even if I consider Aveiro as my city I'm still feeling like a stranger.'
Borja: 'I don't spend much time living a Portuguese life.'
Aija: 'I feel homesick and I miss my culture and my country.'
Liliya: 'Because of the non-adaptation.'
Cristina: 'I do not intend to stay in Newcastle after I graduate. So, I have not put so much effort to integrate within the local community as I would have if my plans were to relocate here.'

As reported by participants, feelings of strangeness, non-adaptation and homesickness may linger throughout the sojourn. As a result, at the end of one year abroad, the host city and its local communities may still come across to sojourners as a distant place with no sense of geographical or emotional attachment.

This was the case of eight sojourners (19.5 %) who felt out of place and/or homesick. Of these sojourners, five were exchange students, two international and one immigrant. Incoming exchange students in Portugal like Borja did not even consider to 'live a Portuguese life'. Equally, Cristina, an international student in the UK, admits she 'didn't put so much effort to integrate within the local community' since she viewed her stay as temporary.

In both cases, student testimonies put into question the extent to which mobile students deem integration a primary social need. One would be naturally inclined to assume that integration in local communities would be stronger for international than for exchange students given that the stay of the former is usually thought of as long-term, whereas for the latter it is short-term. Notwithstanding the different academic pursuits of international and exchange students, the exchange student group in Portugal spent exactly the same time abroad as the majority of their international counterparts who were pursuing a Master's degree in the UK.

Recalling, then, one of the key questions discussed at the outset of the book, in Chapter 2 – Can student mobility modalities be only distinguished by an academic pursuit? – at least the importance mobile students ascribe to integration in the local community appears to be more likely influenced by the temporary duration of their stay than the pursuit of an academic endeavour per se. It is possible that the perception of a limited period of time abroad hampers integration processes. But it is also possible that feelings of non-adaptation linger in longer stays as the maladaptation of Liliya, an immigrant in Portugal, demonstrates.

In exploring Theme B – Cityness – theories of sociology of space render themselves useful. In fact, Theme B is inspired by the notion of Cityness proposed by the sociologist Saskia Sassen (2010a, 2010b) to refer to the communal experience of the city as a site of continuous and open social intersections. Building on this notion, Cityness is used in this book to convey participant appropriation of host cities and their urban life, but without necessarily emphasising social proximity to the local community. Gathering 12 participant responses (29.3%), this theme is illustrated by the following 5 excerpts.

Belén: 'I adapted well to this city and to its beaches.'

Aamu: 'Aveiro is a nice city and if only I would have more local friends this would definitely feel like home.'

Agnë: 'I spent a lot of time in Aveiro. I know all the streets. I have my favourite meals, drinks. I know workers in the shops, cafés, university. So, in this way I feel like here is my home. After all the trips it is very nice to come back to Aveiro.'

Cheng: 'I've familiarised myself with the city.'

Dong: 'The living conditions in Newcastle are cosy and clean even at the school dormitory. So, we can mostly feel at home. However, from a psychological perspective, maybe it is still hard to participate in the activities that normal British do.'

Unlike those participants who felt uprooted, these five sojourners perceive their host cities as familiar places. They are able to map out the urban space into topological subunits, identifiable areas and favourite places. Notwithstanding the development of a sense of geographical familiarity with Aveiro (Portugal) and Newcastle (England), participants did not convey feelings of strong social proximity. Familiarisation with the local community is primarily explained through the passage of time (Cheng), appropriation of the urban space (Bélen, Aamu) or both (Agnë). Significant interactions with others or social relations are not mentioned as key factors to appropriation of Aveiro or Newcastle.

By contrast, participants who expressed rootedness reported both physical and social proximity. This was the case of 21 participants (51.2%) who felt rooted through others (Theme C).

Lucia: 'I feel quite a home, because my family is numerous and so far I had a good experience living in Portugal.'

Guo: 'Friendly environment and people, quite similar to my hometown. Newcastle is not a busy town.'
Karol: 'When I was in my home country for Christmas break I was looking forward to come back "home" and to my "*Erasmus* family".'
Regina: 'More than Newcastle, it is my neighbourhood. It is familiar and made me feel at home. Also, I have really good flatmates.'
Tanja: 'Mostly, because of the long period of my stay – I know my way around the city, have my local shops, supermarkets, favourite cafes. And I have also found good friends here which contribute to a feeling of being rooted (more than I would feel like if I were alone).'

As sojourner testimonies show, host cities are no longer apprehended as strange places, but as social entities which gained meaning through readiness for exploration and significant interaction with others. Participants learned their ways around their host cities, as highlighted by Tanja. In doing so, what was, before, meaningless became a familiar place with favourite areas and shared memories. This proximity was only possible through social relations, i.e., by making 'good friends [who] contributed to a feeling of being rooted' (Tanja). Considered together, excerpts demonstrate that the city is not merely a physical or topological unit, but a condition and symbol of human relations.

Given this backdrop, sojourner appropriation of host cities and their local communities can offer clues to where sojourners stand in adaptation processes. Figure 5.5 illustrates the relationships between the three generated themes according to sojourners' positioning on an imaginary adaptation continuum wherein Uprootedness represents lower stages of adaptation, and Rootedness higher.

Those participants who are rooted to the local community through others are likely to feel more adjusted because interaction was paramount to feeling at home in the local community.

In the middle of the continuum, one finds participants for whom Aveiro and Newcastle became familiar through proximity to the urban space. Naturally, there is the chance that Others were also a significant element of spatial appropriation, but were omitted in participant discourse. Even if we cannot infer from responses under Cityness that sojourners apprehend their hosts cities through others and meaningful interaction, it is extremely unlikely that space was not socially constructed. After all, as argued by human geographers like David Harvey (1996),

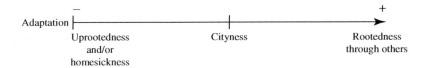

Figure 5.5 Adaptation continuum.

'a space is a site of relations of one entity to another and it therefore contains "the other" precisely because no entity can rest in isolation' (p. 261). The theme Cityness should, therefore, be envisaged as a hybrid category which, despite emphasising the urban realm, does not necessarily exclude socio-spatial relations.

Triangulation of these qualitative data with scores attributed by sojourners to the extent they felt at home provides fuller information regarding the accuracy of my interpretation. To this end, a mixed methods matrix testing differences between participant scores, through application of the Kruskal–Wallis test, is given in Table 5.5. The aim is to integrate quantitative and qualitative inferences to produce a more comprehensive understanding of sojourners' integration in the host cities and their local communities (please recall Chapter 3).

Sojourner scores of the extent to which they felt at home in Aveiro and Newcastle are consistent with the three themes generated from their justifications. Using the median as our baseline, the scores registered by those participant responses which fell under Cityness and Rootedness through Others are higher than those eight participants who reported Uprootedness and/or homesickness. Moreover, results show differences in the response distribution of the three groups at .05. This result validates the qualitative categories while demonstrating the importance of mixed methods research in using multiple validities to enhance the interpretation of significant findings (Onwuegbuzie & Leech, 2004).

The significant test result does not, however, indicate where the difference lies. As such, we need to tease apart the effect and conduct follow-up analyses comparing every group against every other group (pairwise comparisons). The calculation of post-hoc pairwise comparisons between Uprootedness//Cityness, Uprootedness//Rootedness, Cityness//Rootedness show that only the first two pairs of groups are statistically different. That is to say, the difference between the medians of Uprootedness and Cityness are significantly different, $H(3) = -16.417$, $p = .003$, as well as the medians of Uprootedness//Rootedness,

Table 5.5 Mixed methods matrix: extent to which sojourners felt at home

Qualitative data	Quantitative data				Mixed methods characteristics	
Themes	Min	Max	Mdn	χ^2	Priority & timing	Use of adjunct
Uprootedness and/ or homesickness	1	2	2.00			
Cityness	2	4	3.00	16.450*	QUAN+qual	Qualitative: Triangulation & complementary
Rootedness through others	2	4	3.00			

Note. (n = 41; 100%); number of valid quantitative and qualitative responses
*Significant at $p>0.05$; χ^2 = chi-square, Kruskal–Wallis Test
Adapted from Sandelowski (2000); QUANT = priority was given to quantitative data; + Concurrent timing

$H(3) = -17.952$, $p = .000$. The only pair that did not yield a significant effect was Cityness//Rootedness. This result supports the interpretation I made earlier regarding Cityness in that the omission of others in participant discourse may not be indicative of the role they play in sojourners' adaptation to the local community. Hence the hybridism of this theme which, although emphasising the geographic dimension of the urban space, may not necessarily exclude socio-spatial relations.

To summarise, this section demonstrates that sojourner social relations and interactions with others are a key element of adaptation and integration in the local community. After all, the 'development of intercultural relationships takes place at the dynamic experiential interface between environmental affordances and students' agency' (Kudo et al., 2019, p. 473). Sojourners seem to have led a fulling social life largely independent from the host local community. However, in missing out this social element of cultural immersion, sojourners may have also stayed at the doorstep of adaptation, away from rich intercultural interactions with hosts. Ultimately, and as pointed out by Aamu, an exchange student in Portugal, it is by 'having more local friends that the local community can definitely feel like home'.

Summary

As in the preceding chapter, Chapter 5 aimed to demonstrate the analytical power of an interdisciplinary approach in producing a more comprehensive and systematic understanding of student mobility. In the current chapter, this understanding was centred on sojourners' adaption to host cultures, the cities and local communities they navigated within.

Spatial and cultural adjustment were at the heart of the chapter and discussed by interspersing social support theory and theories of sociology of space and, to some extent, urban anthropology. Empirically, quantitative and qualitative inferences were brought together by integrating multiple measures and validities. It was sought, in this way, to approach spatial and cultural adjustment in student mobility with greater breadth and depth of insight. To this end, the following variable groupings were brought together: (a) Living conditions, (b) Social networks and social support, (c) Social activities and host culture facilities and (d) Integration in local communities. Together these different facets of culture adjustment allowed insight into how sojourners stake out the spatial conditions of their host cities and local communities during their socio-cultural transitions.

Findings have also demonstrated that these transitions (e.g., linguistic, cultural, social, professional) are not only multidimensional in terms of individual agency, but also in terms of the symbolic capital of the places sojourners inhabit. Thus, while Chapter 4 forefronted where sojourners were transitioning from, Chapter 5 comes to expand this understanding by showing where they are transitioning into (and to what effects). After all, student mobility is bound by time, culture and place.

Box 5.1 – Reflective questions and/or points of Chapter 5

To help you review critically the content of this chapter, ask yourself the following questions and discuss them with colleagues from other disciplines.

1. This chapter has identified variables related to adaptation abroad, including *living conditions, preferred social activities* and *host culture facilities, social networks and social support,* and *integration in the local community.*
   1.1. What other variables or facets can you think of?
2. While the previous chapter has demonstrated how a given disciplinary theory can shape our categories of analysis, this chapter has shown why the identification of the variables of interest should precede disciplinary allegiances.
   2.1. What sort of assumptions would you be led to make about student mobility, had you started with a preset theoretical framework (or research agenda) instead of the variables of interest?
3. The interdisciplinary element in this chapter was brought about by juxtaposing different theories and concepts which demonstrated that the experience of adaptation abroad is bound by people and place.
   3.1. To understand the social dimension of adaptation, I have employed the notions of *intercultural learning, communities of practice* and *social support theory.* To what extent would I have captured the dual condition of learning through social participation in study abroad had I not interspersed these theories and concepts?
   3.2. To what extent can urban sociological and anthropological theories help you to capture the role of place in student mobility?
4. Does the integration of different (and at times, conflicting) disciplinary perspectives aid your understanding of student mobility as a complex whole? If so, why? If not, why not?
   4.1. And, to what extent can integration (at conceptual and methodological levels) help bridge the gap between theory and practice in study abroad?
5. As you noticed, the application of the Kruskal–Wallis test allowed me to realise the limitations of using one data type to understand a complex problem.
   5.1. If you are conducting research, what analytical techniques can you think of to help better understand your topic?

Appendix 5.1

This questionnaire is part of a research project developed by Dr. Joana Almeida and aims to understand international students' opinion about studying abroad. Your participation is very important to me. Please, answer individually, honestly and remember that there are no right or wrong answers.

Thank you in advance for your participation. **Confidentiality** of each survey is guaranteed. Your name at the top of this survey is for clarification purposes only as I will be the only person who will have access to the **identification number** attributed to each survey.

0. Profile

Name: _____

I. Living conditions

1. Can you describe your living conditions during your study abroad in Portugal/ the UK? Please **tick (✓)** the option(s) that best suit(s) you.

   ☐ Shared private accommodation ☐ University residence halls ☐ Other (Specify: _____ _____)

   1.1. Who did you live with? Please **tick (✓)** the option(s) that best suit(s) you.

   ☐ Other international or exchange students ☐ Other foreign people ☐ Other (Specify: _____ _____)

   ☐ Portuguese[1]/British[2] students ☐ Other Portuguese[1]/ British[2] people

Adaptation 175

II. Friendships and social networks

2. Who did you **most commonly spend time** with during your study abroad? Please **tick (✓)** the option(s) that best suit(s) you.

☐ Other international or exchange students

☐ Portuguese/British students

☐ Language tandem partner

☐ Other foreign people

☐ Other Portuguese/ British people

☐ Other (Specify: _____ _____)

3. On average, how many **exchange or international friends** did you make?

_____

4. On average, how many **Portuguese[1]/British[2] friends** did you make? _____

    4.1. How would you describe the process of making friends with Portuguese[1]/British[2] people? Please **circle the number** that best reflects the **level of difficulty** felt.

    ❶ (No extent) ❶ (Small extent) ❷ (Moderate extent) ❸ (Large extent) ❹ (Great extent)

    4.2. Why is it so? _____

    _____

    _____

5. Which of the two groups (exchange/international or local students) would you describe as your **friendship group** during your study abroad period?

☐ Exchange/International students

☐ local students (Portuguese[1]/British[2])

    5.1. Why is it so? _____

    _____

    _____

III. Host culture facilities

6.[1] Which of the following activities from the Erasmus Student Network (ESN) Aveiro did you participate in?

☐ Magusto

☐ ESN Movie nights

☐ Trips around Portugal

☐ Christmas with Portuguese families

☐ Language tandem

☐ Easter with Portuguese families

☐ International dinners

6.[2] Which of the following activities from the Globe Café (by Friends International) did you participate in?

☐ Weekly dinners   ☐ English conversation groups   ☐ Globe trips around the UK

☐ Cultural nights (e.g., Indonesian night)   ☐ English classes   ☐ Other activities (e.g., ruby, basketball match, trampoline)

7.[2] Were you involved with or attended events from international student associations or societies other than the Globe?
☐ Yes (Specify which:_____) ☐ No

8. What **facilities** did you use to familiarise yourself with the Portuguese[1]/ British[2] culture?

☐ Newspapers and magazines   ☐ Theatre   ☐ Street markets

☐ Literature   ☐ Cinema   ☐ Sports

☐ Media (television, radio)   ☐ Night clubs or bars   ☐ Travelling around Portugal[1]/the UK[2]

☐ Music   ☐ Cafés[1]/Pubs[2]   ☐ Meeting people in the streets

☐ Museums   ☐ Restaurants   ☐ Other (Specify: _____ _____)

9. To what extent do you now feel at home in the local community (Aveiro[1]/ Newcastle[2])? Please **circle the number** that best suits you.

0 (No extent) **1** (Small extent) **2** (Moderate extent) **3** (Large extent) **4** (Great extent)

9.1. Why is it so? _____

_____

_____

IV. Language and intercultural learning

10. How do you rate your motivation to learn the English language? Using a scale of **0 (no motivation)** to **5 (very high motivation)**, rate yourself by circling the level of motivation that best suits you. **0 1 2 3 4 5**

10.1. What is your English language proficiency **now**? Please **tick (✓)** the level that best suits you. ☐ Beginners ☐ Intermediate ☐ Advanced

11. How do you rate your motivation to learn cultural and intercultural issues? Using the previous scale, rate yourself by **circling the level of motivation** that best suits you.

    ⓪   ①   ②   ③   ④   ⑤

12. What kind of advice would you give future mobile students in order to maximise their intercultural gains during their stay abroad? _____

    _____

    _____

V.¹ Intercultural competence

13. In the first semester I asked you to rate yourself on a scale of **0 (no competence)** to **5 (very high competence)** in each of the following sentences. Please **rate yourself now**.

Awareness

While in Portugal/in the UK I became aware of ...

differences between my own language and the Portuguese¹/English² language	⓪ ① ② ③ ④ ⑤
differences between my own culture and the Portuguese¹/English² culture	⓪ ① ② ③ ④ ⑤
my stereotypes to these differences	⓪ ① ② ③ ④ ⑤
how I behave differently according to the Portuguese¹/English² culture	⓪ ① ② ③ ④ ⑤
how Portuguese/English people see me (their opinion about me)	⓪ ① ② ③ ④ ⑤

---

1 Question 13 is an adaptation of the Assessment of Intercultural Competence Questionnaire (YOGA format) developed by the Federation of Experiment in International Living (FEIL). Available at www.worldlearning.org

178 Applications of an interdisciplinary approach

Attitudes

While in Portugal/in the UK I ...

could make friends among Portuguese[1]/English[2] people easily and find opportunities to meet them	⓪ ❶ ❷ ❸ ❹ ❺

used the Portuguese[1]/English[2] language in my daily life (on and off campus), even with other co-nationals (friends who speak your language)　⓪ ❶ ❷ ❸ ❹ ❺

followed the rules and standard behaviours of the Portuguese[1]/English[2] culture (e.g.,[1] I greeted everyone with two kisses); (e.g.,[2] I greet everyone with a handshake)	⓪ ❶ ❷ ❸ ❹ ❺

could deal with the frustrations caused by the different habits of Portuguese[1]/English[2] people (e.g.,[1] Many Portuguese people have a specific sense of punctuality); (e.g.,[2] English people can express themselves in an apologetic or less straightforward manner)　⓪ ❶ ❷ ❸ ❹ ❺

Skills

While in in Portugal/in the UK I ...

in situations of misunderstanding, I could identify if the misunderstanding is personal or cultural when I don't understand Portuguese[1]/English[2] people	⓪ ❶ ❷ ❸ ❹ ❺

could think about the Portuguese[1]/English[2] cultural-perspective to help me in situations in which I seem to offend a Portuguese/English person or done something wrong　⓪ ❶ ❷ ❸ ❹ ❺

was able to relate and contrast the Portuguese[1]/English[2] culture with my own	⓪ ❶ ❷ ❸ ❹ ❺

used specific strategies which facilitated my adaptation and help me not feeling out of place (e.g., I try to find someone to talk about my cultural experience)　⓪ ❶ ❷ ❸ ❹ ❺

used specific strategies to learn the Portuguese[1]/English[2] language and culture (e.g., I did a language exchange/ tandem with a(n) Portuguese/English student)	⓪ ❶ ❷ ❸ ❹ ❺

Adaptation 179

Knowledge

While in Portugal/in the UK ...

could understand what culture means and identify its components ⓪ ❶ ❷ ❸ ❹ ❺

could compare important historical and socio-political aspects of my culture with the Portuguese[1]/English[2] culture ⓪ ❶ ❷ ❸ ❹ ❺

recognised some of the essential norms and taboos of the Portuguese[1]/English[2] culture (greetings, dress, behaviour, etc) ⓪ ❶ ❷ ❸ ❹ ❺

recognised signs of feeling out of place in the Portuguese[1]/English[2] culture and know strategies for overcoming them ⓪ ❶ ❷ ❸ ❹ ❺

developed some techniques to maximise my learning of the Portuguese[1]/English[2] language and culture ⓪ ❶ ❷ ❸ ❹ ❺

VI. Study abroad experience

14. How do you rate your overall study abroad experience in Portugal/the UK? Please **circle the number** that best reflects your view.

❶ (Poor) ❷ (Fair) ❸ (Good) ❹ (Very Good) ❺ (Excellent)

14.1. Why is it so? _____

_____

_____

15. What were the **highs** and **lows** of your study abroad experience in Portugal/ the UK? Please point out the **3 highest** and **3 lowest points** you have experienced, for each giving your responses in **ascending order of importance**.

	Highs	Lows
−	_____	_____
	_____	_____
+ ↓	_____	_____

180 Applications of an interdisciplinary approach

16. Would you consider studying abroad again?

☐ Yes (Specify:_____) ☐ No

16.1. Why? _____

Thank you for your collaboration!
Dr. Joana Filipa Almeida

Note to readers: For conciseness, the questionnaire administered to exchange and international students in Portugal and the UK is presented here jointly. Where examples or situations differed, these cases were marked with [1] and [2], respectively.

Notes

1 Private rental properties in central urban areas that are either self-managed by commercial operations or jointly managed through leasing arrangements with higher education institutions. These properties are usually apartment blocks with individual en-suite bedrooms, communal kitchens, lounges, launderettes. Other standard features include: swipe-card access, on-site security staff and CCTV and, sometimes, even gyms and swimming pools (Hubbard, 2009).
2 The terms British and English were used interchangeably by the students to refer to England and not necessarily the sovereign state of the UK and its four countries: England, Wales, Scotland and Northern Ireland.
3 Note that the question ascertaining friendship groups differed slightly in the immigrant post-experience questionnaire by incorporating the open-ended category 'Other' in addition to the categories 'Immigrants' and 'Hosts'. The underlying reason was that the dichotomy between peer and host friends was not so watertight in the case of immigrants. It was, therefore, decided to add the additional open-category 'Other' to understand what other sources of social support these participants had.
4 Pure social support studies often measure the multi-level association between different sources and functions of social support.
5 Cafés' are coffeehouses serving light meals, coffee and other refreshments. They are an important site for socialisation in Portugal. Pubs are commercial establishments selling alcoholic drinks and light meals or snacks, and a primary source of socialisation within British culture.

References

Almeida, J., Fantini, A. E., Simões, A. R., & Costa, N. (2016). Enhancing the intercultural effectiveness of exchange programmes: Formal and non-formal educational interventions. *Intercultural Education, 27*(6), 517–533.

Bochner, S., McLeod, B. M., & Lin, A. (1977). Friendship patterns of overseas students: A functional model. *International Journal of Psychology, 12*(4), 277–294.

Cohen, S., & Wills, T. A. (1985). Stress, social support and the buffering hypothesis. *Psychological Bulletin, 98*(2), 310–357.

Coleman, J. A. (2015). Social circles during residence abroad: What students do and who with? In R. Mitchell, N. Tracy-Ventura & K. McManus (Eds.), *Social interaction, identity and language learning during residence abroad* (pp. 33–51). Amsterdam: European Second Language Association.

Freed, B., Segalowitz, N., & Dewey, D. (2004). Context of learning and second language fluency in French: Comparing regular classroom, study abroad and intensive domestic immersion programs. *Language Acquisition, 26*(2), 275–301.

Garmendia, M., Coronado, J. M., & Ureña, J. M. (2012). University students sharing flats: When studentification becomes vertical. *Urban Studies, 49*(12), 2651–2668.

Harvey, D. (1996). *Justice, nature and the geography of difference*. Edinburgh: Edinburgh University Press.

Hubbard, P. (2009). Geographies of studentification and purpose-built student accommodation: Leading Separate Lives? *Environment and Planning A: Economy and Space, 41*(8), 1903–1923.

Isabelli-García, C. (2006). Study abroad social networks, motivation and attitudes: Implications for second language acquisition. In M. A. Dufon & E. Churchill

(Eds.), *Language learning in study abroad contexts* (pp. 237–258). Clevedon: Multilingual Matters.

Kashima, E. S., & Loh, E. (2006). International students' acculturation: Effects of international, conational, and local ties and need for closure. *International Journal of Intercultural Relations, 30*(4), 471–485.

Kudo, K., Volet, S., & Whitsed, C. (2019). Development of intercultural relationships at university: A three-stage ecological and person in-context conceual framework. *Higher Education, 77*, 473–489.

Lave, J., & Wenger, E. (1991). *Situated Learning: Legitimate peripheral participation.* Cambridge: Cambridge University Press.

Malecki, C. K., & Demaray, M. K. (2005). What type of support do they need? Investigating student adjustment as related to emotional, informational, appraisal, and instrumental support. *School Psychology Quarterly, 18*(3), 231–252.

Malet Calvo, D. (2018). Understanding international students beyond studentification: A new class of transnational urban consumers: The example of Erasmus students in Lisbon (Portugal). *Urban Studies, 55*(10), 2142–2158.

Montgomery, C. (2010). *Understanding the international student experience.* Basingstoke: Palgrave Macmillan.

Murphy-Lejeune, E. (2002). *Student mobility and narrative in Europe: The new strangers.* London: Routledge.

Onwuegbuzie, A. J., & Leech, N. L. (2004). Enhancing the interpretation of "significant" findings: The role of mixed methods research. *The Qualitative Report, 9*(4), 770–792.

Sandelowski, M. (2000). Focus on research methods. Combining qualitative and quantitative Sampling,data collection, and analysis techniques in mixed-method studies. *Research in Nursing & Health, 23*, 246–255.

Sassen, S. (2010a). The city: Its return as a lens for social theory. *City, Culture and Society, 1*(1), 3–11.

Sassen, S. (2010b). Cityness: Roaming thoughts about making and experiencing cityness. *Ex Aequo, 22*, 13–18.

Schartner, A. (2015). You cannot talk with all of the strangers in a pub': A longitudinal case study of international postgraduate students' social ties at a British University. *Higher Education, 69*(2), 225–241.

Smith, R. A., & Khawaja, N. G. (2011). A review of the acculturation experiences of international students. *International Journal of Intercultural Relations, 35*(6), 699–713.

Ward, C., Bochner, S., & Furnham, A. (2001). *The psychology of culture shock.* Hove: Routledge.

Wenger, E., McDermott, R., & Snyder, W. (2002). *Cultivating communities of practice: A guide to managing knowledge.* Boston, MA: Harvard Business School Press.

Wills, T. A. (1991). Social support and interpersonal relationships. In M. S. Clark (Ed.), *Prosocial behaviour: Review of personality and social psychology* (Vol. 12., pp. 265–289). Newbury, CA: Sage.

Young, T. J., Sercombe, P. G., Sachdev, I., Naeb, R., & Schartner, A. (2013). Success factors for international postgraduate students' adjustment: Exploring the roles of intercultural competence, language proficiency, social contact and social support. *European Journal of Higher Education, 3*(2), 151–171.

Chapter 6

Outcomes and transformations

About Chapter 6

As in the two previous chapters, Chapter 6 addresses the practical applications of an interdisciplinary approach to student mobility by exploring the outcomes and transformations accruing from the stay abroad of the 50 sojourners in this book.

The transformative power of the study abroad experience is often translated into two broad dimensions – academic and personal – or in a finer categorisation of personal, academic, cultural and linguistic achievements, as reflected in early *Erasmus* surveys (see Teichler & Maiworm, 1997). More than 20 years have elapsed since Teichler and Maiworm's study, but the relative importance of the expected academic gains in the face of other study abroad domains remains vague across European higher education discourses and policy agendas (although see Chapter 1 for reference to studies in the US which report academic gains). This is especially true for credit-seeking student mobility insofar as academic recognition is often taken as a synonym for academic achievement.

184 Applications of an interdisciplinary approach

Considering the relative lack of clarity between participant metrics and learning outcomes, it is unsurprising that the three major learning domains of study abroad are often subsumed under individual accounts of personal maturation when distinctions need to be made. Hence the division of the current chapter into three parts: (1) Personal (2) Language and (3) Intercultural outcomes. The first part refers to participant assessment of the study abroad experience and the relative value they assign to it. Language and intercultural outcomes, in turn, address sojourner linguistic and intercultural learning gains. While the main organising principle for data analysis in this chapter is the threefold division of sojourners, in the second and third sections (Language and Intercultural outcomes, respectively) the original case study analysis will be employed (please recall Chapter 3). This analysis relates to the intercultural intervention which the group of exchange students and highly skilled immigrants were subjected to. That is, the *Campus Europae* students (Case Study A) and the mixed group of *Erasmus* students and highly skilled immigrants (Case Study B). In the international student group (Case Study C), an intercultural intervention was not implemented.

As in the previous two chapters, quantitative patterns will be complemented with qualitative data. Quantitative data stem both from the pre- and post-experience questionnaires administered to all 50 sojourners. Qualitative data refers to relevant open-ended questions in these instruments, a focus group and an individual interview conducted with the Portuguese language teacher who observed the intervention. The aim is to ascertain the (external) impact of the intervention other than on the participants themselves (internal impact).

To conclude, a summary of the main key points is provided. As in previous chapters, reflective questions and/or points (see Box 6.1) are provided at the end of the chapter.

Personal outcomes

Living amidst another culture can produce varying learning and developmental outcomes, depending, among other things, on the relative weight of the stay abroad in sojourners' lifelong journey and how they interpret the experiences lived abroad (i.e., their meaning-making).

Cognitive, intra and interpersonal domains are honed by stimuli and challenges posed by the different everyday routine in an unfamiliar setting. Naturally, experiences vary across individuals. As such, understanding sojourners' assessment of the stay abroad can provide clues to how they experience living and studying in another country. Thus, this section describes sojourner ratings of the overall study abroad experience (stay abroad for the immigrant participants) and the grounds for these scores, based on a closed and an open-ended question in the post-experience questionnaire, respectively.

While in this section I will not delve into sojourner psychosocial development per se, valuable insights into sojourner feelings and thoughts of the overall experience abroad will be shared, including the relative importance of self-development in the face of other domains.

Outcomes and transformations 185

Table 6.1 All sojourners: ratings of the sojourn experience

	Exchange		International		Immigrants	
Sojourn experience	N	%	N	%	N	%
(1) Poor	–	–	–	–	–	–
(2) Fair	1	4.5	–	–	–	–
(3) Good	2	9.1	2	10.5	3	33.3
(4) Very good	12	54.5	11	57.9	4	44.4
(5) Excellent	7	31.8	6	31.6	2	22.2
Total	22	100.0	19	100.0	9	100.0

Most sojourners deemed their experience very good. The mean values assigned by sojourners are: 4.14 (SD = 0.77) for exchange students, 4.21 (SD = 0.63) for international students and 3.89 (SD = 0.78) for immigrants.

Although sojourner ratings are similar, this does not necessarily mean they faced the same challenges. As noted in previous chapters, the experiences of mobile students (exchange and international) and immigrants are distinct, first and foremost because their entrance into the host culture is marked by different types of sojourns and socio-professional roles.

As discussed earlier in Chapter 1, study abroad is usually linked to a range of learning and developmental outcomes: from the three key learning domains abroad (academic, linguistic and intercultural) to personal growth and identity, from the build-up of cultural and social capital to the development of an enriched employability skillset and transferable skills (see Jones, 2013 for the latter).

These multiple and mutually reinforcing learning and developmental domains are not only vital for a globalised workplace, but also for students' lifelong learning journey. Which domain is more worthy of note opens room for ample discussion. A possible way to shed light on this array of outcomes is to look at sojourners' perceptions and the abroad domains they choose to forefront. With this goal in mind, in the next couple of pages I will categorise sojourners' justifications for the quantitative assessment of their overall experience into type of gains or achievement. From the analysis of 46 valid responses, the following learning and developmental domains emerged.

Of these responses, 24 emphasised primarily one single domain, namely: (a) personal, (b) academic and (c) socio-cultural. The remaining 22 responses combined two or more domains, including the following:

1. Personal and socio-cultural (Theme D);
2. Personal and professional (Theme E);
3. Personal, academic and socio-cultural (Theme F);
4. Academic and socio-cultural (Theme G);
5. Personal, academic, sociocultural, linguistic and professional;
6. Academic and linguistic (Theme H);
7. Academic, socio-cultural and linguistic (Theme I).

The frequency distribution of all nine categories is illustrated by Figure 6.1.

Results from participant self-assessment of the stay abroad (for immigrants) and study abroad (for mobile students) accord, to some extent, with the research literature forefronting developmental outcomes as a major benefit of living and studying abroad (e.g., Jones, 2010a; Mellors-Bourne, Jones, Lawton, & Woodfield, 2015; Papatsiba, 2005; Severino, Messina, & Llorent, 2014; Teichler, 2004; Tsoukalas, 2008).

Of the 41 mobile students in this book, 31 (67.4%) emphasised the transformative power of study abroad in fostering personal growth and/or maturation, often translated into an ability to take control on one's life-path in a reflexive way (Papatsiba, 2005). Or, as espoused by human developmental psychology theory, an 'ability to author one's thinking, feelings, and social relating [that] is inherent in successful functioning in adult life' (Baxter Magolda & King, 2007, p. 492). That is, self-authorship. The following four verbatim quotations contextualise the personal domain of studying abroad (Theme A) in the words of sojourners.

Jürgen: 'I would probably not be quite original if I said that it was one of the best experiences in my entire life.'
Zhi Ruo: 'Broadened my perspective of life.'
Andresz: 'Principally, because there was a lack of bad experiences. Study allowed me to change some patterns I had at home. I could look/define myself in new ways.'
Cristina: 'It has been a great living experience, particularly at the personal level. I could understand many aspects of my personality better and became more independent as well.'

Life abroad can be a catalyst for identity change as demonstrated by Andresz and Cristina, an exchange and an international student, respectively. The cognitive dissonance produced by living and studying in a different *cultural milieu* invites

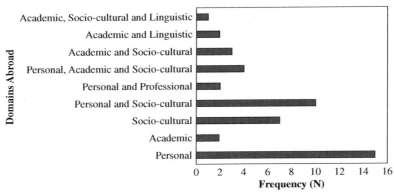

Note. (n=46; 100%)

Figure 6.1 All sojourners: learning and developmental domains abroad.

Outcomes and transformations   187

sojourners to develop their own purposes and meanings. In this process, these young adults may redefine their identity in new ways as evidenced by Andresz's testimony. Learning is situated in a life-altering experience (Jürgen) prompting sojourners to turn inwards and developing a growing awareness of the self, i.e., the intrapersonal dimension in human developmental theory (Kegan, 1994). This renewed internal identity while not overly dependent on others can be also triggered by relationships with 'different cultural' Others (i.e., the interpersonal dimension). Hence the overlap between the personal and social domains of study abroad, with the social likely to include a cultural component. After all, social relations abroad are often mediated by a cultural element as shown by the ten responses in the Personal and socio-cultural domain (Theme D).

Jane: 'In learning so much from independence and meeting so many interesting people.'
Tanja: 'Because I have grown a lot personally and have made really good friends.'
Elinah: 'Made very many friends from everywhere. Tried so many different foods, tried so many experiences and travelled a lot in the UK and Europe.'
Belén: 'Because I live with my husband, I like Aveiro a lot and I am happy.'

As discussed elsewhere (Severino et al., 2014), inner psychological processes of identity formation can be interwoven with the social dynamics of socio-cultural contexts. Moreover, the postponement of entry into adulthood among today's youth can harness the transformative power of study abroad as a defining moment in mobile students' lifelong journey. For immigrant participants like Belén, whose age range is considerably higher, identity formation is unlikely to be at stake but rather there is a sense of personal fulfilment. Not surprisingly, the Personal and professional domain (Theme E) only overlaps for (two) immigrant participants for whom the personal realm was on equal footing with professional fulfilment.

For mobile students, personal development takes many guises (e.g., independence, identity formation, maturation, intellectual development, yearning for novelty, emotional self-resilience, personal fulfilment) and can act both as a pre-departure (see Chapter 4) and a resulting motivation. While constructing their role in the host society, mobile students further their sense of exploration and commitment in a personal narrative wherein self-, academic- and socio-cultural development may be equally important; or as put by Killick (2015), a narrative wherein questions of the lifeworld, alterity and learning are key to the development of global students. This intricate amalgam of learning and developmental domains is brought forward by four mobile students who emphasised the personal, academic and socio-cultural domains of studying abroad (Theme F).

Jeane: 'I love Portugal. I was very happy about the studies and I made friends. I have grown up a lot.'
Krisha: 'I met interesting people, studied under experienced professors, explored new places and had new experiences.'

Dong: 'Independent living and problem-solving skills are fully used when I'm living abroad. Not only passed the school mission, but also made many local and international friends when travelling around the country.'

Nikola: 'Studying abroad allowed me to meet people from all over Europe. It was a nice opportunity for self-development, but the theoretical subjects of studies were a little disappointing.'

As discussed previously in Chapter 4, personal development can go hand in glove with academic drivers for international and exchange students alike, although their initial expectations may not necessarily match the outcomes of the experience. This is particularly evident in the testimonies of exchange students like Nikola for whom the academic side of studying abroad was mostly negative. In fact, of the 12 responses under the academic domain (either alone or combined), the responses given by exchange students tended to depict the academic realm with negative undertones, in contrast with international students. Four opinions, two by exchange students (Juan and Łukasz) and two by international students (Ying and Chao) illustrate these differences in viewpoints.

Juan: 'Because you don't study more and you can know more people from different cultures.'

Łukasz: 'I had some problems to understand lectures in Portuguese. Also, my university didn't give me 30 ECTS for the Master's dissertation. So, I had to focus on some courses instead of focusing on my project.'

Ying: 'The length of the study programme is too short. That is why I didn't circle "excellent". The experience gave me a critical perspective to see my country's education and lecturers here are more supportive than those in China.'

Chao: 'Excellent study methods and facilities provided by the university. Friendly people, almost same culture. Clean city.'

Juan appears to see study abroad as 'time off' from his studies, allowing exchange students to experience their 'new' life in a different country fully. In Łukasz's opinion, the novelty of living away from home does not seem to compensate his disappointment with the academic side, nor the underlying language obstacles. On the contrary, international students (Ying and Chao) appear to be happy with the education received abroad. In fact, whereas exchange students tended to depict their studies as a 'low', international students considered the academic part a 'high'. The divide between exchange and international students regarding the academic realm of study abroad raises two questions introduced in Chapters 1 and 2:

> To what extent are credit-seeking students learning enough academically while abroad? Are academic learning outcomes abroad sufficiently positive?

As discussed in Chapter 2, the ambiguous framing of the educational nature of credit-seeking student mobility in European higher education has taken central stage in shaping public perception of the expected value of credit-seeking student mobility. The fact that students like Juan see studying abroad (for academic credits) as a gap year may not be mere personal rhetoric, but also a reflection of broader European policy and higher education discourses which as yet have not set the bar for educational provision in study abroad programmes like *Erasmus* and *Campus Europae*. Not that the psychosocial development stimulated by these programmes is irrelevant, but if student mobility is to be deemed by the EU to be 'learning mobility', expectations regarding achievement in all learning domains should be clarified and acted upon. This is all the more important since outcomes can be interrelated and growth in one domain can affect (positively or negatively) growth in another. This premise is validated by the overlap between the academic and linguistic domains (Theme H).

Łukasz: 'I had some problems to understand lectures in Portuguese. Also, my university didn't give me 30 ECTS for the Master's dissertation. So, I had to focus on some courses instead of focusing on my project.'
Kinga: 'Very good because of learning Portuguese, but not so good about learning my field of studies.'

The experiences of Łukasz and Kinga demonstrate that language learning has both the potential to harness and hamper academic achievement. For Łukasz, host language proficiency emerged as a barrier to academic success. Kinga, in turn, depicted the possibility to learn Portuguese positively with no apparent relation to academic achievement, although the latter was also deemed negatively. Finally, academic, socio-cultural and linguistic domains (Theme I) can be interrelated, even if less frequent among our responses.

To summarise, this section showed that the stay abroad can result in divergent learning and developmental outcomes. These outcomes can vary by type of sojourn but also according to sojourner characteristics, including their meaning-making structures and experiences in the host culture. Sojourners reaped positive learning and developmental outcomes across five major domains: Personal, Academic, Socio-cultural, Linguistic and Professional. While the first four domains are transversal to all three sojourner groups, the fifth refers to immigrant participants only. Additionally, not all sojourners reaped positive gains in all domains. Exchange students, in particular, reported negative experiences in academic and language attainment. In this sense, while a wealth of research suggests positive outcomes of study abroad, the evidence base in this section lends support to the claims of a few North-American studies (e.g., Twombly, Salisbury, Shannon, & Klute, 2012) questioning the extent to which these outcomes are sufficiently positive. Two corollary questions follow from this statement:

Why are not academic outcomes of study abroad in European higher education actively looked into? Is it simply lack of sufficient empirical evidence or is our premise biased from the outset?

Applications of an interdisciplinary approach

The literature review in Chapter 1 indicated that the academic side of studying abroad is largely under-researched in European post-secondary education (see Learning domains abroad). The voices of exchange students in the current chapter revealed some disappointment with education provision abroad. Their claims come to remind us that the interrelationships between outcomes in study abroad and the conditions hindering growth in certain outcomes need to be probed further. Language outcomes are no exception, as discussed next.

Language outcomes

A commonly expected learning outcome of study abroad in European higher education is improved language proficiency.

Notwithstanding the expectations for optimal language learning abroad, many second language acquisition (SLA) studies have demonstrated that while the effect of studying abroad on language proficiency gains is generally positive, it can be mitigated by intra- and extra-linguistic factors (e.g., Dufon & Churchill, 2006; Freed, 1995; Isabelli-García, 2003; Jackson, 2008; Kinginger, 2009; Mitchell, Tracy-Ventura, & McManus, 2017, 2015) – please recall the discussion in Chapter 1.

To understand the language learning development of the 50 sojourners in this book, this section compares two closed questions from the pre- and post-experience questionnaires ascertaining sojourner levels of host language proficiency at the beginning (see Figure 6.2) and end of the sojourn (see Figure 6.3), respectively. In the case of the exchange student and immigrant groups, this quantitative data set is supplemented by qualitative data from: (a) an additional closed question in the post-experience questionnaire eliciting their motivation to learn language issues, (b) the follow-up focus group with the *Campus Europae* students and (c) an interview with their Portuguese language teacher who assisted to the intercultural intervention.

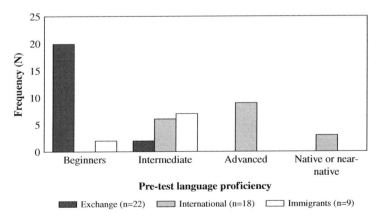

Figure 6.2 All sojourners: host language proficiency in the pre-experience questionnaire.

The vast majority of exchange students were at beginners level (n = 20; 90.9%) at the outset of the sojourn. Only two exchange students assessed their proficiency intermediate. This was the case of two *Erasmus* students who were speakers of other Romance languages. All *Campus Europae* students deemed their host language proficiency beginners. International students departed from a more advanced skill level: six were intermediate speakers, nine advanced and three natives or near-natives. Likewise, immigrant participants were at a more advanced level than exchange students but not as advanced as international students. Seven immigrants deemed their proficiency intermediate, against two participants who considered it beginners.

Figure 6.3 illustrates sojourner self-assessment of host language proficiency at the end of the sojourn.

The comparison of pre- and post-experience scores (see Figures 6.2 and 6.3) breaks down two popular myths widely discussed in the SLA literature: (a) that one becomes fluent in the target language by simply studying abroad (Dufon & Churchill, 2006; Freed, 1998) and (b) that those with lower pre-departure proficiency levels would stand to gain the most (Dufon & Churchill, 2006). Looking at the language gains of our sojourners, three patterns stand out at the end of sojourn:

1. Most exchange students stayed at beginners level (n = 14), with only six students considering to have progressed to an intermediate proficiency at the end of sojourn;
2. Most international students deemed their proficiency intermediate (n = 9) in the post-experience questionnaire, as opposed to advanced in the pre-experience questionnaire;
3. Immigrants maintained their self-assessment, with the majority remaining at the intermediate level.

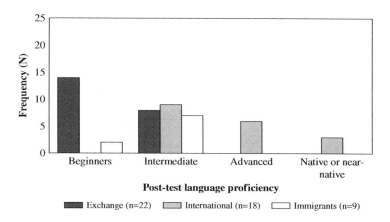

Figure 6.3 All sojourners: host language proficiency in the post-experience questionnaire.

192 Applications of an interdisciplinary approach

It should be noted that exchange students and immigrant participants received intermediate language instruction (B1 as set out in the *Common European Framework of Reference for Languages* – please recall Endnote 9 in Chapter 2), and all but one was formally awarded this proficiency level at the end of the sojourn. For *Campus Europae* students (Case Study A), there were actual programme design expectations that students would reach B1 level after one year of cultural immersion (please recall Chapter 3, Box 3.1). For this reason, I will discuss this case study in more detail.

Before entering this discussion, a remark should be made about between-group differences, specifically, the more stringent self-assessment of international students at the end of the academic year. While exchange students and immigrant participants maintained their assessment of language proficiency levels (beginners and intermediate, respectively), in the international student group there were three participants who considered to have dropped from advanced to intermediate language proficiency at the end of the sojourn. The following questions arise:

> Is this decrease a true decrease in language competence (due to negative learning experiences, for instance)? Or is it the result of inflated self-assessment? Is it possible that sojourners rate themselves more stringently at the end of the sojourn, given the realisation of the difference between their actual and perceived language proficiency?

In the end, the more we know, the more we know what we do not know. Or, as argued by Krueger and Dunning (2009), 'people tend to hold overly favorable views of their abilities in many social and intellectual domains' (p. 1). This can be the case of language learning. Studies in SLA have, in fact, raised this very question. To wit, Allen (2002), on an investigation on the development of listening comprehension skills of 25 study abroad participants in a summer programme in France, observed that the performance self-assessment of three learners in certain tasks decreased in the post-test. The researcher attributed this decrease to greater learner awareness of the challenges of interacting with native speakers.

There is naturally the possibility that our result stems also from within-group individual differences in proficiency gains. The collected data are insufficient to provide an answer, especially because I did not follow the group of international students in the formal language classroom, as opposed to exchange and immigrant participants. The possibility to follow the latter two groups in the language classroom enabled me to pin down other variables related to classroom instruction and learner characteristics that may come into play in language learning abroad. One of these variables is the motivation to learn a language (Table 6.2).

Scores in Table 6.2 show that the greater language achievement of *Erasmus* students and the highly skilled immigrants (Case study B) over *Campus Europae* students (Case Study A) is reified by higher motivational levels of the former over the latter. The distinct motivational dispositions of the two groups suggest that learners who experience success in language learning become more motivated to

Table 6.2 Campus Europae, Erasmus and highly skilled immigrants: motivation to learn language issues

	M	SD	Mdn	Min	Max
Language motivation					
Case A (n = 19)	2.63	1.26	2	1	5
Case B (n = 11)	4.18	0.87	4	2	5

learn, whereas those experiencing failure become less motivated. This finding is line with SLA study abroad researchers who have demonstrated that study abroad learners who have a strong motivation to succeed are better positioned to make the most of opportunities for language and intercultural learning (e.g., Beaven & Spencer-Oatey, 2016; Isabelli-García, 2006; Jackson, 2008, 2018).

Our scores do not, however, tell us much about the reasons for the dissimilar results. The analysis of the focus group with *Campus Europae* students and the interview with the Portuguese language teacher shed insight into (some of) the variables that may account for these differences. These variables are summarised in Figure 6.4 according to data gleaned from the two interviews.

Several variables may have mitigated host language acquisition among *Campus Europae* students. Those brought forward by the students are represented by black arrows in Figure 6.4, whereas those forefronted by the Portuguese language teacher are marked by grey arrows. Whenever variables were brought forward by the two groups of interviewees, both arrows are given. This is the case of (d) language proficiency, (e) motivation and (g) programme design features.

To start with, let us look at the variables forefronted by the students only. Learner anxiety (Theme A) is related to the affective dimension of language

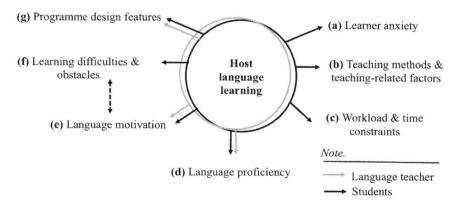

Figure 6.4 Campus Europae students: host language learning variables.

194 Applications of an interdisciplinary approach

learning – in this case, Portuguese. It encompasses feelings and/or emotional reactions of uneasiness, apprehension or discomfort towards learning the host language. According to psychosocial learning theory, anxiety can be defined as 'state of anticipatory apprehension over possible deleterious happenings' (Bandura, 1997, p. 137). This state of anxiety can fluctuate during the stay abroad and hinder the achievement of certain goals – linguistic, in our case. The outcome self-assessment of *Campus Europae* students' language proficiency indicates that their anxiety levels were high at the end of the sojourn. Interestingly, the possibility of learning another language was their most frequent motivation to study abroad at the start of the sojourn (see Chapter 4, Figure 4.2). What was a motivation before, became demotivation and anxiety over the course of study abroad as voiced by the students themselves.

Interviewer: 'How was the process of learning Portuguese for you? Did you find many obstacles? Was it disappointing, frustrating or stimulating?'
Andresz: 'I like the Portuguese language very much. It sounds very pleasant, and I just like it, and I would like to know it, but the big disappointment were the classes.'
Karol: 'It's basically the same, because it was really, really, really disappointing! I started having classes in my home country before coming here. It was fine, it was nice, but then there was … I am now speaking about *Campus* programme … then, there were … the meetings. You were supposed to learn the language during the holidays.'

Student retrospective assessment of the language learning process reflects some frustration in its actualisation and little reduction of anxiety levels after one year of cultural immersion. This accords with some SLA literature which despite showing that anxiety typically decreases during the stay abroad also cautions that it can remain high due its situational nature (e.g., Allen, 2002; Tanaka & Ellis, 2003). According to Andresz and Karol, their lack of motivation is a direct result of the formal learning process, i.e., the Portuguese classes. The frustration towards the pedagogical realm of host language learning may be also related to workload and time constraints (Theme C), as well to specific programme design features of *Campus Europae* (Theme G) as noted by Karol.

Karol: 'and unfortunately it is not possible, because our online meetings started when we really didn't feel yet going, we were inside of our studies, we had exams, we had internships. We didn't really want, because holidays were coming. We had to earn money to come here. We didn't feel at all yet *Erasmus* … and we had many obligations and then there were millions of mails – do this, do the online course, we should meet! I was like very, very against, I didn't do it … I tried, I started, but then it wasn't possible.'

According to Karol, this state of anxiety goes back to the first step of the language learning process, i.e., the online course offered by the *Campus Europae*

Outcomes and transformations 195

programme (see Chapter 3, Box 3.1). The timing of the online course did not match students' academic workload and timetable (Theme C) and led to student distress. The second step, the intensive face-to-face course at the host institution, led to similar feelings, as Bartek explains.

Bartek: 'It was too fast. Six hour per day of intensive course … Ok, we could learn, but after these six hours we came back home and we didn't do nothing unfortunately because we were totally exhausted!'

The rapid movement between the two first steps of language learning (targeting A1 and A2 proficiency levels, respectively) and the number of learning hours had a snowball effect, as Andresz elucidates.

Andresz: 'I think the Portuguese programme is not well constructed and it is not taught as I think it should, but well … It has not started from the beginning very well, it's then hard to get it right.'

While expressing his viewpoint, Andresz touches upon another variable – Teaching methods and teaching-related factors (Theme B). This variable is also highlighted by another three colleagues.

Jan: 'I cannot see the point of knowing and studying ten different tenses … and basically not knowing any vocabulary. Of course, you can say: Come on, you can learn vocabulary on your own!'
Karol: 'We are not at all at the B1 level, maybe A2. We cannot speak with people! For example, we don't have listening exercises and then we have, suddenly, listening in the exam. We don't talk we just do exercises, mainly grammar, not vocabulary.'
Kinga: 'Just grammar, grammar, grammar!'

According to students the adopted pedagogical approaches were inappropriate and focused on grammar acquisition in detriment to oral production and vocabulary acquisition. This mismatch between teaching approaches and student learning needs may have also negatively influenced participant language proficiency and the effort invested in language learning (Theme D). Hence the quantitative scores yielded by the post-experience questionnaire, with 73.6 per cent of *Campus Europae* students considering to have a proficiency lower than intermediate (despite attending a B1 language course). These results were also discussed in the interview with the Portuguese language teacher.

Interviewer: 'I asked the students to rate their language proficiency and 73.6 per cent rated themselves at beginners' level. Of this percentage, 47.3 per cent considered their level to be A2. Does this result surprise you? How do you see it?'
Language teacher: 'Bearing in mind that these results refer to the end of the second semester and that the students should answer a B1 proficiency level,

it surprises me. Bearing in mind the in-class work developed by the students, the assignments done, it doesn't surprise me.'

Students' assessments of their proficiency levels were not entirely unexpected to the Portuguese language teacher in view of student classwork and learning difficulties – Theme F.

Language teacher: 'Well, I think that from the outset we all have our abilities and our difficulties, and from that we can already realise that there are people who might have greater empathy with a foreign language than others. That's a starting point.'

In addition to student learning difficulties, other obstacles may have hindered exchange students' language learning, namely: (1) learner characteristics, namely individual empathy and/or attitudes towards foreign language learning, (2) communication in own language, (3) daily communication in a lingua franca and (4) intense social life.

Language teacher: 'Then, there's also another important question which concerns the fact that a class is composed of a reasonable number of students, but the majority belongs to the same country of origin. Thus, they can continue communicating in their own language or then in English, as typical of *Erasmus* students. Then we have to say that their social life is another obstacle to learn a language, because sometimes the time which should be spent learning a language is spent in their "social life"... that and the fact that sometimes they are more worried about organising parties, because they have a close relationship with their colleagues who have the same nationality, and this ends up distracting them from what they should be actually doing'

The last aspect pointed out by the language teacher brings to the fore the specific lifestyle of exchange students (see Chapter 4), while calling into question student investment in language learning and the degree of interaction with the host context and native speakers. Communitive interactions between exchange students and hosts are likely to take place in a lingua franca rather than the target language, Portuguese.

In addition to the four learning difficulties and/or obstacles, through much of the interview the Portuguese language teacher emphasised the lack of motivation of students to learn Portuguese – Theme E. When confronted with the quantitative results regarding student motivation to learn Portuguese, the teacher did not seem surprised.

Language teacher: 'It doesn't surprise me because learning a language during one year is an evolutionary process and, as a matter of fact, this class did not seem to be motivated from the outset, nor ready, nor even aware of the language learning process.'

Students like Kinga, on the other hand, consider that it is 'the teacher who is motivating people, generally'. The motivation of second language (L2) teachers to teach and its relationship with student motivation are, in fact, variables that educational psychology, teacher education, applied linguistics and psycholinguistics have brought increasing attention to (see Dörnyei & Ushioda, 2011 for an overview of motivation in L2 teachers). Going back to our study, the statement from the language teacher discloses an important component of 'teacher motivation' – teachers' expectations over their students' learning potential (Dörnyei & Ushioda, 2011). It is, therefore, fair to question the Pygmalion effect of this relationship, i.e., the extent to which *Campus Europae* students were not living 'down' to their teacher's negative expectations.

Finally, exchange programme design features can also mediate language learning, an aspect largely under-researched in European study abroad literature as noted in Chapter 1. Previous excerpts drawn from the focus group disclosed interviewees' frustration regarding the workload and timeline required by *Campus Europae* in the two first stages of the language learning process, i.e., the online and the intensive face-to-face language courses. In other focus groups moments, students considered that the *Campus Europae* language goal of reaching B1 at the end of the sojourn is unreachable.

Karol: 'Doing one level or even two levels in one semester when I was learning languages like French for ten years or eight to reach B2. It's not possible! There's no point! We should learn, in my opinion, until the level we are able to do!'

The Portuguese language teacher also appears to consider the goal somehow unrealistic, but achievable.

Language teacher: 'Feasible, yes. Difficult to attain, also. Realistic maybe not so much. It all depends on the type of students we have. Attaining the B1 proficiency level "yes", but with different proficiency levels, that is, attaining B1 is possible but there's a big difference and we can perceive it later on in the grades students get.'

To summarise, the confluence of variables in Figure 6.4 may have mitigated host language acquisition among *Campus Europae* students, thus demonstrating that study abroad participants do not magically become fluent in a foreign language by being immersed in the host culture. They can stop expending effort or persisting in the enterprise of learning the host language. Their linguistic gains are situationally and temporally dependent, with both intra- and extra-linguistic factors having the potential to influence (positively or negatively) language learning. Or, as put by psycholinguistics, affect and cognition, time and context interlock with the motivations to learn a second language (Dörnyei & Ushioda, 2011). Acknowledging these basic premises is crucial to ensure exchange programmes and language teachers can effectively equip

198 Applications of an interdisciplinary approach

study abroad learners with the necessary linguistic tools to function in a new social setting.

Next, another major learning and developmental domain of study abroad is examined – intercultural outcomes.

Intercultural outcomes

Two major premises hold sway as to how intercultural outcomes are understood by the scholarly community in the twenty-first century. 'Some authors consider intercultural competence as an integrated competence, while others study components of the broader construct' (Twombly et al., 2012, p. 68). Equally, the plethora of intercultural constructs opens up a sea of taxonomies, raising challenges to scholars and practitioners alike on what model to use.

In Chapter 2, I tried to throw light on the flurry of intercultural competence models published since the 1990s by summarising their typological features according to the conceptual pathways proposed by Spitzberg and Changnon (2009) (see Table 2.3). Earlier in Chapter 1, I identified intercultural learning as a major learning domain abroad while noting the increasing calls from interculturalists and study abroad professionals for ongoing intercultural learning support in study abroad, through face-to-face and online pedagogical interventions or both (see Chapter 1, Learning domains abroad).

Having discussed earlier in the book the relevance of intervening in student intercultural learning abroad, in this section I hope to offer readers useful curriculum and assessment guidelines for designing their own face-to-face intercultural interventions. These guidelines draw on an intercultural intervention I developed in Portugal with 31 sojourners, the 19 *Campus Europae* students and the mixed group of the 3 *Erasmus* students and 9 highly skilled immigrants. I will start by outlining the curriculum and assessment guidelines I believe can be transversal to the design of other intercultural interventions. After this discussion, I will go into the particulars of the intervention and the impact it had on the 31 participants.

Curriculum and assessment guidelines

Designing intercultural interventions and other structured educational support to impact sojourner outgrowth on intercultural outcomes requires careful attention to curriculum design. This process and its underlying phases are illustrated in Figure 6.5 as fundamental steps to develop purposeful educational support that optimises intercultural outcomes in study abroad. Together, these four steps offer a roadmap for higher education stakeholders, educators, researchers, study abroad professionals, international educators, language and intercultural instructors or trainers to develop this sort of educational support in their own contexts, with their own learners.

Designing intercultural curricula is a process of continuous refinement that should be clear about its positioning regarding: (a) the underlying conceptions of culture, (b) the targeted construct (e.g., intercultural competence, intercultural maturity, intercultural sensitivity, etc.) and (c) the adopted learning theories (e.g., transformative, experiential, social-constructivist). In those cases where the adopted construct is intercultural competence, another element should be also clarified: (d) the adopted notion of competence. For instance, is competence understood according to a behaviourist approach centred on performance? Or does it couple knowledge with performance? Or even, knowledge and performance along with the capacity to undertake a given role and learners' perception about that same role?

In terms of the process itself, not only does each step in Figure 6.5 build on the previous, but the sharing of results (Step 4) can trigger new refinements that can add to and/or revise the stock of knowledge available, or simply internally revise the approaches inherent to the first three steps. While bearing in mind previous efforts, an important lesson cannot be forgotten – that every time a new cycle begins, learner needs, the type of sojourn and the cultural contexts learners transition *from* and *into* (home and host contexts) need to be taken into account. Another crucial aspect of this cycle are the conceptions of teaching and learning which will ultimately affect how intercultural curricula are designed (Step 2) and delivered (Step 3). For instance, the adopted learning theories in the intervention I developed in Portugal are experientially based on the assumption that: (1) sojourners learn best when they learn through experience; (2) deep learning abroad needs to be experiential, developmental, holistic and dialectic (Passareli & Kolb, 2012). Whatever approach to learning readers decide to adopt, it should be commensurate with the targeted construct. In my intervention, the adopted construct is Fantini's (2006) model of intercultural communicative competence

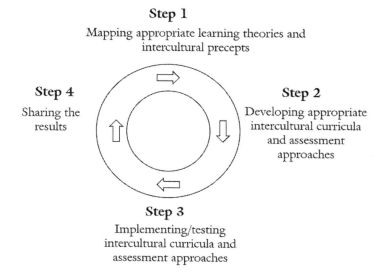

Figure 6.5 Intercultural curriculum development, adapted from Suskie (2009).

which is premised on the notion that language and (inter)cultural learning are inextricably linked.

In addition to the three foundational precepts of an intercultural intervention (i.e., the notion of culture, the targeted construct and the adopted learning theories), there is an additional element that can help bridge the gap between the intervention and broader higher education internationalisation processes. This element is the dialectic movement between formal, non-formal and informal intercultural learning and sharing in study abroad. By formal intercultural learning I mean learning that is intentional and leads to some form of certification (e.g., an intercultural intervention offered as a credit-bearing course). By non-formal intercultural learning I mean learning which, despite entailing some degree of structure, is not tied up to formal educational requirements (e.g., extra-curricular activities promoting interculturality on campus). My use of informal learning, in turn, refers to learning which is not structured or planned nor intentional from the learner's standpoint, involving learning that accrues from life experience or situations.

In short, intercultural interventions can achieve greater transformative power when they are designed as a sequence of learning experiences that build off the formal, non-formal and informal continuum in cumulative and interactive ways. That is to say that rather than seeing formal, non-formal and informal intercultural learning as mutually exclusive categories, I see them as positions on a learning continuum on which intercultural interventions should draw.

Going back to an argument made in Chapter 2, if student mobility is meant to grow out of the processes of internationalising higher education, optimising its intercultural outcomes can (and should, in my view) be extended to those who do not study abroad, not just the mobile minority. An increasing number of scholars in Europe and elsewhere have drawn attention to this gap through concepts like internationalisation at home (Beelen & Jones, 2015), which intentionally draws on intercultural learning opportunities within local contexts, campus internationalisation (Green & Olson, 2003), internationalisation of the curriculum (Leask, 2015) or pedagogy (Ryan, 2013) and enhanced interaction between mobile and local students (Leask, 2009).

Notwithstanding the burgeoning calls for social inclusivity in international higher education, the role extra-curricular activities can play in nurturing interculturality on campus and helping mobile and local students mix and mingle still merits more attention. In Europe in particular, European-wide student services have an enormous potential to reach out to a large number of students and assist higher education institutions in harnessing the diversity of the student body as a learning resource and a mechanism for cross-cultural integration. Let us say the reader is interested in designing a formal intercultural intervention in a structured environment like the academic classroom, the multiplier effect of this intervention can be maximised and extended to other students through non-formal learning activities on campus and enhanced links to the local community. Two good examples are the activities offered by two volunteer organisations, in Portugal and the UK, and fostering intercultural sharing among academic and local communities (Chapter 5, Table 5.4).

Finally, good curriculum guidelines are inseparable from good assessment guidelines, with the latter having a double function – that of (a) monitoring and assessing how well student learning goals are achieved throughout an intervention and (b) judging the effectiveness of the intervention in reaching its overarching goal and/or mission. Simply put, aspect (b) entails the programmatic evaluation of interventions. But let us frame these two aspects within the process of planning, implementing and aligning the teaching and assessment frameworks. One possible way to align these frameworks is to design our intercultural intervention according to a type of approach to curriculum and assessment design called 'backward design' (Wiggins & McTighe, 2005). Figure 6.6 illustrates the broader sequence of aligning curricula and assessment frameworks while outlining the three-stage approach of a 'backward design' proposed by Wiggins and McTighe (2005) (on the left of the figure).

The planning and implementation stages (Steps 1 and 2 in Figure 6.6) refer to the process of setting up and aligning the instructional design and assessment framework of an intervention. Ensuring this alignment from the outset may be facilitated by deriving the curriculum from the desired learnings. That is, by: (1) identifying the desired learning results first, to then (2) determine acceptable evidence and (3) plan learning experiences and instruction (Wiggins & McTighe, 2005).

Stated another way, we start by 'diagnosing' participants' intercultural learning needs (*needs assessment*) to determine their stages of intercultural development and consider the learning goals of the intervention and curriculum expectations. I find it useful at this stage to ascertain student areas of interest for intercultural learning (through a focus group or a questionnaire for example). After determining where

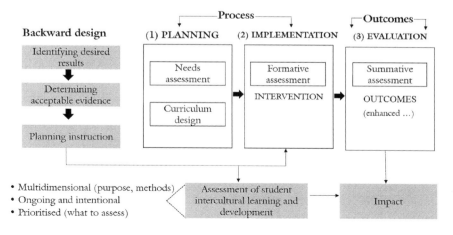

Figure 6.6 Teaching and assessment frameworks.

202 Applications of an interdisciplinary approach

the 'intervention is headed', it is necessary to define which evidence is acceptable for assessing the desired learnings. At this stage, it might be necessary to prioritise the aspects of our intercultural construct that need to be assessed as suggested by Deardorff (2015). The desired learnings will then be assessed as the congruence between *teaching objectives* and *student learning outcomes.*

In the case of my intervention, this involved defining clear teaching objectives and measurable indicators across the four competence areas of intercultural communicative competence – Attitudes, Skills, Knowledge and Cultural awareness,. That is to say, my intended learning outcomes should translate into greater levels of intercultural communicative competence of participants in any of these areas (ideally, in all four). In this way, the learning outcomes communicate an integrated and holistic view of the intervention following contemporary approaches to teaching and assessment in higher education (Biggs & Tang, 2011). With clearly defined intended learning outcomes and assessment evidence, we can then plan the instructional design.

The programmatic evaluation of our intervention (Step 3) is also part of the broader sequence in Figure 6.6, but may extend it. To elaborate further, Step 1 lays out the effective ways for designing our intervention, followed by its implementation in Step 2 (hence both steps being subsumed under Process in Figure 6.6). In this step, a *formative assessment*, focused on defining, monitoring and determining how well student learning goals are achieved during the intervention, is conducted. The *summative assessment* of student intercultural learning informs the programmatic evaluation of our intervention by providing a baseline measure for determining its effectiveness – that is, its internal and external value: the internal value to the participants themselves by measuring the impact of the intervention upon their intercultural gains; the external value to those who, while outside the intervention, might have a legitimate interest in it and help us assess its usefulness to learners other than those who benefited directly from our intervention.

To summarise, instructional and assessment structures of intercultural interventions should be designed as integrated frameworks following a constructively aligned outcomes-based approach to teaching and learning (Biggs & Tang, 2011). Simply put, it is about beginning our intervention with a clear conception of its larger purposes (or mission) and expected learning outcomes. Hence a type of assessment that ought to be ongoing, intentional, multidimensional, multipurpose, multimethod and tailored to student learning needs and the instructional contexts. In the end, an important measure tells us the relative success of our efforts – the impact of our interventions upon the intercultural gains of its participants. This is discussed next.

The intercultural intervention

As elaborated by Vande Berg, Paige and Lou (2012), purposeful intercultural pedagogy is designed to enhance students' intercultural learning during the study

Outcomes and transformations 203

abroad cycle (before, during and after). In the case of the intervention I designed, this enhancement should translate into the greater intercultural communicative competence of the 31 participants. Naturally, the impact of an intervention cannot be understood without an overview of its design and implementation. This overview is provided next, followed by a discussion of the intercultural gains reaped by participants due to the effect and/or fundamental changes induced by the intervention.

Overview

The intercultural intervention I developed was delivered as a sequence of eight two-hour modules, over the course of one academic semester, to support and enhance sojourner intercultural learning during their stay in Portugal. Implementation occurred in two intermediate language classrooms of Portuguese, one attended by *Campus Europae* students and the other by the mixed group of *Erasmus* students and highly skilled immigrants. Known by participants as 'intercultural seminars', the intervention was implemented by myself in Portuguese, using English as an auxiliary language of instruction.

The theoretical foundations for the intervention draw on: experiential learning theories; conceptions of culture that attend to its objective and subjective dimensions as well to regularity and variability of social groupings; and an holistic conception of competence whereby knowledge and performance are coupled with learners' perceptions about their role in a given context and their capacity to undertake this very role (Bowden & Marten, 1998). The targeted construct, as I mentioned before, is Fantini's (2006) model of intercultural communicative competence which depicts intercultural competence as a set of 'complex abilities needed to perform *effectively* and *appropriately* when interacting with others who are linguistically and culturally different from oneself' (Fantini, 2006, p. 1, italics in the original). Intercultural communicative competence was, thus, operationalised as a cultural-linguistic construct embodying the necessary abilities to undertake the role of intercultural speaker and/or mediator as required by the context of interaction.

The teaching and assessment frameworks were designed around the fourfold modelling of competency areas in Fantini's (2006) model – i.e., Attitudes, Skills, Knowledge and Cultural awareness, the ASK+A framework (see also Fantini, 2019). Each intervention module addressed a specific content area and learning goals. These goals were further broken down into teaching objectives and learning outcomes or indicators for each competency area in Fantini's model. For a more detailed description of the intervention modules and learning outcomes, the reader is referred to Almeida (2017), and Almeida, Fantini, Simões and Costa (2016).

The instructional design integrated theory and research-based content, implemented through experiential activities. The students' host country experience in Portugal and their diverse cultural backgrounds were areas for introspection, comparison, discussion and learning during in-class activities. Using Kolb's (1984)

204 Applications of an interdisciplinary approach

experiential learning cycle, pedagogical activities utilised students' sojourn experiences, followed by reflective observations and abstract conceptualisations.

Impact

To assess the short-term impact of the intervention on participant intercultural gains, I will draw on data from one closed and one open-ended question in the post-experience questionnaire eliciting the extent to which the intervention maximised participant intercultural gains while in Portugal, and justifications for the attributed ratings.

While discussing the impact of the intervention and type of intercultural gains reaped by participants, I will also demonstrate why an integrated use of intercultural models should be carefully weighted and considered. To this end, I will bridge the spectrum of difference between two models of intercultural communicative competence and two developmental intercultural models by weaving in key notions from these four conceptualisations. As noted earlier in Chapter 2, these models are: Bennett's (1986, 1993b) developmental model of intercultural sensitivity, King and Baxter Magolda's (2005) developmental model of intercultural maturity, Fantini's (2006) and Byram's models of intercultural communicative competence. Although Fantini's model was explicitly adopted as the unit of analysis, the other three models aided the understanding of sojourner intercultural development and learning. The two developmental models offered insights into the psychosocial nuances of sojourner intercultural development, whereas Byram's (1997) model clarified the formulation of teaching objectives and the notion of critical cultural awareness.

But let us look at the impact produced by the intervention first (Table 6.3) to then discuss why an integrated use of these four models was needed.

Overall, results underscore the positive (short-term) impact of the intervention on participant intercultural gains, but they also show that this impact was greater in Case study B, i.e., the mixed group of *Erasmus* and highly skilled immigrants. Most *Campus Europae students* (Case study A) consider the intervention

Table 6.3 Campus Europae, Erasmus and highly skilled immigrants: intercultural impact of the intervention

Intercultural gains	Case A		Case B	
	N	%	N	%
(0) No extent	1	5.3	1	8.3
(1) To a small extent	–	–	1	8.3
(2) To a moderate extent	13	68.4	1	8.3
(3) To a large extent	5	26.3	5	41.8
(4) To a great extent	–	–	4	33.3
Total	19	100.0	12	100.0

Outcomes and transformations   205

had a moderate impact (68.4%), whereas Case B participants deem the extent large (41.8%). With regard to lower ratings, two participants in Case studies A and B rated the impact nil, and another participant in Case B small.

Two type of gains emerged from participant justifications (n = 26; 100%) to the attributed ratings, namely: (a) Increased cultural knowledge, (b) Increased cultural awareness, along with (c) Absence or paucity of intercultural cains.

Most participants reported an increase in the knowledge (n = 11; 42.3%) and awareness (n = 9; 34.6%) dimensions of intercultural learning due to the intervention. Six participants (23.1%) considered the intervention had a minor role or may not have contributed to their intercultural gains during the sojourn.

Those 11 participants reporting 'increased cultural knowledge' emphasised the acquisition of new cultural knowledge, culture-specific or general. Culture-specific knowledge refers to the acquisition of information and facts about Portuguese culture as a cultural and social entity. Culture-general knowledge addresses cultures or social groups other than the Portuguese culture (although the culture-general component of the intervention was centred on cultures represented by participants).

Gaëlle: 'It was really interesting to learn things about the Portuguese culture but also about international and European cultures. We really shared a lot of knowledges and I enjoyed it a lot.'

Juan: 'Because I learnt more aspects about the Portuguese culture.'

Jeane: 'I learnt a lot about Portuguese culture and I missed it in the first semester. Without help of Portuguese friends I wouldn't know this much though.'

Martyna: 'Very good idea to create these seminars, I learnt new things about culture. It was interesting.'

Kinga: 'The intercultural interaction is still the most important thing, but the seminars can systematise our knowledge and extend, enrich it.'

These five sojourners considered the intervention or 'intercultural seminars' (as it was known by sojourners) led to an enrichment or systematisation of explicit and implicit cultural knowledge. The transmission of new knowledge happened either through direct exposition of contents (Juan, Martyna) or the interactive sharing in the classroom (Gaëlle). Jeane and Kinga also acknowledge the systematisation of cultural knowledge, but consider procedural knowledge, via social interactions with hosts and diverse Others, the most important thing. Kinga's testimony illustrates well this dichotomy wherein the conjunction 'but' signals the relative weight assigned to the intervention in view of the grandeur of the sojourn.

Increased cultural awareness was the second most frequent gain, representing the responses of nine participants. This enhanced awareness entails the development of a renewed or more complex mindfulness about cultural difference and intercultural situations. Abilities to decentralise (from the self and others), suspend disbelief, reflective thinking, critical evaluation of knowledge and perspective-taking characterise this type of intercultural gain.

Elena: 'I'm familiarised with multiculturalism and I have always had good intercultural relations, but I could never analyse "why". Now, I can.'

Mercedes: 'I acquired new knowledges and I learned about cultural relativism, to suspend judgement, to analyse every situation and learn from it.'

Anfisa: 'In my daily life and when speaking with Portuguese people I already understand some things that before were very strange to me.'

Milosz: I understand few things that before I even didn't care about (connected to interculture).'

Andresz: 'The seminars pointed me to several issues that in other cases would be unconscious or neglected.'

The gains reported by these participants can be posited against intercultural developmental models like King and Baxter Magolda's (2005) model of intercultural maturity which purports that intercultural growth entails a multidimensional development in cognitive, intra- and interpersonal dimensions. Participant responses seem to echo this developmental growth. Milosz and Andresz, for instance, stress a renewed understanding of the world and is diversity (cognitive dimension). The interpersonal domain is emphasised by Anfisa who notes a renewed understanding of relationships between herself and Portuguese Others. Finally, Elena and Mercedes' testimonies encapsulate all three dimensions in that their awareness came through a new understanding of the world and intercultural situations (cognitive domain), of themselves (intrapersonal) and relationships with diverse Others (interpersonal).

Increased cultural awareness also involves critical appropriation of knowledge as noted by Mercedes who highlights the importance of employing complex knowledge in situ to evaluate critically intercultural situations. It is precisely here where the difference between increased cultural knowledge and awareness resides. In the latter dimension, participants pointed out abilities to evaluate arguments and knowledge claims critically while, in the former, information seems to have been processed effectively but it may not have evolved to the level of critical appropriation (nor the ability to ground knowledge in context). In other words, learners may display declarative cultural knowledge, but they may have not reached higher levels of abstraction and synthesis. This is why critical appropriation and reflection are the crux of increased cultural awareness and the leverage for a leap in insight. In Byram's (1997) model of intercultural communicative competence, the superordinate component of intercultural competence is critical cultural awareness. It is possibly through the evolutionary motion of this component that higher-order psychosocial development (like self-authorship) may be attained, and a threshold of competence (implying mobilisation of knowledge, skills and attitudes) is reached. It is here where developmental and communicative models intersect, and the need for integrated models arises. And yet once again, it is about opting for a 'both/and' thinking at the heart of interdisciplinarity to negotiate interpretations from different conceptualisations – of intercultural abilities in this case.

Outcomes and transformations 207

Finally, although the vast majority of participants reported a positive impact, there were also six sojourners who accounted for no or slight gains (23.1%). Five different factors were identified by these participants (Table 6.4).

Among the constraints in Table 6.4 are: (1) similarity between home and host cultures (Jimena and Borja); (2) participant lack of interest for intercultural issues (Saskia); (3) participant previous cultural knowledge or training (Tanja); (4) timing of the intervention (Jonas); and (5) teaching approaches (Jan).

Interestingly, for sojourners like Jimena and Borja it can be argued that the ways in which they made meaning of cultural proximity may have hindered what the intervention had to offer them. Tanja appears to acknowledge the value of the intervention, but deemed it little in view of previously acquired knowledge. With regard to the other two sojourners, Jonas thought the intervention could have brought added-value, were it not for its timing (the intervention was only one semester long). Jan, in turn, considered that teaching methods should target

Table 6.4 Intercultural impact of the intervention: absence or paucity of intercultural gains

Factors	Particips.	Ratings	Excerpts
Similarity between home and host culture	Jimena	0	'In my case in particular, I can adapt and live outside my home country because I have done it before. Also, my culture is very similar to the Portuguese culture.'
	Borja	1	'Despite being useful, I think it wasn't difficult for me, because Portugal is very similar to my home country.'
Lack of interest for intercultural issues	Saskia	2	'That's a matter that I don't spend too much time thinking about. I think in this matter I didn't have gains.'
Previous cultural knowledge	Tanja	2	'I've been studying topics and issues addressed in the seminars before. So, it was not an entirely, new unknown subject. … Nevertheless, the seminars were interesting for me. I just don't think that they influenced me to a great extent in how I perceive the Portuguese culture.'
Timing of the intervention	Jonas	0	'I started integrating to *Erasmus* and Biology department communities before the seminars began. Otherwise, it could have helped me to a medium extent.'
Teaching approaches	Jan	2	'I feel there was a little too much issues about the term culture (the term culture, what is, etc.). Little too much about the culture in general, not about particular cultures.'

Note. Particips. = participants

more specific cultures. Overall, although these participants pointed to individual constraints regarding the intervention, its educational value seems generally appreciated.

Looking into the particular case of Borja, who along with Jimena considered that the intervention had little impact due to similarities between home and host cultures, it is possible to draw further inferences regarding the need for integrated intercultural models. Bearing in mind Borja's intercultural journey and the fact that he considered 'not to spend much time living a Portuguese life' (see Chapter 5), his views are not entirely unexpected. Borja's intercultural development also casts doubt on the unidirectional intercultural development, into poles of ethnocentricity and ethnorelativity, in Bennett's (1986, 1993b) model. To elaborate my argument further, Figure 6.7 represents Bennett's six-stage continuum of worldview configurations into two trajectories. The ethnocentric trajectory is on the left (Denial, Defence and Minimization), and the ethnorelative on the right (Acceptance, Adaptation and Integration).

Like the imaginary Student A in Figure 6.7, Borja appears to hold two contradictory worldviews. On the one hand, he shows no apparent interest for actively engaging with hosts. On the other hand, he sought Otherness among other sojourners, i.e., among the multicultural exchange student community he is part of. According to the six stages of the developmental model of intercultural sensitivity, Borja holds a typical *denial* behaviour in that the host culture is construed in vague ways and neither does he wish to engage with hosts, but with undifferentiated Others. Yet, Borja accepts differences among peers from diverse cultural backgrounds and recognises that one's culture is one of many equally complex cultures. The following question arises:

> How can Borja's developmental path during the sojourn be described through the developmental model of intercultural sensitivity, if two contradictory worldviews (denial and acceptance) are held?

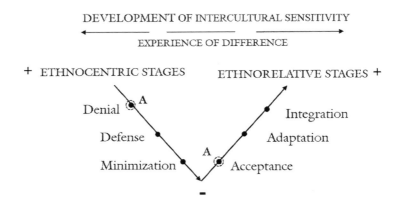

Figure 6.7 Compound development of intercultural sensitivity.

Borja's intercultural journey shows that worldview configurations cannot always be reduced to fixed cognitive structures indicative of certain kinds of attitudes and behaviours. Hence the relevance of opting for relational methods of analysis in bridging different meaning systems. Through comparing, although necessarily briefly, Bennett's (1986, 1993b) and King and Baxter Magolda's (2005) developmental models, we can better understand why Bennett's model fails to break down the ways in which Borja is culturally sensitive and the ways he is not. While both models are concerned with identifying and articulating the progressive steps in achieving an intercultural developmental threshold over time, in Bennett's model these developmental shifts imply a change in worldview configurations. In other words, the emphasis is more on cognitive structures, and less on the interpersonal domain of human development. King and Baxter Magolda's (2005) model, in turn, is centred on a multidimensional growth based on individual capacities across all three developmental domains (cognitive, intra and interpersonal).

Going back to Borja's case, the intra- and interpersonal domains are fundamental to grasp his apparent 'lack of sensitivity' towards the host culture. To elaborate further, Borja's friendship group were other exchange students, and perhaps he was more inclined to discover cultures other than the Portuguese culture through his multinational social network, especially because he considered Spanish (home) and Portuguese (host) cultures to be alike. Borja's journey would, therefore, be exceedingly difficult to describe according to the unidirectional progression purported by Bennett's model and its measurement instrument (the Intercultural Developmental Inventory, IDI).

The linear and scalar nature of Bennett's (1986, 1993b) model is, in fact, one of the major criticisms levelled at it (e.g., Liddicoat, Papademetre, Scarino, & Kohler, 2003; Perry & Southwell, 2011). Even if adult development is accretionary and individuals do not typically regress, there may be stagnation or insufficient progress to cause a developmental shift in one's worldviews. Another criticism of the model is its culture-general nature and assumed cross-cultural transferability (Greenholtz, 2005). This criticism raises two further questions regarding Borja's intercultural journey and the role of language acquisition in it, a crucial feature in Fantini's (2006) and Byram's (1997) models of intercultural communicative competence.

> Is it possible that mobile students follow a distinct intercultural path according to the culture-specific-or culture-general nature of this development? And is language a key differentiating variable?

It seems fair to assume that culture-specific development warrants host language mastery, at least if the sojourner seeks successful (effective and appropriate) interaction with hosts. Culture-general development, as illustrated by Borja and the other exchange students in Portugal, does necessarily demand host language mastery given that interaction will likely occur in a lingua franca, possibly with undifferentiated Others (i.e., their peers).

Applications of an interdisciplinary approach

Need for integrated intercultural models

Having demonstrated the need to intersect different conceptualisations of intercultural abilities, in this section I summarise four key assumptions that bring these four systems of meaning together.

These assumptions form a framework for a more integrated or holistic view of intercultural communicative competence that attends to its behavioural, affective, cognitive and developmental dimensions (see Figure 6.8).

Four premises are illustrated by Figure 6.8 to form a more holistic view of the construct of intercultural communicative competence, to wit:

1. Intercultural communicative competence is a complex and multidimensional competence with core competence dimensions being Attitudes, Knowledge, Skills and Cultural awareness.
2. Intercultural communicative competence is a cultural-linguistic construct which can be culture-general or culture-specific:
   2.1. Culture-specific development requires host language mastery for effective and appropriate interaction with different 'Others' (i.e., hosts);
   2.2. Culture-general development does not necessarily involve host language mastery for effective and appropriate interaction with similar Others (i.e., other sojourners).
3. Intercultural communicative competence is a higher-order developmental process of multidimensional growth in cognitive, intrapersonal and interpersonal domains.
4. Intercultural communicative competence is a competence of qualitative growth whereby mature levels of performance may be related to abilities to decentre from oneself and reflect critically.

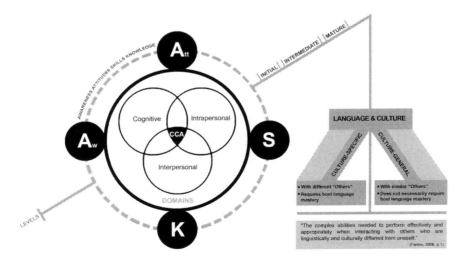

Figure 6.8 Integrated or holistic view of intercultural communicative competence.

Outcomes and transformations   211

The four assumptions presented here are based on participant intercultural development (beyond the impact of the intervention) through a longitudinal multimethod measurement outside the remit of this book. A few words of further contextualisation are, therefore, needed regarding Assumption 2 which conveys the language-culture nexus beneath intercultural communicative development. This nexus can impart both unification and separation. Deeper levels of culture-specific development may warrant host language mastery, at least if sojourners seek successful (i.e., appropriate and effective) interaction with hosts. Culture-general development, on the other hand, does not necessarily involve host language abilities as interaction will likely occur in a lingua franca with sojourner peers. The closely knit social networks formed by the mobile students in this book (the exchange student group in Portugal in particular) are symptomatic of the central role of English during the period of studies abroad, and the compound development that can occur (as in Borja's case). Stated another way, one can be a fluent fool, as asserted by Bennett (1993a), but one can also certainly be a cultural fool. Deeper levels of culture-specific development may occur when one is neither a fluent nor a cultural fool, not least because many rich cultural subtleties are unveiled when one has some degree of host language command.

To summarise, my intention in this section was, through looking at key notions of four intercultural models, to demonstrate the importance of breaking down the different meaning systems inherent to conceptualisations and disciplinary allegiances. Possibly because the different facets of intercultural learning and development have been the focus of particular disciplines, we have paid insufficient attention to how these facets can cohere. Or, as espoused by interdisciplinary research, our efforts have not been concentrated on creating a common ground between different disciplinary insights, when there are parts of intercultural learning and development that are not apparent in disciplinary isolation.

Box 6.1 – Reflective questions and/or points of Chapter 6

To help you review critically the content of this chapter, ask yourself the following questions and discuss them with colleagues from other disciplines.

1. This chapter has identified four types of gains in study abroad (*personal, linguistic, intercultural* and *academic*) and explored how growth (or lack thereof) in one domain can affect another.
    1.1. What other ways can you think of to explore the interrelationships in these learning and/or developmental domains?
    1.2. Can a clearer understanding of these interrelationships help clarifying the contribution of study abroad towards the broader educational endeavour?

2. This chapter has shown that some facets of student mobility (as in intercultural learning and development) are not apparent in disciplinary isolation.

   2.1. In what other domains can the weaving in of different conceptualisations produce a more nuanced understanding of the study abroad experience?

   2.2. And, how can the 'both/and' thinking of an interdisciplinary approach help you negotiate different conceptualisations or interpretations?

3. This chapter has argued that structured educational support is key to optimise the intercultural gains of mobile students. To this end, I developed an intercultural intervention following the curriculum design process in Figure 6.5.

   3.1. If you are to develop intercultural curricula and/or learning materials, take the steps in Figure 6.5 and explain the: (a) underlying conception of culture, (b) targeted construct, (c) learning theories; (d) and, in case your construct is premised on a competence threshold, the adopted notion of competence.

   3.2. In what ways can this process facilitate the design of your curriculum and/or learning materials, and help you clarify the intended learning outcomes?

   3.3. In addition to intercultural interventions and/or orientations, in what other ways can intercultural learning be embedded into study abroad programme design and delivery?

4. This chapter has also drawn attention to the mismatch between mobile students' learning outcomes and study abroad programme design (as in the linguistic underachievement of *Campus Europe* students).

   4.1. In what ways can academics, practitioners and policy-makers collaborate to ensure study abroad programmes are designed around explicit and realistic learning outcomes?

Summary

In Chapter 6, the last chapter of Part II, I have reflected on some of the outcomes and transformations accruing from the study abroad experience. Three types of outcomes were at the heart of the chapter: (a) Personal, (b) Linguistic and (c) Intercultural.

Individual sections have shown that learning and development in these domains can be affected by variables related to the learner but also to external contextual factors. When read together, these sections demonstrate that sojourner gains (or losses) may be interrelated and that learning in one domain can affect growth in another. In these sections, I have also interspersed a number of theories and conceptualisations of intercultural constructs to demonstrate the importance of co-creating meaning through a plurality of viewpoints.

Two other important lessons drawn from Chapter 6 are: the need to (1) design study abroad programmes around explicit and realistic learning outcomes and (2) stop positioning mobile students as passive and unidirectional learners. These two premises have also been emphasised by other study abroad scholars and organisations (e.g., Forum on Education Abroad, 2015; Jackson, 2018; Jones, 2010b; Twombly et al., 2012). The consequences of failing to address the first premise were illustrated by the linguistic underachievement of *Campus Europae* students against the high goals set by the *Campus Europae* programme. The post-sojourn language outcomes of these students were, indeed, underwhelmingly low compared to the programmatic hope and hype.

The second premise is inherent to all three sojourner groups and attuned to the importance of understanding our students' lifeworld. This means closer attention to the student voice and the contribution of study abroad towards students' lifelong learning journey (and the broader educational endeavour). As it turned out, some exchange students seemed to value more the personal realm of the stay abroad, especially because their academic expectations were not met. If this finding holds up to further scrutiny, and in light of other studies on international and European voluntary service (e.g., Jones, 2010a; Kairé, 2018), two question should be asked. To what extent is study abroad fulfilling its educational purposes? If personal development is all there is to credit-bearing schemes, could not other international experiences like volunteering be just or even more effective in fostering deep personal transformations?

References

Allen, H. W. (2002). *Does study abroad make a difference? An investigation of linguistic and motivational outcomes* (Doctoral thesis). University of Wisconsin-Madison. Retrieved from http://works.bepress.com/heatherwillisallen/50/

Almeida, J. (2017). Intercultural seminars: An educational intervention with sojourners at a Portuguese university. In D. K. Deardorff & L. A. Arasaratnam-Smith (Eds.), *Intercultural competence in higher education: International approaches, assessment and application* (pp. 144–150). London: Routledge.

Almeida, J., Fantini, A. E., Simões, A. R., & Costa, N. (2016). Enhancing the intercultural effectiveness of exchange programmes: Formal and non-formal educational interventions. *Intercultural Education, 27*(6), 517–533.

Bandura, A. (1997). *Self-efficacy: The exercise of control.* New York, NY: W. H. Freeman.

Baxter Magolda, M. B., & King, P. M. (2007). Interview strategies for assessing self-authorship: Constructing conversations to assess meaning making. *Journal of College Student Development, 48*(5), 491–508.

Beaven, A., & Spencer-Oatey, H. (2016). Cultural adaptation in different facets of life and the impact of language: A case study of personal adjustment patterns during study abroad. *Language and Intercultural Communication, 16*(3), 349–367.

Beelen, J., & Jones, E. (2015). Redefining internationalization at home. In A. Curai, L. Matei, R. Pricopie, J. Salmi & P. Scott (Eds.), *The European Higher Education Area: Between critical reflections and future policies* (pp. 59–72). Dordrecht: Springer.

Bennett, M. J. (1986). A developmental approach to training for intercultural sensitivity. *International Journal of Intercultural Relations, 10*(2), 179–196.

Bennett, M. J. (1993a). How not to be a fluent fool: Understanding the cultural dimension of language. *The Language Teacher, 27*(9), 16–21.

Bennett, M. J. (1993b). *Towards ethnorelativism: A developmental model of intercultural sensitivity.* Yarmouth, ME: Intercultural Press.

Biggs, J., & Tang, C. (2011). *Teaching for a quality learning at university* (4th ed.). New York, NY: McGraw-Hill Education.

Bowden, J. A., & Marten, F. (1998). *The university of learning: Beyond quality and competence in higher education.* London: Kogan Page.

Byram, M. (1997). *Teaching and assessing intercultural communicative competence.* Clevedon: Multilingual Matters.

Deardorff, D. K. (2015). *Desmystifying outcomes assessment for international educators: A practical approach.* Sterling, VA: Stylus Publishing.

Dörnyei, Z., & Ushioda, E. (2011). *Teaching and researching motivation* (2nd ed.). London: Routledge.

Dufon, M. A., & Churchill, E. (Eds.). (2006). *Language learners in study abroad contexts.* Clevedon: Multilingual Matters.

Fantini, A. E. (2006). About intercultural communicative competence: A construct. *Appendix E.* Retrieved from World Learning. SIT Digital Collections website http://digitalcollections.sit.edu/worldlearning_publications/1/

Fantini, A. E. (2019). *Intercultural communicative competence in educational exchange: A multinational perspective.* New York, NY: Routledge.

Forum on Education Abroad. (2015). *Standards of good practice for education abroad* (4th ed.). Northampton, MA: Forum on Education Abroad.

Freed, B. (1998). An overview of issues ad research in language learning in a study abroad setting. *Frontiers: The Interdisciplinary Journal of Study Abroad, Fall*(9), 31–60.

Freed, B. (Ed.). (1995). *Language learning in a study abroad context.* Amsterdam: John Benjamins.

Green, M., & Olson, C. (2003). *Internationalizing the campus: A user's guide.* Washington, DC: American Council on Education.

Greenholtz, J. F. (2005). Does intercultural sensitivity cross cultures? Validity issues in porting instruments across languages and cultures. *International Journal of Intercultural Relations, 29*(1), 73–89.

Isabelli-García, C. (2003). Development of oral communication skills abroad. *Frontiers: The Interdisciplinary Journal of Study Abroad, IX*(Fall), 149–173.

Isabelli-García, C. (2006). Study abroad social networks, motivation and attitudes: Implications for second language acquisition. In M. A. Dufon & E. Churchill (Eds.), *Language learning in study abroad contexts* (pp. 237–258). Clevedon: Multilingual Matters.

Jackson, J. (2008). *Language, identity and study abroad: Sociocultural pespectives.* London: Equinox Publishing.

Jackson, J. (2018). *Online intercultural education and study abroad.* London: Routledge.

Jones, E. (2010a). 'Don't worry about the worries': Transforming lives through international volunteering. In E. Jones (Ed.), *Internationalisation and the student voice: Higher education perspectives* (pp. 83–97). London: Routledge.

Jones, E. (2013). Internationalization and employability: The role of intercultural experiences in the development of transferable skills. *Public Money & Management, 33*(2), 95–104.

Jones, E. (Ed.). (2010b). *Internationalisation and the student voice: Higher education perspectives*. London: Routledge.

Kairé, S. (2018). *We are in the same boat, yet I am from another culture: The lived experiences of learning in groups during mobility* (Doctoral thesis). Vilnius University. Retrieved from https://www.vu.lt/naujienos/ivykiu-kalendorius

Kegan, R. (1994). *In over our heads: The mental demands of modern life*. Cambridge, MA: Harvard University Press.

Killick, D. (2015). *Developing the global student: Higher education in an era of globalization*. London: Routledge.

King, P. M., & Baxter Magolda, M. B. (2005). A developmental model of intercultural maturity. *Journal of College Student Development, 46*(6), 571–592.

Kinginger, C. (2009). *Language learning and study abroad: A critical reading of research*. New York, NY: Palgrave Macmillan.

Kolb, D. A. (1984). *Experience as the source of learning and development*. Englewood Cliffs, NJ: PTR Prentice Hall.

Krueger, J., & Dunning, D. (2009). Unskilled and unaware of It: How difficulties in recognizing one's own incompetence lead to inflated self-assessments. *Psychology, 1*, 30–46.

Leask, B. (2009). Using formal and informal curricula to improve interactions between home and international students. *Journal of Studies in International Education, 13*(2), 205–221.

Leask, B. (2015). *Internationalising the curriculum*. London: Routledge.

Liddicoat, A. J., Papademetre, L., Scarino, A., & Kohler, M. (2003). *Report on intercultural language learning*. Canberra: Department of Education, Science and Training.

Mellors-Bourne, R., Jones, E., Lawton, W., & Woodfield, S. (2015). Student perspectives on going international Retrieved from https://www.britishcouncil.org/sites/default/files/iu_bc_outwd_mblty_student_perception_sept_15.pdf

Mitchell, R., Tracy-Ventura, N., & McManus, K. (2017). *Anglophone students abroad: Identity, social relationships, and language learning*. London: Routledge.

Mitchell, R., Tracy-Ventura, N., & McManus, K. (Eds.). (2015). *Social interaction, identity and language learning during residence abroad*. Amsterdam: European Second Language Association.

Papatsiba, V. (2005). Student mobility in Europe: An academic, cultural and mental Journey? Some conceptual reflections and empirical findings. In M. Tight (Ed.), *International relations (International perspectives on higher education research)* (Vol. 3, pp. 29–65). Bingley: Emerald Group Publishing Limited.

Passareli, A. M., & Kolb, D. A. (2012). Using experiential learning theory to promote student learning and development in programs of education abroad. In M. Vande Berg, R. M. Paige & K. H. Lou (Eds.), *Student leaning abroad: What our students are learning, what they're not, and what we can do about it* (pp. 137–161). Sterling, VA: Stylus Publishing.

Perry, L. B., & Southwell, L. (2011). Developing intercultural understanding and skills: models and approaches. *Intercultural Education*, 22(6), 453–466.

Ryan, J. (2013). *Cross-cultural teaching and learning for home and international students*. Oxon: Routledge.

Severino, S., Messina, R., & Llorent, V. J. (2014). International student mobility: An identity development task? *International Journal of Humanities and Social Science*, 4(3), 89–103.

Spitzberg, B. H., & Changnon, G. (2009). Conceptualizing intercultural competence. In D. K. Deardorff (Ed.), *The Sage handbook of intercultural competence* (pp. 2–52). Thousand Oaks, CA: Sage.

Suskie, L. A. (2009). *Assessing student learning: A common sense guide* (2nd ed.). San Francisco, CA: Jossey-Bass.

Tanaka, K., & Ellis, R. (2003). Study-abroad, language proficiency, and learner beliefs about language learning. *JALT Journal*, 25(1), 63–85.

Teichler, U. (2004). Temporary study abroad: The life of Erasmus students. *European Journal of Education*, 39(4), 395–408.

Teichler, U., & Maiworm, F. (1997). The Erasmus students' experience: Major findings of the Erasmus evaluation research project. Retrieved from http://bookshop.europa.eu

Tsoukalas, J. (2008). The double life of Erasmus students. In M. Byram & F. Dervin (Eds.), *Students, staff and academic mobility in higher education* (pp. 131–152). Newcastle upon Tyne: Cambridge Scholars Publishing.

Twombly, S. B., Salisbury, M. H., Shannon, D. T., & Klute, P. (2012). Study abroad in a new global century: Renewing the promise, redifining the purpose. *ASHE Higher Education Report*, 38. San Francisco, CA: Jossey-Bass.

Vande Berg, M., Paige, R. M., & Lou, K. H. (2012). Student learning abroad: Paradigms and assumptions. In M. Vande Berg, R. M. Paige & K. H. Lou (Eds.), *Student leaning abroad: What our students are learning, what they're not, and what we can do about it* (pp. 3–28). Sterling, VA: Stylus Publishing.

Wiggins, G. P., & McTighe, J. (2005). *Understanding by design* (2nd ed.). Alexandria, VA: Association for Supervision and Curriculum Development.

Part III

Implications of an interdisciplinary approach

Chapter 7

Conclusions

About Chapter 7

This concluding chapter addresses the implications of an interdisciplinary approach to understanding student mobility comprehensively.

The first section of the chapter summarises the key messages of the preceding six chapters and the practical applications of the interdisciplinary approach in which they are anchored. Having done so, I reflect upon the limitations of the research journey in Part II of this volume. In the closing section, I return to the book's central argument: that an agenda for theorising student mobility should be interdisciplinary. Organised into dichotomies, this final reflection paints a forward vision by polarising ten fundamental premises or leverage points for further reasoning and critical evaluation of the existing body of knowledge about student mobility in European higher education. This evaluation is substantiated by the book findings and urges specific actions with regard to research, practice and policy in student mobility.

Book summary

Based on the overview of the research landscape of student mobility in European higher education in Chapters 1 through 3 – against the conceptual, methodological and educational foundations of an interdisciplinary approach – it was possible to dialogue across a range of disciplines and theories painting this very landscape. Together, these three chapters demonstrated that student mobility is an area of study in which a vast stock of disciplinary literature has been accumulated, only a modicum of which was reviewed in the first part of this book.

My main goal in Part I was to invite readers to explore the foundations for approaching student mobility from an interdisciplinary perspective. Chapters 1 and 2 reviewed some of the literatures in which this plurality of disciplinary understandings is sourced by charting the variables characterising student mobility. In doing so, I sought to reverse the prevailing normative thinking about student mobility, insofar as the application of disciplinary frameworks usually precedes the identification of the variables of interest. Chapters 1 and 2, in contrast, used variables as focal points for bridging disconnected literatures and, thus, reveal the disciplinary parts of student mobility research and scholarship.

Among the disciplines and subdisciplines identified in Chapters 1 and 2 are: applied linguistics, language education, psychology, sociology, anthropology, human geography, general education, comparative and international education, intercultural education, to name but a few. While these disciplines tend to investigate different parts of student mobility, there may be areas of overlap. That is, cases where the variables of interest may be the same (as in the example of social networks approached from sociological, psychological and linguistic standpoints – see Chapter 1). But even in such cases, perspectives differ.

In student mobility, as in other areas of multidisciplinary interest, readers should create a common ground between conflicting disciplinary views to speak with a joint voice on a problem of mutual interest. Deconstructing disciplinary angles (and their stakes on reality) is crucial to gain an integrated understanding of student mobility as a complex whole. Hence the conceptual diagram in Chapter 1 (reproduced here in Figure 7.1) and the interplay between the part and the whole.

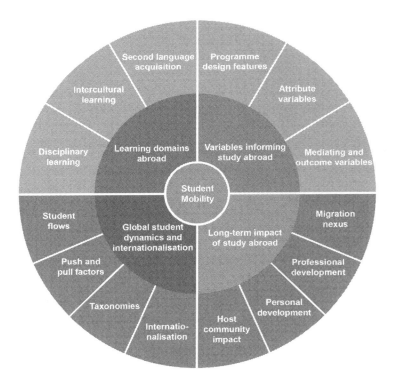

Figure 7.1 Conceptual diagram of student mobility research and scholarship in European higher education.

The interdisciplinary diagram can be used as a tool that gives structure and direction to the process of researching or understanding student mobility in European higher education while providing a framework for developing practice. By pinning down relevant literature by research foci, the diagram can assist readers in identifying different facets of student mobility.

For readers conducting research on student mobility (either established academics or postgraduate students), the diagram can provide a useful guide at different points of the research process. At the outset of a research project, researchers can use the diagram to guide literature searches and define their problem or research question with greater systematicity and reflexivity (aware that there can be insights from more than one discipline). Additionally, readers new to the field of education abroad can use this tool in conjunction with Box 1.1 in Chapter 1 to find relevant sources of specialised information on the internationalisation of higher education and education abroad.

In more advanced stages of the research process, readers can use the conceptual diagram to revisit their work. The practical applications of the diagram at this stage are: to help readers to identify knowledge gaps and disciplinary biases in their own work; and to evaluate the insights and theories gathered and ascertain if they can be integrated, or even, if additional literature searches are needed.

From a practitioner and policy-making perspective, the conceptual diagram can facilitate cross-fertilisation between *research*, *practice* and *policy* by systematising relevant pockets of information about student mobility. In centring around variables of interest instead of disciplinary frameworks (and lexicon), the tool encourages a problem-based dialogue that can leverage joint agendas to a quality study abroad experience.

More than anything else, I see the interdisciplinary approach in this book as a way to foster an active dialogue across various disciplines and stakeholders. Let us take as an example the piece of the conceptual diagram addressing programme design components (Box 1.3, Chapter 1). This facet of student mobility is strongly linked to the professionalisation of education abroad as evidenced by the professional resources available on the topic, albeit primarily from a North-American perspective – e.g., NAFSA's *Guide for Education Abroad* (Wiedenhoeft, Hernandez, & Wicke, 2014) or *The Guide to Successful Short-term Programs Abroad* (Chieffo & Spaeth, 2017) and the Forum on Education Abroad *Standards of Good Practice* (Forum on Education Abroad, 2015). Less well-known among faculty and scholarly communities in European higher education, study abroad programme design demonstrates how important it is to break down different types of knowledge (whether deriving from academic research or professional practice) to facilitate communication among the several actors in education abroad.

Overall, the main functions of the conceptual diagram are, to: (1) assist literature searches, (2) identify relevant disciplines and theories (to understand student mobility), (3) ascertain lacunas in knowledge or overlooked scholarship, (4) recognise the limits of our own reasoning and/or disciplinary emphasis and (5)

222 Implications of an interdisciplinary approach

bridge the gap between research, practice and policy. In becoming more mindful of our own disciplinary biases and the efforts of other disciplines to understand student mobility, we open the door to find new meanings, assemble new sets of solutions and create knowledge in socially responsible and reflective ways. Opening this door requires not only incorporating conceptual insights from different disciplines and literatures, but also strong analytical skills, to which I turned my attention in Chapter 3.

The subject of this chapter was the operational foundations of an interdisciplinary approach to think broadly about student mobility. This was done in three regards, by: (1) exploring the linkage between disciplinary methods and theories in student mobility research and scholarship, (2) demonstrating the analytical power of mixed methods in providing fuller and more evidenced-based responses to student mobility and (3) relating the philosophical outlooks shared by mixed methods and interdisciplinary research, and the role of integration in both literatures.

The first part of the chapter summarised common research methodologies and methods to investigate student mobility. Additionally, this summary identified major methodological setbacks and improvements of European student mobility research and scholarship from the 1990s to the present day. This overview may help readers conducting investigations on student mobility to make informed decisions about methodological approaches. By having a good working knowledge of the methodological challenges permeating the field of education abroad, researchers can resolve with greater focus and efficacy the procedural obstacles encountered during the research process. Moreover, this awareness is crucial to convey how the methodological features of our studies sit within the broader methodological content area of the field of education abroad and how the findings we arrived at can contribute to improve its practice.

In the second part of Chapter 3, particular attention was paid to the explanatory power of mixed methods in enabling a more relational account of student mobility through the same integrative habit of mind advocated by interdisciplinary research. This habit of mind requires evaluating knowledge claims between and across disciplinary domains, as well as the supporting empirical evidence and methods employed.

In mixed methods, as in interdisciplinary research, the synthesis inherent to the integration of different insights is generally considered central to the research process. Within mixed methods, this involves blending in quantitative and qualitative inferences through strategies and/or elements like the ones identified in Chapter 3. These strategies can assist researchers in developing their own mixed methods studies and explaining the added value of mixed approaches. Among these strategies are: (1) frameworks or terminology to explain the reasons for mixing methods, (2) procedural diagrams to illustrate research steps and/or activities, (3) research designs to plan out mixed methods studies, (4) data analysis strategies to integrate quantitative and qualitative data, (5) metaphors to describe the process of integrating data analyses and (6) the integration of 'competing'

Conclusions   223

epistemologies or paradigms. Conducting mixed methods research takes considerable time and effort, primarily because of the difficulty in mastering multiple methods but also due to the vast specialised literature and lexicon. The overview of mixed methods in Chapter 3 offers an initial roadmap (particularly to readers new to this approach) to take stock of essential literature on mixed methods and some of its key concepts and pressing issues. Naturally, a more advanced knowledge of mixed methods is outside the remit of this book.

Assuming that the foundational substructure within which student mobility is housed should be interdisciplinary, the second part of the book – Practical applications – laid out ways in which (some of) the theories identified in Part I can be interspersed to develop a more holistic analysis of student mobility in European higher education. The cultural immersion experiences of 50 sojourners in Portugal and the UK were at the heart of the three chapters that formed Part II – Chapters 4 to 6.

In coming to examine these experiences from various disciplinary lenses, insofar as possible for a single researcher, different theoretical frames were combined to provide sustained responses to questions raised by the chronological instances of the sojourn, specifically, Pre-departure (Chapter 4), Adaptation (Chapter 5), and Outcomes and transformations (Chapter 6). The questions brought about by the chronological unfolding of the sojourn of *exchange students, international students* and *highly skilled immigrants* led, in turn, to more general questions about student mobility in European post-secondary education. The process involved a dialectic interplay between theories, methods and sojourner voices that attests to the explanatory power of interdisciplinarity. Reading through the chapters made the fit between theoretical foundations (Part I) and practical applications (Part II) of an interdisciplinary approach become progressively visible.

Chapter 4 offered a retrospective examination of variable groupings characterising the sojourn pre-departure stages: (1) Language biography, (2) Motivations, (3) Mobility capital and (4) Steps into mobility. Together these variable groupings assessed (part of) the stock of dispositions, skills and social habits sojourners accumulated before the stay abroad. In terms of the practical applications for readers, these variable groupings can be used as broad units of analysis to guide other studies entailing a retrospective examination of sojourner experiences and skills that may have a bearing on the period of studies abroad. Likewise, the pre-experience questionnaire in Appendix 4.1 can serve as a tool to benchmark and operationalise pre-sojourn variables. While some of the variables in the questionnaire may be situational, others may resonate with the experiences of other sojourners engaged in the same type of sojourn in other European higher education contexts. Hence the need to pilot and adapt this instrument to the contexts and sojourners under scrutiny.

In the theoretical perspective, sociological, second language acquisition and intercultural learning theories were combined to consider the experiences of the 50 sojourners in this book against quantitative and qualitative data. Overall, sojourner accumulated cultural and social capital (Bourdieu, 1979) and its correlation to intercultural development was more alike between highly skilled immigrants and international students. Yet, the logic of *exercise*, which is also inherent to this capital, through the notion of *habitus*, showed that the social dimension abroad was experienced in more similar ways by exchange and international students. Sharing a young age range and marked by an agenda of active experimentation, both student groups deemed the 'yearning for novelty' a top motivation to study in Portugal and the UK. For international students, this impetus went on a par with academic learning and the prestige of world-class universities. Exchange students, in turn, emphasised international career prospects and the possibility of learning a foreign language. The motives of immigrants were naturally different and related to family reasons and/or professional added-value.

The initial period abroad is followed by an adjustment phase, firmly anchored in socialisation processes and the routes taken by sojourners to enter host societies. This phase was narrated in Chapter 5 by deploying theories from sociology, psychology and education to integrate quantitative and qualitative data. Concepts and/or notions from sociology of space, social support and situated learning theories were paramount to develop the qualitative categories that broke down sojourner experiences of adaptation. The social construction processes sojourners engaged in were captured through the following variable groupings: (a) Living conditions, (b) Preferred social activities and host culture facilities, (c) Social networks and social support and (d) Integration in the local community.

As in Chapter 4, these groupings can be used as broad units of analysis to ascertain the variables characterising the different phases of the sojourn experience, in this case the in-country phase. The post-experience questionnaire in Appendix 5.1 shows possible ways to operationalise these variables. It should be noted, however, that due to the one-academic-year time frame of the two empirical studies, the post-experience questionnaire measured both sojourners' in-country experiences and the outcomes reaped. The possibility of running a study with greater longitudinal scope would enable a more fine-grained grasp of changes happening in the long run.

With regard to the key findings of Chapter 5, what stood out as the most striking finding for me (possibly, not the same as to the reader) was that the *duration* of the cultural immersion and the *host context* appeared to have a more prominent role in sojourners' adaption than the '*strangeness of the situation*' (Murphy-Lejeune, 2002) and sojourners' *context of entry* (as students or migrants). This is not to say that the ways sojourners entered host societies were irrelevant for their adaptation. For instance, the socio-professional roles of immigrant participants enabled the formation of social networks minimally extended to hosts, even if language and social hurdles were experienced by all three groups.

The *duration* of the stay abroad emerged quite strongly among exchange and international students given that most of them were immersed for a limited time period (one academic year). The return home loomed on the horizon for both student groups, even if the academic purposes of their stays differed. Possibly

Conclusions 225

because of this, peer social networks were more actively sought by mobile students than immigrant participants, although the 'international bubble' was common to all.

The sheer social intensity of a stay abroad limited in time was made visible through the social activities mobile students engaged in with their peers. These activities took place in 'multilingual and lingua franca environments' (Mitchell, Tracy-Ventura, & McManus, 2017) reified by the tightly knit social networks formed solely of student travellers. Resembling 'communities of practice', in that learning occurred through social co-participation (Lave & Wenger, 1991), peer communities were a source of positive intercultural learning as documented by other study abroad studies (e.g., Montgomery, 2010; Schartner, 2015; Young, Sercombe, Sachdev, Naeb, & Schartner, 2013). However, Chapter 5 also challenged this assertion, since these closely knit communities may also mitigate sojourner culture-specific gains.

There is a dual condition in learning from social co-participation in study abroad. The communities of practice formed by mobile students can function as a 'shelter' against feelings of isolation and a source of culture-general learning, but also as a 'fence' hampering actual socialisation between sojourners and hosts and, by implication, culture-specific learning. The negative effects of the latter came to the fore due to the different host contexts of the two student groups, namely because the host language (Portuguese) and the language of communication and identification (English) were not the same for exchange students.

In missing out culture-specific elements of the stay abroad, sojourners may have stayed at the doorstep of adaptation, away from rich intercultural interactions with hosts. Sojourner integration into the local communities of Aveiro (Portugal) and Newcastle (UK) was characterised by a fulfilling social life, but largely independent from the host community.

To probe further into sojourner integration into local communities, quantitative and qualitative inferences were brought together by mixing different data types and methods (thematic and statistical). Through the application of the Kruskal–Wallis test, the qualitative themes of sojourner integration into host communities – Uprootedness, Cityness and Rootedness through Others – were triangulated with the ordinal scores attributed by participants to the extent they felt at home in Aveiro and Newcastle.

More importantly, the use of Kruskal–Wallis in Chapter 5 demonstrated how the integration of multiple measures and data sources can enhance interpretations of data. By seeking convergence of results, it was possible to create an upward spiral of data clarification that enlightened the relative positions of three analytical categories on an adaptation continuum (see Figure 5.6). The post-hoc comparisons of these categories helped to clarify the interpretations of the qualitative data set. Of the three combinations, Cityness//Rootedness was the only pairwise comparison which did not yield a statistically significant result. In practice, while before the application of the statistical test I was tempted to conclude (based on the analysis of the qualitative data alone) that Cityness was clearly distinct from

Rootedness through Others, upon realising that the distribution of responses was not significantly different I formed another hypothesis. Cityness was, therefore, placed on the middle of the adaptation continuum in that participant geographic proximity to the host cities did not necessarily exclude socio-spatial relations. As in Rootedness, Others may have been an element of spatial appropriation but were omitted in participant discourse.

To summarise, the application of the Kruskal–Wallis test in Chapter 5 is a practical example of integration in that the quantitative and qualitative data strands produced findings greater than the sum of the parts, thereby shedding light on the nuances of sojourner immersion in host communities. Although I do not have a formula for integrating data analyses, my practical advice to readers is to start by browsing the specialised mixed methods literature in Chapter 3 and re-examining their data to look for problems or questions in which they feel the meshing of data can unfold nuances of student mobility that cannot be captured through one data source or method alone.

Reading on, Chapter 6 disclosed that the evaluation of the sojourn may not necessarily match the expectations of the initial period abroad. Thus, while Chapter 4 showed that exchange students in Portugal were the most plurilingual group, Chapter 6 revealed they were also the group in which expectations of host language proficiency (Portuguese) were largely unmet at the end of the sojourn.

The contrast between pre-departure and resulting motivational dispositions was stark for those exchange students participating in the *Campus Europae* programme. Having departed from low levels of host language proficiency but deeming language learning a top motivation to study abroad, *Campus Europae* students were the sojourners progressing the least linguistically. The mismatch between their language learning outcomes and programme goals demonstrates the negative implications that the absence of a line of inquiry on study abroad programme design may have on student learning. Hence the urge to create a common ground to discuss these sorts of issues among all stakeholders involved in education abroad.

That is also why I made the case (in Chapter 1) for developing multiple-criterion classification schemes of European study abroad programmes. By focusing on programme design components and goals, the learnings of credit-seeking students in European universities would be more readily assessed and acted upon. Educational impact in exchange programmes is all the more important since, within the outcomes in Chapter 6, academic gains were frequently deemed a low by exchange students, thus questioning the default assumption of European student exchange as an inevitable success story. Perhaps in part because credit-seeking student mobility has been a tangible avenue to realise the EU integration project, and in part because *Erasmus+* is also a major funding source of European higher education, centralised monitoring and evaluation systems of credit-seeking students' learning abroad have not been readily assumed by academic nor policy circles.

Within the other learning and developmental domains in Chapter 6 – Personal, Linguistic, Intercultural – it was in the personal realm where positive gains were

Conclusions   227

reaped by all three sojourner groups. Yet, these gains may also hinge upon the relative importance assigned by mobile students (exchange and international) to personal growth and/or maturation in the face of other learning domains. For immigrant participants the personal side of living abroad meant something different, being equated with a sense of personal fulfilment related to family life or professional realisations.

Intercultural outcomes were a mixed blessing for all three sojourner groups. Interwoven with the social dynamics of host societies and friendship groups, as demonstrated by Chapter 5, the discussion in Chapter 6 focused on formal intercultural learning, specifically, on the short-term impact of an intercultural intervention upon the intercultural gains of exchange students and highly skilled immigrants in Portugal. The positive impact of the intervention came to reinforce the increasing calls from interculturalists, study abroad scholars and practitioners for purposeful intercultural pedagogy during the study abroad cycle (for a review see Chapter 1, Learning domains abroad).

In describing the design and impact of the intercultural intervention with the 31 sojourners in Portugal, practical curriculum and assessment guidelines for designing outcomes-based intercultural interventions were defined (see Curriculum and assessment guidelines, Chapter 6). These guidelines should be read in conjunction with the typology of intercultural constructs in Chapter 2 (Table 2.3), since the adopted intercultural construct(s) will have implications for the pedagogical design of the intervention. This does not mean readers ought to be confined to one single intercultural model, especially if they feel one model alone is insufficient to capture the learning and developmental areas targeted by their intervention.

As in interdisciplinary research, finding a common ground between different disciplinary theories and conceptualisations (of intercultural constructs in this case) is essential to produce a fine-grained understanding of complex issues like intercultural learning and development in study abroad. The integrated intercultural model (or framework, to be fair) in Chapter 6 emerged precisely from the difficulty to explain the nuances of participant intercultural learning and development through one model alone. Building on the meaning systems of two developmental and two co-orientational intercultural models, the best elements of these explanations were integrated to form a more holistic framework of participant intercultural development and learning. More importantly, the integration of different conceptualisations demonstrated that in intercultural learning and development, as in other domains of study abroad, some facets are not apparent in disciplinary isolation.

Limitations

As in any scientific inquiry, there are limitations to research findings or issues that were perhaps not explored in as much depth as they deserve. Two important points should be underscored.

First, and with regard to the two empirical studies underpinning this book, the qualitative selection method of a sample of 50 sojourners should be acknowledged. While relying on a sample that cannot numerically capture the diversity of the mobile student experience in an equally heterogeneous European higher education, the breadth of variables sought, along with the richness of responses, and how they relate to existing theory and research across disciplines, contributed to advancing an interdisciplinary understanding of student mobility. Hence the balance sought between the theoretical foundations (Part I) and practical applications (Part II) of an interdisciplinary approach.

There is always a compromise in the methodological decisions made during a research journey. In opting for probabilistic samples we test patterns based on a finite number of combinations, but it may come at the expense of losing sight of the individual realities of those we investigate. Equally, a qualitative approach centred on participant voices may fail to capture bigger picture issues. For instance, I am cognisant that the examination of student mobility primarily from the point of view of the sojourner limited the understanding of the country-specific and institutional realities that mediate sojourner experiences. Not that the macro- and meso-level dynamics infused by the national and institutional contexts are irrelevant; they are important indeed and the data would benefit from further investigation from this perspective. Despite this limitation, it was by putting sojourner narratives at the centre of Part II of the book that I was able to move back and forth between the variables under scrutiny and relevant theories (and their disciplines). Ultimately, it was the dialectic interplay between the two inquiry-guided studies and the links with existing theory and research that enhanced the scope of the book.

The second point I want to make concerns the composite conceptual architecture of the book and the risks of working at the borders of multiple disciplines. Two immediate risks are appropriating work from disciplines in an uncritical manner and underestimating the complexity interdisciplinarity entails.

Naturally, I cannot go into the same the depth as experts in the individual disciplines employed in this book, but at the same time it is this engagement with various disciplines that leads to new forms knowledge. Conscious of the limitations of proposing an interdisciplinary approach based on the insights of one individual, I still came to the conclusion that the awareness raised would compensate for the limitations of my own reasoning and academic background.

As asserted by Repko and Szostak (2017) 'Interdisciplinary research is a process where the necessarily incomplete research of one scholar is built upon by others. No research is ever completely comprehensive' (p. 121). It is in this sense that I see the contribution of this book – as a step towards a collaborative dialogue between all of us who are interested in furthering knowledge about student mobility and improving education abroad; stated another way,

Conclusions   229

a step towards developing a dialogue in which disciplines are not normative umbrellas where we shelter under a shared opinion oblivious to the efforts of others.

Looking towards the future

In my mind, a retrospective examination of any academic book should bolster a prospective outlook by instilling in readers a desire to look forward and seek out new grounds based on the set of trails mapped out during the reading journey. To paint a forward vision, this section offers an evaluation of the book's contributions to an interdisciplinary agenda for theorising student mobility in European higher education and, through it, more informed ways to improve education abroad.

Throughout the writing of *Understanding Student Mobility in Europe: An Interdisciplinary Approach* I have demonstrated that within student mobility research and inquiry, the present need is for collaborative knowledge production which integrates adventurousness of disciplinary perspectives, breadth of application and clarity of implications for further research and practice. Different variables or facets of student mobility were brought together in this volume via an interdisciplinary approach. In defining variables as the lines of demarcation, it was possible to trace the conceptual and methodological range of reference of student mobility research and scholarship, identify blind spots and questions falling between the cracks. The many discussion questions threaded throughout the book highlighted some existing contradictions in student mobility theory and practice.

Building on these questions, in this closing section I tabulate ten sets of dichotomies to form premises that may serve as starting points to leverage an interdisciplinary agenda for understanding student mobility in European higher education. In coming to see the dichotomies of each premise not as separate categories but as ends of a continuum with different positions in between, the reader will be more likely driven by the 'both/and' thinking underpinning a comprehensive understanding of student mobility.

Figure 7.2 sketches out the dichotomies of each premise. Because these premises were brought about by individual book chapters, on the left of Figure 7.2 the reader can find the identification of chapters alongside the corresponding premises. All ten premises are explained at length afterwards (both in terms of the implications and applications for further research, practice and policy).

As recurrent throughout the book, my explanations are as concerned with contextualisation as with perspective-taking, two fundamental aspects of interdisciplinarity (Repko & Szostak, 2017).

230 Implications of an interdisciplinary approach

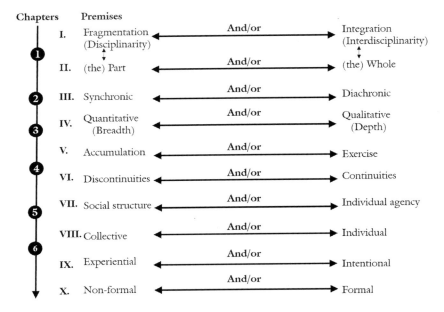

Figure 7.2 Major dichotomies of an interdisciplinary approach to understand student mobility.

These explanations sit also within my views of the current state of the art of knowledge on student mobility in European higher education and are, at times, presented with a sceptical bent. To the reader, I leave the following reflective questions:

1. What is your interpretation of the need for an interdisciplinary approach to advance the current body of knowledge on student mobility?
2. In what ways can this approach help bridge the gap between theory and practice in education abroad?
3. Where would you position yourself on each continuum with regard to the dichotomies presented in Figure 7.2?
4. Does your position reflect a specific disciplinary emphasis?
5. Are there any other dichotomies you would add?

Premises I and II: the part (fragmentation) and the whole (integration)

As discussed in Chapters 1 and 2, the mid-1990s in Europe witnessed the start of disciplinary interest in post-secondary student mobility. The zeitgeist of interest in the last and current decades in particular led to fast-developing repositories of knowledge, but with it also came fragmentation and polarisation of understandings (Premise I).

Conclusions 231

The contributions by interested disciplines have tended to specialise in different parts and/or variables of student mobility without necessarily looking at the totality of the study abroad experience. Seeing the parts in relation to the whole is, however, as important as seeing the whole in relation to its constituent parts (Premise II). In being able to promote a broader dialogue between the various wings of knowledge, the practice of interdisciplinarity allows researchers and practitioners alike to better appreciate the nuanced complexities of student mobility.

More importantly, fostering synergies between diverse perspectives and systematising multiple pockets of knowledge is crucial to advance an agenda for theorising student mobility as an area of study and professional practice. Developing this joint agenda can, in turn, facilitate the identification of fundamental considerations for policy-making (at national/institutional/sector levels) on what constitutes a quality study abroad experience in contemporary European higher education. This includes considerations regarding the design and delivery of study abroad programmes (discussed later on in Premise IX).

Premise III: synchronic and diachronic perspectives

In addition to systematising and evaluating knowledge claims on student mobility across interested disciplines, both synchronic and diachronic perspectives should be taken into account. Premise III is anchored in this need to systematise knowledge at a point in and over time – the synchronic and diachronic perspectives, respectively. The typological and chronological synopses in Chapter 2 draw on this complementarity by surveying current modalities and terminologies of student mobility in European tertiary-level education while placing this overview in an historical context.

Although receiving insufficient attention in Europe, historical accounts of student mobility are paramount to trace the evolution of the field and clarify its semantic ambiguities. In North America, study abroad scholars like Hoffa and de Paul showed, through a two-volume history of US study abroad, how the documentation of the past can contribute to bring meaning and coherence to the field (see Hoffa, 2007; Hoffa & de Paul, 2010).

While the brief historical summary in Chapter 2 is far from the impressive overview by Hoffa and de Paul, it allowed me to cut through some of the confusion regarding overlapping typologies and indistinct or misapplied terminology of student mobility in contemporary European higher education.

Among the practical applications of Chapter 2 is a taxonomy that can be used by education abroad scholars, practitioners and policy-makers for categorising different types of student mobility according to key descriptors, namely: (1) Academic purpose, (2) Nature (of the academic movement), (3) Direction, (4) Duration and (5) Level of study. A practical illustration of this taxonomy across six types of (physical) student mobility is provided in Table 2.1. This application is, by no means, exhaustive and leaves a further challenge – to expand this glossary through the joint efforts of education abroad scholars, practitioners and policy-makers. It is critically important that all three stakeholder groups work together on a set of agreed-upon definitions, especially because different terms permeate academic, practitioner and policy circles.

Premise IV: breadth and depth

The fourth premise of an interdisciplinary agenda for theorising student mobility points to an enhanced awareness of methodological options. The implications brought about by this premise address research practice and are, therefore, of primary interest to academics.

Chapter 3 made the case for the unmatched ability of mixed methods in heightening our awareness of the synergies between methods and results. Hence the importance of cross-validating results using multiple methods. Opting for quantitative methods will generally allow for breadth through deductive approaches, while a qualitative approach will seek depth or knowledge generated inductively. Both approaches are important and useful, and both have strengths and limitations. An interdisciplinary approach to student mobility should be open to quantitative and qualitative methods as, in many cases, a more balanced use between the two may be key to capturing the complexity of this multifaceted phenomenon.

It is in this middle ground position that I believe student mobility research and scholarship is still missing. Furthering this middle-ground methodological stance can further education abroad as a mature area of study producing sound empirical evidence to support its claims. In encouraging education abroad scholars to look at both quantitative and qualitative research, mixed methods can bolster the development of rigorous research agendas of the methodological content area of the field. Five major advantages are: (1) assessing the robustness and validity of existing studies, (2) orienting scholars new to field of education abroad, (3) establishing the field as a mature area of inquiry (beyond anecdotal accounts of student experiences and single-institution case studies), (4) developing research that is overtly evidence-based and (5) setting methodological directions for future research.

Premise V: accumulation and exercise

The logic of accumulation and exercise in Premise V was made clear through the application of Bourdieu's theory of capital in Chapter 4. Simply put, evidence in this chapter has shown that neither the experiences sojourners engaged in before the stay abroad nor those furthered while abroad can be ignored. Individual agency in student mobility is made of an accumulated capital, but also of desires and actions related to the lived experience abroad. As demonstrated by Chapter 6, these desires can change as the sojourn unfolds and students alter their actions as they encounter new stimuli and challenges abroad.

In terms of practical applications, Premise V urges education abroad researchers and practitioners to reconceptualise study abroad as an integrated experience in individuals' lifelong learning journeys. This involves looking at *discontinuities* and *continuities* of student trajectories and learning with respect to past and present, both in terms of research measurement and outcomes assessment.

For researchers, this implies accounting for pre-mobility variables and determining their bearing on the study abroad experience. For education abroad practitioners and educators (whose students include mobile students), the implementation of ongoing assessment is fundamental to ascertain how well student learning goals are achieved and can be improved. This also brings implications for policy-making, namely in clarifying who retains the locus of control over monitoring and evaluation systems of student learning abroad. The incorporation of these systems into the design and delivery of the *Campus Europae* programme, for example, could have mitigated the linguistic underachievement of the *Campus Europae* student group in Portugal. Implementation of these systems is crucial for defining realistic learning outcomes and ensuring its clear evaluation (beyond ad hoc initiatives of faculty).

Premise VI: discontinuities and continuities

Another way to balance out the dichotomy of Accumulation//Exercise (Premise V) is questioning whether our emphasis is on *continuities* or *discontinuities*, not only in time but also in space. Two key points are worth underscoring with regard to the implications of failing to address *continuities* and *discontinuities* of student mobility in time (present/past/future) and space (here/there).

First of all, the isolation of student mobility as an enclave in time has, to some extent, underestimated the link between sojourners and the broader educational journey, not so much in terms of their future aspirations (scrutinised in the migration nexus literature, see Chapter 1) but in past mobility trajectories, specifically, the implications that early mobility experiences may have on the learning gains of mobile students in higher education. This lacuna permeates the disconnect between the internationalisation of secondary and higher education, an emerging research topic (e.g., Baiutti, 2019; Rizvi, 2017; Van Gaalen & Freiertag, 2018) that promises to receive renewed attention in European policy debates through the realisation of a European Education Area.

The second point addresses the space logics underpinning student mobility. Students' individual agency is embedded in social space and its dynamics (see Chapter 5).

The incorporation of findings from recent research in human geography, sociology of migration and urban anthropology, exploring the role of place in student mobility, may shine new light on this overlooked aspect of the student experience (see Chapter 1, Long-term impact of study abroad). Equally, recent literature on the internationalisation of higher education is providing valuable insights into the local realities underpinning internationalisation processes and student mobility (e.g., de Wit, Gacel-Ávila, Jones, & Jooste, 2017; Jones, Coelen, Beelen, & de Wit, 2016). Other international educators like Larsen (2016) assert the significance of shifting to a post-structuralist spatial analysis to rethink processes and effects in student mobility.

234 Implications of an interdisciplinary approach

The immediate implications for research and practice are the need to think relationally about the socio-spatial forms of student mobility by combining multi-layered units of analysis that attend to macro/micro dynamics, the global/local, space/place, time/place and emic/etic perspectives.

Premise VII: social structures and individual agency

As noted in Chapter 4, the balance between *social structures* and *agency* is a long-standing debate in sociology, but also a conundrum in student mobility research and scholarship.

Building on the two previous premises, Premise VII segues into our discussion on the time, space and place logics underpinning student mobility. The current premise puts into perspective the relation between social structure and individual agency. The emphasis on either side of the continuum has implications for the ways the study abroad experience is conceptualised, and the role of student agency in the construction and reconstruction of this very experience. Finding a point of balance between structure and agency, as advocated in modern social theory, is essential to developing a more nuanced understanding between student agency and the influence of the socio-structural contexts students transition *from* and *into*. In the end, privileging agency over structure or vice versa may shape how we look at and interpret student mobility.

Premise VIII: collective and individual

The eighth point of our agenda builds on the previous premise by drawing attention to the balance between the *collective* and *individual* aspects of the study abroad experience.

Teasing out the effect of the peer group in study abroad can clarify the role of group dynamics in enabling and constraining actions and outcomes of studying abroad. As Chapters 4 and 5 have demonstrated, there were close connections between the group life of mobile students and the ways they apprehended host contexts. Chapter 6 added to this analysis by showing that group processes can also influence the outcomes of the experience.

Looking at the study abroad experience longitudinally, it is interesting to note that although it often starts as an individual experience it quickly becomes a group experience in which group dynamics shape part of the opportunities and outcomes accruing from the stay abroad. In a comparison between European and North-American study abroad, de Wit (2002) deemed the former an indivual unsupervised experience, and the latter collective and supervised given the abundance of faculty-led study abroad programmes in the US.

The longitudinal examination of the student experiences in this book shows that while study abroad can, indeed, start as an individual experience (although some institutions give students the opportunity to meet beforehand), it is likely to end as a collective experience. This is particularly true for exchange students.

Probing further into group procesess abroad can throw light on the interactions and learnings taking place in mobile student groups, the areas in which educators and institutions can intervene (for example, to enhace interaction between domestic and mobile students) and the use of group dynamics to harness interculturality on campus. For instance, institutional internationalisation at home agendas could build on these synergies to offer extra-curricular activities for intercultural development in and outside the academic classroom. In contemporary European higher education, we often come across valuable non-formal activities promoted by student and local organisations (like the ones in Chapter 5), or even informal initieaves by personally organised student groups, which could be maximised through their incorporation into institutional internationalisation strategic plans.

Premise IX: experiential and intentional

Chapter 6 questioned how much of the study abroad experience should be left to student devices (*experiential*) and how much of it should be *intentional*.

Part of the meaning of studying abroad will remain with 'student travellers' themselves, but there is also a great deal that can be investigated and acted upon. Since this book has demonstrated that the current emphasis is on the experiential end of Premise IX, in the following pages I outline practical suggestions or recommendations for making the value of study abroad more purposeful. These recommendations are organised into different domains – policy, research and practice – and specify the targeted student population, i.e., exchange students, international students or both (referred to as mobile students as in the rest of the book), as follows:

For policy: to define, develop and enact: (1) language policies that establish the language of instruction for exchange students (in non-Anglophone countries) and provision of appropriate language support, (2) centralised evaluation systems and standards for assessing exchange students' learning (assessment standards for academic learning are paramount given the current ad hoc practices across European post-secondary institutions), (3) teacher training and/or faculty capacity building for teaching mobile students, (4), support systems for integrating mobile students and enhancing interaction with their domestic counterparts (e.g., the incorporation of non-formal intercultural activities into institutional strategizing);

For research and practice: to: (1) develop orientations throughout the study abroad cycle (see Curriculum and assessment guidelines, Chapter 6), (2) embed these orientations into study abroad programme design and delivery, (3) support and monitor the study abroad experience (e.g., through the allocation of an advisor or tutor), (4) pilot the length of time required to attain varying levels of host language proficiency (to avoid unrealistic learning goals as in the *Campus Europae* programme), (5) define plausible and articulated learning goals that take into account the duration of the period of studies abroad and type of programme, (6) connect and align research and practice in education abroad and in the design and delivery of quality exchange programmes.

At a time when mobile students are part and parcel of the daily life of post-secondary institutions, bringing benefits to academic and civic communities alike, it is imperative to ensure that the benefits to the students themselves are as positive as we would like to believe or as warranted by the investment. Hopefully, the recommendations offered here can encourage further discussions on what constitutes a quality study abroad experience in contemporary European higher education, and contribute to shifting the focus from an increase in participation to purposeful educational impact.

Premise X: non-formal and formal

The tenth and last premise of an interdisciplinary agenda for theorising student mobility concerns the articulation between the non-formal and formal learning dimensions of study abroad, often set in opposition, as Chapter 6 has shown.

At student level, the lived experiences of sojourners have, at times, diverted our attention from the work that still needs to be done to make the formal educational value of student mobility (particularly credit-seeking) clear and rewarding. Within the formal, non-formal and informal learning continuum, more synergies should be sought for an enhanced study abroad experience. Within the institutional realm, the disconnect between formal and non-formal activities has, to some extent, overlooked student learning on university campuses and links to local communities. Valuable initiatives developed by student unions, support services and local organisations go frequently unnoticed by higher education institutions (leading sometimes to their discontinuation as I argued elsewhere – Almeida, Fantini, Simões, & Costa, 2016). By the same token, the competencies gained by the students themselves through participation in non-formal activities (to which they also contribute) are often overlooked.

At policy level, this separation is evident in the ways learning mobility has been operationalised in supranational and intergovernmental agendas of the EU and the Council of Europe. Youth mobility opportunities in the context of non-formal learning typically fall within the scope of the youth sector of the Council of Europe, whereas most formal mobility opportunities are bound to EU education and training programmes and *Erasmus+* in particular (although this compartmentalisation was softened with the streamlined architecture of *Erasmus+*, see Chapter 2). Aware of this level of fragmentation, the two institutions have, since the 2000s, promoted increasing cooperation in the youth field with joint efforts like the first *Framework for European Cooperation in the Youth Field* (2002), tools for the recognition of competencies (e.g., the Youth Pass) or platforms for increasing dialogue between stakeholders in the youth sector (e.g. the *European*

Platform on Learning Mobility in the Youth Field, created in 2011). In part, this division derives from historical reasons, with the Council of Europe posited as the first intergovernmental organisation to address (non-formal) learning mobility at European level (Friesenhahn, Hanjo Schild, Wicke, & Balogh, 2013; see also Chapter 2 and Endnote 6).

Despite these valuable efforts, there is still a high level of fragmentation in the available information within and across these two institutions, as well as a divide between those who conduct research and those who deliver study abroad and, therefore, between formal and non-formal learnings in student mobility in Europe.

To summarise, the ten premises in this concluding chapter aimed to enlighten major contradictions in theory and practice of student mobility in European higher education. Tackling these contradictions involves a joint enterprise between the range of relevant disciplines and stakeholders involved in education abroad. It is this very collaboration that can heighten our understanding of student mobility and raise awareness of the limits of our own reasoning and disciplinary biases. In embarking on this writing journey this has, indeed, been one of the greatest gains I have reaped.

As in any other journey, there are limitations to the sort of trails walked as they reflect my ability and inability to navigate across certain disciplines, methods and languages. And yet, if the set of trails mapped out in this book lead readers to want to chart new ground, to blaze a new set of trails with a renewed awareness of their own positioning, I will be happy to say 'my hopes have been met'.

References

Almeida, J., Fantini, A. E., Simões, A. R., & Costa, N. (2016). Enhancing the intercultural effectiveness of exchange programmes: Formal and non-formal educational interventions. *Intercultural Education, 27*(6), 517–533.

Baiutti, M. (2019). *Protocollo di valutazione Intercultura*. Pisa: ETS.

Bourdieu, P. (1979). *La distinction. Critique sociale du jugement*. Paris: Les éditions de Minuit.

Chieffo, L., & Spaeth, C. (2017). *NAFSA's guide to successful short-term programs abroad*. Washington, DC: NAFSA: Association of International Educators.

de Wit, H. (2002). *Internationalization of higher education in the United States and in Europe: A historical, comparative, and conceptual analysis*. Westport, CT: Greenwood Press.

de Wit, H., Gacel-Ávila, J., Jones, E., & Jooste, E. (Eds.). (2017). *The globalization of internationalization: Emerging voices and perspectives*. London: Routledge.

Forum on Education Abroad. (2015). *Standards of good practice for education abroad* (4th ed.). Northampton, MA: Forum on Education Abroad.

Friesenhahn, G. J., Schild, Hanjo, Wicke, H.-G., & Balogh, J. (2013). Introduction: Learning mobility and non-formal learning. In G. H. Friesenhahn, H. Schild, H.-G. Wicke & J. Balogh (Eds.), *Learning mobility and non-formal learning in European contexts: Policies, approaches and examples* (pp. 5–8). Strasbourg: Council of Europe Publishing.

Hoffa, W. W. (Ed.). (2007). *A history of US study abroad: Beginings to 1965* (Vol. I). Carlisle, PA: Frontiers and the Forum on Education Abroad.

Hoffa, W. W., & de Paul, S. C. (Eds.). (2010). *A history of US study abroad: 1965-Present* (Vol. II). Carlisle, PA: Frontiers and the Forum on Education Abroad.

Jones, J., Coelen, R., Beelen, J., & de Wit, H. (2016). *Global and local Internationalization*. Rotterdam: Sense Publishers.

Larsen, M. A. (2016). *Internationalization of higher education: An analysis through spatial, network and mobilities theories*. New York, NY: Palgrave Macmillan.

Lave, J., & Wenger, E. (1991). *Situated Learning: Legitimate peripheral participation*. Cambridge: Cambridge University Press.

Mitchell, R., Tracy-Ventura, N., & McManus, K. (2017). *Anglophone students abroad: Identity, social relationships, and language learning*. London: Routledge.

Montgomery, C. (2010). *Understanding the international student experience*. Basingstoke: Palgrave Macmillan.

Murphy-Lejeune, E. (2002). *Student mobility and narrative in Europe: The new strangers*. London: Routledge.

Repko, A., & Szostak, R. (2017). *Interdisciplinary research: Process and theory* (3rd ed.). Thousand Oaks, CA: Sage.

Rizvi, F. (2017). School internationalization and its implications for higher education. In H. de Wit, J. Gacel-Ávila, E. Jones & N. Jooste (Eds.), *The globalization of internationalization: Emerging voices and perspectives* (pp. 18–26). London: Routledge.

Schartner, A. (2015). You cannot talk with all of the strangers in a pub': A longitudinal case study of international postgraduate students' social ties at a British University. *Higher Education, 69*(2), 225–241.

Van Gaalen, A., & Freiertag, S. (2018). Is there a gap to bridge between internationalization in secondary and higher education? In D. Proctor & L. E. Rumbley (Eds.), *The future agenda for internationalization in higher education* (pp. 199–211). London: Routledge.

Wiedenhoeft, M., Hernandez, M., & Wicke, H.-G. (2014). *Guide to education abroad for advisers and administrators* (4th ed.). Washington, DC: NAFSA.

Young, T. J., Sercombe, P. G., Sachdev, I., Naeb, R., & Schartner, A. (2013). Success factors for international postgraduate students' adjustment: Exploring the roles of intercultural competence, language proficiency, social contact and social support. *European Journal of Higher Education, 3*(2), 151–171.

Index

Page numbers in **bold** indicate tables. Page numbers in *italic* indicate figures.

Academic Cooperation Association (ACA) 11–12, 33, 92
academic learning 22, 26, 73, 75, 80, 123, 188, 224, 235; *see also* disciplinary learning
academic purpose 57–58, 60, 80, 224, 231
academic recognition 21, 25, 70–71, 183
academic value (of student mobility) 21, 25, 72–73, 75, 80
adaptation 3, 28–29, **78**, 117, **127**, 127–128, 132, 145, 149, *149*, 160–161, 170, *170*, 172–173, *177*, 178, 208, *208*, 223–226; non- 168–169
Allen, H. W. 192, 194
Almeida, J. 19, 55–56, 77, 141, 146, 165, 174, 180, 203, 236
Anquetil, M. 19, 93
Association of International Educators (NAFSA) 12, 24–25, 221
attribute variables *27*, 27, 30, *41*, 91, *220*

Barber, E. 10
Baxter Magolda, M. B. **78**, 78–79, 186, 204, 206, 209
Beaven, A. 17, 19, 67, 193
Bennett, M. J. **78**, 78–79, 204, 208–209, 211
Berry, J. 28, **78**
Bierwiaczonek, K. 29
Bochner, S. 28, 152, 161
Bologna Declaration 68

Bologna Process 5, 68, 71–72, 76, 81n4, 81n5; *see also* European Higher Education Area (EHEA)
Borghetti, C. 19, 67
Bosley, G. 19
Bourdieu, P. 79, 126, 130, 138–139, 223, 232
Bredella, L. 77
Brewer, E. 24–25
Bryła, P. 37, 91
Byram, M. 10, 12, 17, 19, 24, 67, 73, 76–79, **78**, 204, 206, 209

Cairns, D. 34, 36–37, 61–62, 73, 91, 93, 135
Campus Europae programme 73, 99, 102, 103–104 (Box 3.1), 119–120, 133, 136, 140, 184, 189–195, **193**, *193*, 197–198, 203–204, **204**, 213, 226, 233, 235
Caracelli, V. J. 98
Carroll, J. 17, 19, 57
Changnon, G. 77–79, 198
Coleman, J. A. 17, 19, 26, 66–67, 75–76, 157
Common European Framework of Reference for Languages (CEFR) 76, 81n9, 104, 146, 192
communities of practice 17, 162, 164, 225
Comp, D. 14, 23
Comparative and International Education 17, 34, 89, 220
Costa, N. 19, 77, 165, 203, 236
Creswell, J. W. 91, 94–95, **95**, 98–99, 101, 107

240 Index

cultural barriers 155, 157

Cunningham, K. 24

curriculum: design and integration 22, 24, 30; intercultural curriculum development and assessement 198–202; *see also* study abroad programme design features

data: analysis 98, 104, 117, 133, 184, 222, 226; collection 33, 88–90, **95**, 96, 98–99, 101, 106

Deardorff, D. K. 12, 19, 23, 73, 77, 78, 202

de Paul, S. C. 231

Dervin, F. 10, 12, 19

deVellis, R. F. 127–128

development: personal 20, 36, 37–38, *41*, 74, 122, *123*, 124, 143, 187–188, 213, *220*; professional 34, 36, 39, *41*, *220*

de Wit, H. 12–13, 23, 34, 55, 61, 66, 69, 73, 233–234

disciplinary learning 15, *16*, 25, *41*, 72, *220*

double/multiple degrees **63**, 65; *see also Erasmus Mundus Joint Master Degrees*

Dunning, D. 192

Dwyer, M. M. 22, 90

Engle, J. 23

Engle, L. 23

Erasmus+: duration of the period abroad 62; statistics of 32, 42n5; structure of 72, 81n8

Erasmus Mobility Quality Tools (EMQT) 25

Erasmus Mundus 19, 62–65, 71, 81n8

Erasmus Mundus Intercultural Competence (EMIC) 19

Erasmus Mundus Joint Master Degrees (EMJMD) 62–65

Erasmus programme 4, 53, 60–61, 65, 73–74, 90, 104

Erasmus Student Network (ESN) 4, 12, 25, 35, 41n1, 92, 121, 150, 162, 165, 175

EURODATA studies 33, 57, 91; I 33, 92; II 33, 61, 92, 121, 147n2

European Credit Transfer and Accumulation System (ECTS) 70, 188–189; *see also*European Community Course Credit Transfer System

European Higher Education Area (EHEA) 68, 71–72, 81n5, 125

European Union (EU) 5, 20, 21, 23, 25, 31–33, 35, 37, 53, 58, 60, 65, 67–72, **74**, 75–77, 81n6, 92, 102–103, 124–125, *125*, 126, 143, 189, 226, 236

European University Association (EUA) 12, 33, 65, 92

Facilitating Student Mobility's Service including Quality Insurance Dimension (FASQUAD) 25

Fantini, A. E. 17, 19, 77–79, **78**, 128, 165, 199, 203–204, 209, 236

Fetters, M. D. 98

Field, A. 104, 128, 130

field work **64**, 66

Forum on Education Abroad (FEA) 12, 14, 24, 32, 62, 213, 221

Freed, B. 17, 97, 157, 190–191

Freshwater, D. 98

General Agreement on Trade in Services (GATS) 54

global student dynamics 9, 15, *15*, 30, *31*, 31–32, 35 (Box 1.4), 39, *41*, 92, 220; in Portugal 124, 147n2, 147n3; in the UK 26, 125; *see also* student mobility flows

Graham, W. F. 98

Greene, J. C. 98, 107

Guilherme, M. 77

Harvey, D. 171

higher education: European 1, 3, 9, 11, 14, 21–23, 25, 26, 29, 33, 39, *41*, 53–54, 56, 58, 60–62, **63**, 66–71, 73, 75, 79–80, 81n4, 90, 92, 136, 140, 149, 183, 188–190, 219, *220*, 221, 223, 226, 228–229, 231, 235, 236–237; *see also* European Higher Education Area (EHEA)

Hoffa, W. W. 231

host community impact 35–37, 39, *41*, 41n8, *220*

immigrants: highly skilled 1, 3, 99–100, 102, 105, 110, 119–120, 124, 126, 130, 147n1, 151, 154–155, 166, 168, 184, 193, **193**, 198, 203–204, **204**, 223–224, 227; participants 103, 128, 130–132, 139, 149, 151, 153, 154–155, 157, 159–160, 167, 184, 187, 189, 191–192, 224–225, 227

Index   241

integration: interdisciplinary integration, 5, 6n1, 96, 206, 231; methodological integration 96–98, 106, 222–223

intercultural: learning *16*, 17–21, 23, *41*, 53, 81, 99, 162, 164, 173, 176, 184, 193, 198, 200, 201–202, 205, 211–212, *220*, 223, 225, 227; outcomes 75, 79, 184, 198–200, 227

intercultural communicative competence 17, 77–79, **78**, 93, 199, 202–204, 206, 209–210, *210*

intercultural competence 17, 29, 75–77, **78**, 79–80, 127–128, **128**, 130–131, 144–146, 177–179, 198–199, 203, 206; definitions, terminology/ taxonomies and models 77–78, **78**; integrated intercultural models 210–211, **211**; *see also* intercultural outcomes

Intercultural Educational Resources for Erasmus Students and their Teachers (IEREST) 19–20

intercultural outcomes 75, 79, 184, 198–200, 227

interdisciplinary approach (in student mobility) 1–5, 14–15; applications of 1, 4, 10, 117, 139, 149, 183, 219, 223, 228; conceptual foundations 3, 10, 23, 79, 88, 117, 219; definition of interdisciplinarity 1–3; educational foundations 3, 88, 117, 219; goal of (comprehensive understanding) 2, 96, 104–105, 114; implications of 1, 3, 11, 17, 37, 39, 54, 56, 60, 68, 75, 79, 91, 106, 121, 138, 219, 226–227, 229, 231–234; methodological foundations 3, 117, 219

internationalisation: of the curriculum 200; definitions, terminology and rationales 54–56; of higher education 3–4, 10–11, 13, 30, *31*, 34–35, *41*, 54–55, 124, 200, 221, 233; at home 200, 235; of secondary education 61, 233

Ivankova, N. V. 101, 107

Jackson, J. 17–19, 29, 190, 193, 213
joint degree programmes **63**, 65; *see also Erasmus Mundus Joint Master Degrees*
Jones, E. 22, 23, 56, 73, 77, 185, 186, 200, 213, 233

Kelo, M. 33
Kerouac, J. 118
Killick, D. 187
King, P. M. 78–79, **78**, 186, 204, 206, 209
Kinginger, C. 16, 29, 67, 97, 190
Knight, J. 34, 54–56, 65
Kolb, D. A. 199, 203
Krueger, J. 192
Kruskal–Wallis test 104–105, 171, **171**, 173, 225–226
Krzaklewska, E. 27, 34, 121–124, 135

La Brack, B. 18
language: barriers 29, 155–157, 165; biography 117–119, 130, 139, 141, 223; learning 12, 15, 16, 22, 29, 53, **64**, 67, 73, 76, 97, *118*, 121, 123, 126, 130, 140, 152, 157, **163**, 165, 176, 189–190, 192–193, *193*, 194–197, 226; outcomes 26, 29, 158, 190, 213
Larsen, M. A. 10, 54, 58, 60, 233
Lave, J. 162, 225
Le, E. 89–90
learning abroad 15, 20, 23, 190, 192, 198, 199, 226, 233
learning domains abroad 9, 15–21, *15*, 21 (Box 1.2), *27*, 39, *41*, 72–73, 77, 121, 185, 190, 198
Leonardo da Vinci programme 71–72
level of study 57–58, 60, **63–64**, 66, 80, 81n4, 231
Lifelong Learning Programme 72–74, 81n8
long-term impact of study abroad 9, 15, *15*, 35, 36, 39 (Box 1.5), 90, 92, 151, 233
Lou, K. 18–202

McDermott, R. 162
McTighe, J. 201
Maiworm, F. 20, 25, 35, 70, 89, 92, 121, 123, 183
Maximizing Study Abroad through Language and Culture Strategies (MAXSA) 18
Maxwell, J. 97–99
mediating and outcome variables *27*, 28, 30, *41*, *220*
migration: nexus 36, 36, 39, *41*, 90, 92, 97, *220*, 233; skilled 37, 100, 110n4; student 34, 38

242 Index

mixed methods 3, 88, 93–101, **95,** 106, 110n2, 171, **171,** 222–223, 226, 232; mixed methods and interdisciplinarity 95, 98; *see also* methodological integration
mobility capital 27, 30, 37, 91, 117–118, *118,* 126–128, **127, 129,** 130–132, 139–140, 163, 223
Montgomery, C. 93, 162, 164, 225
Morse, J. M. 101
motivations: to study abroad 17, 27, 117–118, *118,* 120–126, *123, 125,* 138–140, 143, 157–158, 176–177, 187, 190, 192–194, **193;** to learn the host language 17, *193,* 196–197, 223–224, 226
multidisciplinarity: definition of 2
Murphy-Lejeune, E. 10–12, 27, 37, 67, 89–93, 121, 123, 126–128, **127,** 131–132, 138–140, 163, 224

National Academic Recognition Information Centres (NARIC) 70
Niehaus, L. 101
Nordplus Higher Education Programme 32, 42n4

Ogden, A. 4, 13–14, 23, 89–90
Onwuegbuzie, A. J. 94, 105, 171
Oosterbeek, H. 90
Organisation for Economic Co-operation and Development (OECD) 12, 31, 59

Paige, R. M. 18, 20, 202
Papatsiba, V. 12, 37, 61, 68, 72, 93, 186
Parey, M. 90
Plano Clark, V. L. 91, 94–95, **95,** 98–99, 101
pre-departure 3, 15, 18, 30, 117–121, 127, 139–140, 191, 223, 226
programme design features (in study abroad) *27,* 30, *41,* 193–194, *193,* 197, *220;* curriculum design and integration 22, 24, 30; grading policies and recognition of studies 22, 25, 30; intercultural interventions, trainings and/or orientations 19–21, 22–23, 30; opportunities for contact with hosts 22, 26, 30; programme duration 22–23, 30; programme evaluation

and assessment 22–23, 30; type of housing 22, 26, 30
push-and-pull factors 30, *31,* 32, 35, *41,* 41n8, 122, *220*

Repko, A. 2, 6n1, 96–97, 106, 228–229
residence abroad 19, **64,** 66–67
Residence Abroad Matters 19, 67; *Interculture Project* (ICP) 19; *Learning and Residence Abroad* (LARA) 19; *Residence Abroad Project* (RAPORT) 19
Risager, K. 77
Rodrigues, M. 36–37, 41n6, 90–91
Rust, V. 89–90

Sassen, S. 169
second language acquisition (SLA) 15–16, 22, 26, *41,* 89, 97, 121–122, 157–158, 190, *220,* 223
Simões, A. R. 19, 77, 165, 203, 236
Snyder, W. 162
Socrates programme 70–71; I **74,** 75; II 71–72, **74,** 81n7
sojourners: Aamu 169, 172; Agnë **107,** 159–160, 169; Aija **107,** 168; Alexei **109,** 159; Andresz **108,** 159–160, 186–187, 194–195, 206; Andrzej **134,** 135; Anfisa **109,** 157, 206; Bartek **108,** 133, **134,** 135, 195; Belén **109,** 159, 169, 187; Borja **108,** 168, 207–209, **207,** 211; Chao **109,** 188; Cheng 169; Cristina **109,** 133, **134,** 137–138, 152, 168, 186; definition of 109n3; Dong **109,** 134, **134,** 137–138, 169, 188; Elena **109,** 158, 160, 206; Elinah **108,** 157, 187; Felix **108,** 156; Gaëlle **108,** 168, 205; Guo 170; Interviewer 194–195; Jan **108,** 133, **134,** 135, 195, 207, **207;** Jane **109,** 156, 187; Jeane **107,** 187, 205; Jimena **109,** 160, 207–208, **207;** Jonas **108,** 207, **207;** Juan **108,** 188–189, 205; Julija 158; Jürgen **108,** 133, **134,** 135, 186–187; Karol **108,** 133, **134,** 135, 156, 170, 194–195, 197; Kinga **108,** 133–136, **134,** 157, 165, 189, 195, 197, 205; Krisha **109,** 187; Language teacher 195–197; Liliya **109,** 168–169; Lin **109,** 159–160; Lucia **109,** 160, 169; Łukasz **107,** 188–189; Maja **107,** 156; Martyna

107, 205; Mercedes **109**, 156, 206; Milosz **108**, 206; Nikola **108**, 156, 188; Paula **108**, 160; Regina **109**, 159–160, 170; Saskia **108**, 207, **207**; Tanja **108**, 170, 187, 207, **207**; Tao **109**, 137; Ying **108**, 133–134, **134**, 136–137, 157, 188; Yuwei **108**, 157; ZhiRuo **108**, 186
Spitzberg, B. H. 77–79, 198
Statistical Office of the EU (EUROSTAT) 31, 41n3
steps into mobility 117–119, *118*, 131–134, 139–140, 163, 223
Stick, S. L. 101, 107
Streitwieser, B. T. 4, 10–13, 89–90
student mobility in Europe: credit-seeking 56, 57, 58–61, **63–64**; degree-seeking 57, 58–62, **63–64**; flows 12, *31*, 31–33, 35, *41*, 124, *220*; history of 68–72; research and/or scholarship 1, 9–13, 38, *41*, 89–90, 92–93, 106, 220, *220*, 220–222, 229, 232, 234; *see also* taxonomies
Szostak, R. 2, 6n1, 96–97, 106, 228–229

taxonomies of student mobility 28, 30, *31*, 33–35, *41*, *220*, 231; applied taxonomies 60–68, 80–81; typological synopsis 56–59
Teichler, U. 10, 12, 20, 25, 32–35, 37, 55, 57, 59, 61–62, 70, 81n3,

89, 92, 121, 123–124, 147n2, 183, 186
transdisciplinarity: definition of 2–3
Tsoukalas, J. 37, 135–136, 186

UNESCO Institute for Statistics (UIS) 31, 41n2, 53
United Nations Educational, Scientific and Cultural Organisation (UNESCO) 12, 31
Urias, D. 13

Vande Berg, M. 14, 18, 20, 23, 202
Van der Wende, M. 70
Van Mol, C. 10, 30, 32, 34, 36–37, 93
variables informing study abroad 9, 15, *15*, 22, 27, 30 (Box 1.3), 39, *41*, 136, *220*

Wächter, B. 10–11, 33, 57, 59, 61–62, 91, 124
Waldinger, F. 90
Waldzus, S. 29
Webbink, D. 90
Wenger, E. 162, 225
Wiggins, G. P. 201
Willis, F. 17
Wills, T. A. 159

Yemini, M. 13, 54–55

Zarate, G. 76